FAILING INTELLIGENCE

'For a conflict whose justification turned on weapons of mass destruction, an account penned by Brian Jones, *the* Whitehall expert on the subject at the time, will, from the day of its publication, become and remain a crucial paving stone in any future reconstruction of the road to war in Iraq. It's compelling and depressing stuff.'

Professor Peter Hennessy
Attlee Professor of Contemporary British History
Queen Mary, University of London

FAILING INTELLIGENCE

THE TRUE STORY OF HOW WE WERE FOOLED INTO GOING TO WAR IN IRAQ

Brian Jones

biteback

First published in Great Britain in 2010
Dialogue, an imprint of
Biteback Publishing Ltd
Heal House
375 Kennington Lane
London
SE11 5QY

ISBN 978-1-906447-11-3

10 9 8 7 6 5 4 3 2 1

A CIP catalogue record for this book is available from the British Library.

Set in Adobe Garamond Pro by Soapbox
Printed and bound in Great Britain by CPI Cox & Wyman, Reading, RG1 8EX

CONTENTS

PART IV: CONCLUSION

ACKNOWLEDGEMENTS

I am indebted to many professional colleagues in the civil service and beyond whose knowledge and experience, contributed over many years, has had an indelible influence on this book. None more so than those I worked with on the Defence Intelligence Staff, especially in my own branch. I cannot name many names but 'my chemical warfare expert' has a special place in a group of special people. I also thank those busy officials in Whitehall who have been additionally burdened by having to review drafts of this book to provide security clearance.

An important part of it has been made possible by the generosity of Hamish Killip and Rod Barton, two brave weapons inspectors. Without the tragic death of a third, David Kelly, much of the information on which this book is based might not have entered the public domain. I would also like to mention the encouragement and occasional direct input of Ian Dye, Alex Danchev, Michael Herman and Chris Ames. A number of people in the press and wider media have played an important part and, although it may be unfashionable to say so, my experience of their profession has been overwhelmingly positive.

I am grateful to Michael Smith, first for identifying this as a book worth publishing, and for the help I then received from him and his colleagues Jonathan Wadman and James Stephens at Biteback.

The support of my wider family throughout this entire experience has been very important. More specifically, the encouragement and humour of my sons, Ceri and Gavin, has been vital. Finally, I would like to acknowledge the load, predominantly emotional, shared with my wife, without whose courage, resolution, advice and occasional rage, none of this would have been possible. It is to her that I dedicate this book.

ABBREVIATIONS

ADI NBC ST	Assistant director of intelligence for nuclear, biological and chemical weapons, scientific and technical – the title of my post in the DIS in September 2002
BIG	Butler Implementation Group
BWC	Biological and Toxin Weapons Convention (sometimes BTWC)
'C'	Head of MI6
CBDE	MoD Chemical and Biological Defence Establishment at Porton Down
CBW	Chemical and biological warfare
CDE	MoD Chemical Defence Establishment at Porton Down (subsequently CBDE)
CDI	Chief of defence intelligence (head of the DIS)
CIA	Central Intelligence Agency
CIG	Current Intelligence Group, an ad-hoc inter-departmental committee of officials which produces an assessment for approval by the JIC
CWC	Chemical Weapons Convention
CX	Reports issued by MI6 (Secret Intelligence Service), often highly classified
DCDI	Deputy chief of defence intelligence (head of the DIAS)
DIAS	Defence Intelligence Analysis Staff (of the DIS)
DIS	Defence Intelligence Staff (of the MoD)
DIST	Director of Intelligence (Scientific and Technical)
DTI	Department of Trade and Industry
FAC	Foreign Affairs Committee (parliamentary select committee)
FCO	Foreign and Commonwealth Office
GCHQ	Government Communications Headquarters (Britain's signals intelligence agency)
IAEA	International Atomic Energy Agency

IIS	Iraqi Intelligence Service
ISC	Intelligence and Security Committee (of parliamentarians reporting to the Prime Minister)
JARIC	Joint Air Reconnaissance Interpretation Centre
JIC	Joint Intelligence Committee, which authorises top-level assessments
MI5	Security Service
MI6	Common name used to describe the Secret Intelligence Service
MoD	Ministry of Defence
MRE	Microbiological Research Establishment at Porton Down ('closed' 1979)
NOFORN	US security marking denying foreign access to information
NPT	Nuclear Non-proliferation Treaty
OD Sec	Overseas and Defence Secretariat of the Cabinet Office
Report X	Highly sensitive and compartmented intelligence on Iraqi WMD from MI6 received/issued on or about 11 September
SIS	Secret Intelligence Service, often known as MI6
UN	United Nations
UNMOVIC	UN Monitoring, Verification and Inspection Commission
UNSCOM	UN Special Commission, to eliminate Iraq's biological and chemical weapons and missiles
WMD	Weapons of mass destruction

PEOPLE

Barton, Rod	Australian intelligence official and weapons inspector
Blair, Tony	British Prime Minister (1997–2007)
Blix, Dr Hans	Head of UNMOVIC (1999–2003), previous head of IAEA
Blunkett, David	British Home Secretary (2001–4)
Braithwaite, Sir Rodric	Former JIC chairman and FCO diplomat
Bush, George H. W.	US President (1989–93)
Bush, George W.	US President (2001–9)
Butler, Lord	Former head of civil service, chairman of 2004 review of intelligence on WMD
Caldecott, Andrew, QC	Legal representative for BBC at Hutton inquiry
Campbell, Alastair	Prime Minister's head of communications at No. 10
Cheney, Dick	US Vice President (2001–9)
Chilcot, Sir John	Chair of the Iraq inquiry (2009–10), member of Butler Review Committee, retired senior civil servant
Clinton, Bill	US President (1993–2001)
Cook, Robin	British Home Secretary (1997–2001), leader of the House of Commons (2001–3). Died 2005
Cragg, Tony	Deputy chief of defence intelligence (1999–2003)
Davis, Prof. Christopher OBE	Retired surgeon commander and former biological warfare analyst
Dayton, Maj. Gen. Keith	Head of Iraq Survey Group
Dearlove, Sir Richard	Head of MI6 ('C')
Deverill, Brig. John	First head of British contingent of Iraq Survey Group
Dingemans, James, QC	Counsel for Hutton inquiry
Dowse, Tim	Senior FCO official

Duelfer, Charles   Chief investigator, Iraq Survey Group (2004–5)
Ehrman, Sir William   Senior FCO official
Freedman, Prof.   Member of Iraq Inquiry Committee
Sir Lawrence
French, Air Marshal Sir Joe Chief of defence intelligence (2001–3)
Gilligan, Andrew   Journalist, defence correspondent, once of BBC's
                             Today programme
Greenstock, Sir Jeremy   British ambassador to the UN
Hewitt, Gavin   BBC news correspondent
Hoon, Geoff   British Defence Secretary (1999–2005)
Howard, Martin   Deputy chief of defence intelligence (2003–5)
Humphrys, John   Veteran broadcaster, presenter of *Today* programme
Hutton, Lord   Law lord who conducted an inquiry into David
                             Kelly's death
Inge, Field Marshal Lord   Member of the Butler Review Committee
Jones, Prof. R. V.   First director of scientific and technical
                             intelligence
Kamil, Hussein   Iraqi general, son-in-law of Saddam Hussein
Kay, Dr David   Chief investigator, Iraq Survey Group (2003–4)
Kelly, Dr David, CMG   Microbiologist, biological weapons inspector
Killip, Col. Hamish   Inspector and adviser on WMD
(retired)
Lamb, Patrick   Deputy head of Counter-Proliferation Department,
                             Foreign Office
Libby, J. Lewis 'Scooter'   Aide to Vice President Cheney and leading
                             'neocon'
Lyne, Sir Roderic   Member of Iraq Inquiry Committee, former
                             UK diplomat
Manning, Sir David   Prime Minister Blair's foreign policy adviser
                             and head of OD Sec (2001–3); UK ambassador
                             to US (2003–7)
Manningham-Buller,   Director general, MI5 (2002–7, previously
Baroness   deputy DG)
Mates, Michael   Conservative MP and member of both ISC and
                             Butler Review Committee
Meyer, Sir Christopher   UK ambassador to US (1997–2003)
Morrison, John   Deputy head of DIS (DCDI) until 1999,
                             subsequently investigator for ISC until 2004

Murphy, Paul	Chair of ISC (2005–8)
Omand, Sir David	UK intelligence and security coordinator (2002–5), previously permanent secretary at Home Office, director of GCHQ and policy director at MoD. Member of JIC
Osama bin Laden	Leader of al-Qaida network of terrorist organisations
Pasechnik, Vladimir	Defector from Soviet biological warfare programme
Pearson, Dr Graham	Director general of CDE and CBDE until 1995
Powell, Jonathan	Prime Minister Blair's chief of staff
Rice, Condoleezza	US National Security Advisor (2001–5); Secretary of State (2005–9)
Richards, Sir Francis	Head of GCHQ and JIC member
Ricketts, Peter	UK policy director at Foreign Office
Ritter, Scott	Former officer in the US marines who was a chief inspector for UNSCOM
Rumsfeld, Donald	US Defence Secretary (2001–6)
Rycroft, Matthew	Prime Minister Blair's personal secretary
Scarlett, John	Chairman of JIC, former MI6 intelligence officer, later head of MI6 or 'C'
Short, Clare	UK secretary for international development (1997–2003)
Straw, Jack	UK Foreign Secretary (2001–6)
Sumption, Jonathan, QC	Legal representative for the government at the Hutton inquiry
Taylor, Ann	Chair of ISC (2001–5) and member of the Butler Review Committee
Tenet, George	Director of central intelligence and head of CIA (resigned 2004)
Thatcher, Margaret	British Prime Minister (1979–90)
Walker, Sir John	Air marshal (retired) and former CDI
Ware, John	Senior presenter, *Panorama* (BBC TV)
Watts, Susan	Science correspondent, *Newsnight* (BBC TV)
Wells, Bryan	Head of Proliferation and Arms Control Secretariat, MoD
Wolfowitz, Paul	US deputy Defence Secretary (2001–2005)

TIMELINE

1990

August   Iraq invades Kuwait.

1991

January   An international coalition organised by President George H. W. Bush begins military operation Desert Storm to eject Iraq from Kuwait (essentially completed by end February).

April   Ceasefire agreed – UN Security Council Resolution 687. UNSCOM formed and with IAEA undertakes inspections in Iraq. Chemical weapons found, nuclear programme uncovered.

1993

January   President Clinton replaces Bush.

February   First attack on World Trade Center, New York City.

1995

March   Sarin attack by Aum Shinrikyo sect on Tokyo subway in Japan. (Draws attention to previous nerve gas attack in Matsumoto in 1994.)

August   General Hussein Kamil leaves Iraq, leading to more extensive Iraqi admissions on biological warfare and the nuclear programme.

1996

June   According to Scott Ritter, CIA supports a failed coup attempt against Saddam.

1997

May   New Labour led by Tony Blair wins UK general election.

October	Iraq refuses to deal with US inspectors working for UNSCOM. All inspections suspended. Intense diplomatic activity resolves dispute.

1998

March	According to Scott Ritter, American attempt to stimulate confrontation with Iraq ends in failure.
May	India and Pakistan conduct underground nuclear tests.
August	Al-Qaida attacks US embassies in west Africa. US missile strikes conducted against Sudan and Afghanistan. Iraq withdraws cooperation with UNSCOM and IAEA.
December	Inspectors withdrawn from Iraq. Operation Desert Fox conducted.

1999

December	UNMOVIC replaces disbanded UNSCOM.

2001

January	George W. Bush replaces Clinton as President.
11 September	Terror attack on US.

2002

29 January	George W. Bush in State of the Union address declares his objectives are to eliminate the threats posed by terrorists and by regions that seek weapons of mass destruction.
11 March	Vice President Cheney visits Downing Street. A number of relevant policy-related papers and memos prepared at about this time were leaked in 2004.
5/6 April	Tony Blair in an NBC interview states: 'We know that [Saddam] has stockpiles of major amounts of chemical and biological weapons.'
6–7 April	Blair visits Bush at Crawford, Texas.
1 June	Bush declares doctrine of pre-emption.
23 July	Blair's Downing Street meeting (briefing paper and memo leaked in 2005).
29 August	Bush approves 'goals, objectives, strategy' of war on Iraq. Donald Rumsfeld orders operation Southern Focus.
3 September	Blair announces: 'There will be a dossier soon.'
6–7 September	Blair meets Bush at Camp David.

24 September	Dossier published.
10–11 October	US Congress gives Bush war powers.
November	UN Security Council Resolution 1441. UNMOVIC inspectors in Iraq.

2003

29 January	Bush's State of the Union address.
7 March	UNMOVIC inspectors out.
16 March	US–UK draft second UN resolution on Iraq abandoned.
17 March	Bush gives Saddam final ultimatum.
18 March	Blair wins House of Commons support for military action.
20 March	Invasion.
6 April	UK forces enter Basra.
7 April	US forces take control of central Baghdad.
9 April	Televised toppling of Saddam's statue in Firdaus Square.
1 May	Bush declares major fighting over.
7 & 12 May	David Kelly talks on phone to Susan Watts.
22 May	Kelly meets Andrew Gilligan at Charing Cross Hotel.
29 May	Gilligan's *Today* broadcasts; Kelly, in New York, speaks with Gavin Hewitt; Blair visits Iraq.
30 May	Kelly talks on phone to Susan Watts and sends email.
1 June	Gilligan's article in *Mail on Sunday.*
2 & 4 June	*Newsnight* broadcasts by Watts.
5 June	Kelly in Iraq.
15 June	*Observer* article on 'mobile biological warfare labs'.
19 June	Gilligan gives evidence to FAC.
25 June	Alastair Campbell gives evidence to FAC.
28 June	Campbell appears on *Channel 4 News*.
2 July	MoD informed about Kelly.
3 July	FAC report on decision to go to war with Iraq completed.
7 July	FAC report released.
8 July	Kelly 'agrees' to press release and it is issued (no name). I write to DCDI about FAC report.
9 July	(Wednesday) Kelly named in some papers. MoD confirms name.
c. 12 July	UK's Iraq Survey Group civilian contingent deploys to Iraq.
15 July	Kelly gives televised evidence to FAC.
16 July	Kelly appears before ISC in closed session.

17 July	(Thursday) Gilligan recalled by FAC in closed session; Kelly sets out on 'suicide walk'.
18 July	(Friday) Kelly's body found; Blair orders Hutton inquiry; DCDI (Martin Howard) signs off Geoff Hoon's brief for ISC inquiry.
19 July	Kelly post mortem.
20 July	BBC announces Kelly was Gilligan's source.
22 July	Hoon, CDI and DCDI give evidence to ISC.
1 August	Lord Hutton 'opens' inquiry.
11 August	Witnesses begin appearing before Hutton.
3 September	I give evidence to Hutton.
4 September	Hutton Part I closes.
10 September	ISC report issued.
15 September	Hutton Part II opens.
24 September	Hutton Part II closes.
3 October	Iraq Survey Group issues interim report.
mid-December	David Kay leaves Baghdad; Rod Barton arrives in Baghdad.

2004

19 January	Howard visits Barton in Baghdad.
c. 21 January	Iraq Survey Group video conference, London/Washington/Baghdad.
23 January	Kay resigns from Iraq Survey Group.
28 January	Kay gives evidence to Congress; Hutton report published.
c. 15 February	Charles Duelfer, new Iraq Survey Group leader, arrives in Baghdad.
8 March	John Scarlett's 'nuggets' to Baghdad Iraq Survey Group.
c. 18 March	Iraq Survey Group video conference, London/Washington/Baghdad.
c. 23 March	Barton resigns. In the preceding few days two other senior Iraq Survey Group members, Hamish Killip and John Gee, had resigned.
21 April	I give evidence to Lord Butler's review.
7 July	Senate Intelligence Committee report on Iraq published.
14 July	Butler report published.
30 September	Iraq Survey Group final report published.
2 November	Bush re-elected US President.

2005

5 May	Blair re-elected UK Prime Minister.
7 July	London Underground and bus bombings.

2007

27 June	Blair resigns; Gordon Brown becomes Prime Minister.

2009

15 June	Brown agrees to Chilcot inquiry.
24 November	Chilcot public hearings begin establishing a framework.

2010

12 January	Inquiry begins Phase 2 and a more inquisitorial approach.
8 March	Public hearings suspended for general election.
29 June	Public hearings resume. During the interim the Inquiry Committee had visited US and interviewed a number of people and held private hearings in UK.
30 July	Public hearings concluded. Final report anticipated at the end of the year.

PREFACE

I was born in the blitzed city of Bristol towards the end of the summer of 1944, as the age of nuclear weapons was dawning. Before I was a year old there had been three atomic explosions, the Second World War had ended and George Orwell had christened the evolving conflict of ideologies between west and east as the 'Cold War'.

In July 1945 the Americans exploded the first nuclear device at a site in New Mexico they called Trinity. Three weeks later, three days apart, two atom bombs were dropped on Japan, incinerating tens of thousands of civilians in Hiroshima and Nagasaki. Those three shots were the starting pistols for a nuclear arms race; and the world was in the icy grip of a Cold War that was to last forty years.

The Soviet Union exploded its first atom bomb at about the time I went to infant school in 1949. By the end of a miserable decade, the earth's atmosphere was contaminated for an eternity by minute quantities of man-made radioactive particles. I was unaware of these momentous events or, indeed, of the more primitive chemical weapons that had occasioned the general issue of 'gas masks' during the war.

My childhood was punctuated by announcements about atomic power and atomic weapons. The news on television and in the papers brought an awareness of 'mushroom clouds' marking the progress 'Ike' and 'Uncle Joe' were making in their developing race, first with atom bombs and next with hydrogen bombs. Somewhere amongst it all there must have been celebrations as well as criticism when Britain joined the notorious club. But when our first nuclear weapons became 'operational' in the mid-1950s, at about the time I went to secondary school, it passed me by. Nor was I aware that the government coincidentally decided to abandon Britain's chemical weapons and biological weapons programmes and capabilities.

In 1962 I went off to Cardiff University to study metallurgy. In my first weeks there, the world held its breath as Kennedy's United States and Khrushchev's Soviet Union confronted each other over ballistic missiles in

Cuba. Thoughts of a nuclear holocaust were dragged from the backs to the fronts of our minds. Four minutes was all the warning we might get and suddenly this was a potent symbol of the fragility of our lives, and they were never quite the same again.

On graduation in 1965 I landed a PhD contract with the United Kingdom Atomic Energy Authority to study a new zirconium alloy that was under development for the construction of nuclear power reactors. That summer, I went to work for a few weeks at the Chalk River Nuclear Laboratory on the banks of the deep Ottawa River in Ontario, where I was able to learn something about nuclear reactors. Little, if anything, was said about nuclear weapons. Canada did not have any and, although I picked up vague hints of earlier links with the Manhattan Project, that was not something I took much interest in.

In 1968 I was awarded my doctorate and started my first job, returning to Canada as a research and development scientist at the brand new but remote Whiteshell Nuclear Research Establishment in Manitoba, about 80 miles north of Winnipeg. In 1973 I returned with my young family to Britain to continue my career in research and development with the Ministry of Defence. Through the eight years I was involved with the nuclear power industry, nuclear weapons was not a subject that seemed at all relevant to me. The negotiation during that time of the Nuclear Non-proliferation Treaty was something else that passed me by. I had even less reason to be aware of President Nixon's decision that America would abandon its biological and toxin weapons and press for a convention to ban them.

In 1973 I became a member of the scientific civil service at the Admiralty Materials Laboratory (AML) on the south coast of England. The AML was one of numerous Ministry of Defence research and development laboratories that existed at that time. I studied structural materials for submarines, including Polaris, which brought me closer to the world of nuclear weapons. However, the weapons were fairly incidental to my work and we had virtually no contact with the Atomic Weapons Research Establishment at Aldermaston, which dealt with the bomb behind a screen of security that was much more exclusive than our own.

On Salisbury Plain in Wiltshire, about 40 miles from the AML, were two other establishments of which I was only vaguely aware, partly because they related most strongly to the army. They were both at Porton Down; one was called the Chemical Defence Establishment and the other the

Microbiological Research Establishment. My interest in what they did was stimulated only briefly when an unfortunate employee at the latter had an accident which attracted the attention of the national press. He inadvertently injected himself through his rubber glove with something described as 'green monkey disease' for which there was no known cure, and he could not be saved. I remembered wondering at the apparent potency of such a disease and about its terrible potential as a weapon. However, I assumed someone somewhere was taking due account of such things and returned my briefly distracted focus to issues that were much closer to the nuclear deterrent that was the cornerstone of our defence.

I loved being an R&D scientist, but the MoD was gradually reducing the amount of in-house research it funded. I moved on to take charge of a facility that provided technical support and advice on naval aircraft for the Fleet Air Arm. During this period, whilst on a management course, I briefly met Dr David Kelly, another middle-ranking civil service scientist. I recollect that I found him quite hard going but I did learn that he had only recently joined the MoD. He had been recruited at an unusually senior level to lead the microbiology work at the Chemical Defence Establishment. I would understand later that this was part of an attempt to recover expertise in biological defence that had been lost when the MRE closed in 1979, but for the moment the significance of that escaped me. I had no reason to suppose our paths would ever cross again.

In the autumn of 1986 I was visited at my laboratory by a senior Whitehall scientist. He had come to persuade me to move on to a job in Whitehall in intelligence. The prospect of working in central London was not appealing, but I thought a job in intelligence might be interesting. I had previously had slight contact with that world and was intrigued by the experience and thought the suggestion worth exploring.

A few weeks later, I had a peculiar interview with the director general of scientific and technical intelligence in London. The job on offer was to organise and manage a group of about fifteen assorted scientists who analysed intelligence on a range of subjects including my specialism of 'structural materials'. The director general described the range of the work of 'Defence Intelligence 53', which would be my branch, and almost as an afterthought he mentioned that a couple of 'desks' covered chemical warfare and biological warfare. He said that he was not allowed to tell me much about the work because I did not have the higher security clearances necessary. Unfortunately they could not begin the expensive process by which I would gain these clearances unless I committed myself to the job: Catch-22. I talked to some of the staff who would work for me and their enthusiasm was obvious and infectious. I was a little concerned about the CBW element of the branch because I knew nothing about these subjects. However, I rationalised that it would represent only a small proportion of my responsibility and these were not matters that were of great significance to MoD – the MRE at Porton Down had recently closed down. I accepted the appointment, subject to detailed security checks.

'Positive vetting' for security clearance is a slow and complicated process that takes months to complete. Whilst it was in process I had a heart attack. It was a great shock, not least to my wife and teenage sons. Thankfully it turned out to be relatively mild. I was in hospital for a week and then sent home to recuperate. I recovered quickly, went back to work within a month or so and was able to take up my new job in the Defence Intelligence Staff on 13 July 1987. By that time, after several months of diet and exercise, I was fitter than I had been for years. I needed to be.

I was surprised to suddenly find myself immersed in the strategic security of Britain by virtue of the two desks in my branch that I had too readily relegated as 'also-rans'. I had not fully understood that biological and chemical warfare are the poor relations to nuclear warfare in an unholy trinity that some called 'weapons of mass destruction' or 'WMD'.

For ten years my main focus was to be on biological and chemical weapons. I found that not only did I have to overcome my own initial ignorance about them, but I also had to tackle that of many of my colleagues in intelligence and the wider Whitehall community. Britain had ceased its interest in the offensive potential of CBW in the technologically juvenile 1950s. Visibility of them was lost in the glare of the new nuclear weapons that had just been deployed. After this it was only a tiny part of the intelligence community and a few hidden experts at Porton Down that gave even the scantest attention as to how increasingly advanced and sophisticated versions of biological and chemical weapons might be used against the United Kingdom.

When, in the mid-1990s, in the wake of the Cold War and the collapse of the Soviet Union, my job embraced nuclear weapons intelligence, I expected that widespread unfamiliarity would be much less of a problem. We had possessed nuclear weapons since the 1950s and applied advances in technology to improve their design as the years passed. As a result, we had modified and updated our perception of how they might be used.

However, although a broader familiarity with nuclear weapons did exist, in the 1990s it remained frozen in a Cold War mindset. The real issues associated with the nascent threats arising from nuclear proliferation and the evolving world order remained obscured by visions of mutually assured destruction in a nuclear winter which would surely have followed a confrontation between superpowers.

Ironically, all of the issues I had wrestled with since 1987, misconceptions about WMD and confusion about the capability of intelligence, came together as my career ended in 2003. This took the form of a war the declared objective of which was to disarm Iraq of its WMD and, coincidentally perhaps, to remove Saddam Hussein from power. The war proved to be a disastrous misjudgement. There were no WMD and Saddam's terrifying totalitarian regime was replaced for many years by an environment no less terrifying. Meanwhile, Britain and the world was left more confused than ever about WMD and increasingly sceptical about the threat they might pose, and the value of arms control. It is my purpose in this book to reflect on how that came about and to highlight the important lessons to be learned from the experience.

Central to my purpose is the need to dispel some of the confusion about the weapons involved and about how intelligence and government should work. I begin by explaining the reasons for my own initial misconceptions about WMD since that might chime for others who, from a distance, continue to struggle to understand their relevance. A description of how the mists of my ignorance were slowly lifted might help explain some of the nuances of this difficult subject. And the problem we experienced in explaining the related strategic issues to a mainly sceptical and uninterested Whitehall audience might cast some light on why so many errors of judgement were made and why they have been concealed for so long.

PART I

CONTEXT

CHAPTER ONE

1987–90: Intelligence, chemical warfare
and biological warfare

Joining Intelligence

I was transferred to the Defence Intelligence Staff (DIS) in July 1987. At
that time its headquarters occupied one corner of a floor in the massive
green-roofed MoD Main Building on Whitehall. However, a sizeable
chunk, including the Scientific and Technical Directorate, was housed in
the Metropole Building, about a hundred yards away on Northumberland
Avenue. Once a grand hotel, the Metropole had now been reduced, behind
its original facade, to the utilitarian standard typical of most government
building. It looked as though it had suffered even further since Professor
R. V. Jones, the first ever director of scientific and technical intelligence,
took up his job almost forty years earlier.[1]

Over the first months, I was introduced to a world that would fascinate
and frustrate me for the rest of my career and beyond. In all that time I
never stopped learning about the mysterious and sometimes perplexing
community of intelligence in which I found myself. What is more, the
range of scientific and technical subjects in which I was involved was
now so wide and complicated that there would always be elements that
remained a mystery to me. And Whitehall and its politics were unlike
anything I had ever imagined.

Intelligence is something that few people have thought about in a more
than superficial way. It is often presented as a subject of mystery, adventure
and romance. Authors, playwrights and film makers exploit its exciting
facets. However, such things are just a small part of the real intelligence
world. It is difficult to represent the laborious, office-bound process of
intelligence analysis and assessment as a subject to occupy the interest of
the casual observer.

In the DIS we were the analysts of all available information (all-source) on foreign military matters. All-source includes secret intelligence supplied by the 'intelligence agencies' or 'collectors' as well as any other information we could get from diplomatic and attaché reports, liaison with foreign intelligence services, academic journals and the news media. I quickly learned that the DIS was the only large group of dedicated intelligence analysts in the UK government, and hence the recipients of the largest amount of 'raw' secret intelligence from the agencies. It was part of the MoD and funded by it. Its main function was to evaluate the military capabilities and intentions of potential enemies of Britain in order that our military services could be shaped, trained and equipped to do their job and to reduce any risks they might encounter. If our forces were in action then information for their immediate requirements and safety was the highest priority.

Apart from that, at the strategic level, the Warsaw Pact led by the Soviet Union was the only identified threat to our national security. It had the military capability and the perceived intention to expand communism into western Europe and across the world. It was by far the most technologically advanced and militarily powerful potential enemy we had and in the field of scientific and technical intelligence it was the dominant driver for our work.

There were other security risks. The Falklands war had occurred a few years earlier. The IRA was a persistent thorn in Britain's side and a constant disruption during my first decade in Whitehall. Travel was frequently disrupted by bomb threats and once the window of my office was blown out. Thankfully we had heeded one of the many warnings received of the impending blasts. On another occasion, a mortar was fired across Whitehall into the garden of 10 Downing Street.

But neither Argentina nor Irish terrorists threatened our national survival or our democracy. The unspoken assumption was that, give or take a few marginal issues, if we were equipped to deal with the Soviet threat we would be able to handle any other military challenge.

The DIS's responsibility to the MoD and the armed forces sometimes brought it into contention with other departments of state that went beyond the inevitable competition for funding from the Treasury. The two main areas were arms control and exports involving technologies which had defence applications. Dealing with such problems, I soon found myself, suitably escorted by a policy chaperone, haunting the offices of various ministers around Whitehall or in the Houses of

Parliament to explain the background to some specific advice we had offered.

None of the other departments of state had dedicated and experienced intelligence analysts and I soon began to realise that this was a fundamental flaw in the organisation, especially when it came to discussing the strategic technical subjects in which my branch was involved. In the scientific and technical area this was much more difficult for the 'gifted amateurs' that other departments relied upon. Consequently, the DIS specialists were an essential component of, and contributor to, the national as well as the departmental, intelligence capability.

Because of this, the priorities in our work were linked with those of the Cabinet Office and the Joint Intelligence Committee, whose function it was to coordinate the various departments with an interest and involvement in intelligence. However, our pan-departmental role and authority on specialist matters tended to be acknowledged by other departments only when our assessment were convenient to their policy requirements. When they were not they would charge us with departmental bias.

The intelligence business has three corners to its eternal triangle – collectors, analysts and customers. The main intelligence collection organisations included MI6 or the Secret Intelligence Service (SIS), which provided intelligence collected from human sources. GCHQ (Government Communication Headquarters) provided intelligence obtained from intercepted messages and signals. The Foreign Secretary was responsible for both MI6 and GCHQ. The Joint Air Reconnaissance and Intelligence Centre (JARIC) provided photographic or imagery intelligence. It was part of the MoD and managed by the DIS. The Security Service, more popularly known as MI5, also provided some intelligence. MI5 belonged to the Home Office but was not strictly speaking a 'collector' of intelligence. Its remit required it often to conduct rapid analysis of the information it collected and to organise an active response to it in the fields of counter-terrorism or counter-intelligence.

Within three months I had attended eye-opening courses organised by each of these organisations to explain the nature of the information they provided, how they obtained some of it, and to point out some of the pitfalls in interpreting it. I quickly formed the impression that each was staffed mainly by extremely professional, competent and imaginative personnel. GCHQ and JARIC were staffed mostly by 'backroom boys', much like ourselves. We received information into our offices and processed it. MI5 was more mysterious and far less visible to us. Its staff seemed to be forever 'out and about' vaguely 'doing things', with one or two liaison people calling in on us occasionally to ask us oblique questions without much context – 'Does the term "such-and such" mean anything to you?' or 'If I were to tell you "pigs might fly" what would you think?' MI5 has an important interface with law enforcement which places certain constraints on any information, including secret intelligence, that might be used in a prosecution. This sometimes acted as a barrier to MI5's total integration with the rest of the intelligence community.

But MI6 were the real thoroughbreds. They acted like the spies in the novels. They knew everyone in Whitehall and were everywhere. They were highly polished in all that they did. They drifted in and out of meetings unidentified or sometimes giving a false affiliation. But they always made sure everyone knew how clever they were. And they were clever. Occasionally over the years, I would leave a meeting with an individual or a team from MI6 with my mind reeling at the brilliance and audacity of some plan they had devised. They would only have told me in order to seek some background advice or to provide important context to information that they had obtained for us. There was always a great deal going on of which I, correctly, remained unaware, but this factor sometimes makes it difficult to be confident as an analyst that you have the best picture available.

As time went by I was to learn that, like their MI5 counterparts, MI6 sometimes organised action as a consequence of the information they received to prevent something happening or confound someone's plan. Often this would be in some far-flung corner of the globe. This was their 'James Bond' role. Acting at or beyond the limits of acceptable diplomatic behaviour, such business was afforded the very highest level of secrecy and security. This was played to maximum effect with the politicians and senior civil servants, demonstrating MI6 as a 'can-do' organisation that made things happen. The population at large expects that such things are being done in its name, forswears the democratic right of detailed oversight, and lends 'the system' an exceptional degree of trust over these matters. It is essential that 'the system' honours that trust.

The other part of the intelligence world I had to get to know was the central intelligence machinery. This was organised within the Cabinet Office and was directly responsible to the Prime Minister, placing him at the head of the intelligence community. It exists to coordinate the community and to ensure that assessments are independent of motives and pressure which may distort judgements. That is, independent of the vested interests of those who collect the intelligence and are likely to be biased in favour of their own input, and of those who will use the product who might be biased to interpret the intelligence to match their own policies or prejudices.

The Joint Intelligence Committee (JIC), which brought together the heads of the various elements of the intelligence community with representatives of the important policy departments that used the intelligence, was both a 'management board' responsible for directing the community and dictating its priorities, and a working committee that approved assessments. A main function of the central machine was to provide ministers and senior officials with coordinated intelligence assessments on a range of issues of immediate and longer-term importance to national interests, primarily in the fields of security, defence and foreign affairs. The assessments the JIC issued were used at all levels of government to guide policy decisions.

The JIC was served by the Assessments Staff, which was part of the command of the committee's full-time chairman and based in the Cabinet Office. It comprised about thirty senior and middle-ranking officials on temporary secondment from other departments for periods of up to three years.

The Assessments Staff was much too small to deal with the full range of subjects and fields of expertise that fall within the scope of the government's intelligence requirement. For example, during the years of my involvement, the Assessments Staff and the JIC often did not include a single technically qualified official. In fact in many areas, including WMD, the Assessments Staff served as little more than a powerful, able and well-informed secretariat for the JIC, marshalling specialist inputs from around Whitehall. As the major repository of all-source intelligence and career intelligence analysts and specialists, the DIS was often the only knowledgeable and experienced contributor to the process. Thus the laudable concept of unbiased assessment was undermined.

Members of the Assessments Staff entered the job with a subconscious bias inherited from the culture of their 'home' departments and perpetuated by their eventual return to those same ranks. Generally their lack of specialist expertise meant they had to rely on others in the intelligence community which, as noted above, was set up on departmental lines. When it came to disputes, the hierarchical nature of Whitehall could be a factor in their resolution, with the

Foreign Office and the Home Office having the bigger 'guns' in the form of the more senior and powerful Cabinet ministers at their head.

The Assessments Staff was led by its chief, who was a member of the JIC in his or her own right. The chief was supported by about half a dozen deputies, each of whom covered a defined geographical or subject area. The central machine would generate assessments. The JIC sometimes asked for an assessment, but the requirement was often triggered by a request from a department to inform a particular policy issue, or support an anticipated meeting such as a summit or conference, or even by some new, important intelligence. In an emergency, an assessment would be done quickly through informal consultation and issued immediately for retrospective approval a few days later by the JIC, which met once a week. More normally a planned programme of assessments stretching into the future was established, continuously revised, dealt with and updated. When necessary planned papers were overridden by matters of greater priority as they arose.

The normal process would be that, with or without the assistance of other departments, the relevant desk officer on the Assessments Staff would draft a provisional assessment and circulate it around Whitehall. It would then be reviewed and debated at a meeting called a Current Intelligence Group. CIGs involve a different group of people for each category of paper, and include middle-ranking intelligence collection and analysis experts in the relevant subject, as well as representatives from the government departments with a policy interest. Under the chairmanship of the appropriate Assessments Staff deputy chief, the CIG would consider the existing draft and work up and usually agree a modified draft assessment that would be sent to JIC members for consideration and minor adjustment before being submitted to the weekly JIC meeting for approval and formal issue.

CIG meetings are of fundamental importance in the British system and, although branch heads from the DIS did not normally attend them, I was initially keen to see some of them in action. For various reasons, including the often contentious nature of my field, I occasionally attended such meetings over the years. Because of their varied constitution and the competing interests of the participants, the dynamics of the meetings could be fascinating. The collectors were always keen to see their own intelligence included prominently in the assessment because it would demonstrate their worth. The customers would generally like to see an assessment compatible with existing or developing policy. Some of the customers, especially those from the Foreign Office which attracts the brightest and the best, displayed debating skills of the highest order to try and fit assessment to policy. From time to time I was filled with admiration, as well as annoyance, at seeing such high flyers, who clearly had little background knowledge, weave complex arguments around the expert contributor to convince the non-specialist deputy to shade a judgement to suite their department's purpose. Scientists fresh from the laboratory and the scientific leading edge were rarely used to debating with non-scientists, let alone such silver-tongued political operators. Until they adjusted, they were first baffled, and then thoroughly frustrated by the experience. Some were so outraged at having their scientific authority repeatedly challenged by people who were transparently ignorant in their field that they gave up in despair. Some became so disenchanted that they walked away from intelligence and quickly returned to the lab. There is little sympathy in Whitehall for those who are not familiar with its arcane ways.

Other devices were used to sway an argument. Early on I was involved in a CIG where the Foreign Office was clearly losing the argument until it was 'rescued' by a representative from MI6, keen to support its paymaster, who suddenly presented the meeting with some new intelligence 'hot off the press'. The rather bluff deputy who was chairing challenged me to change my mind in the light of this new information. Having listened to the evidence, I protested that I could not possibly do so until I had time to have my experts analyse it thoroughly and give it due thought.

'You can do it by the morning,' I was told.

I said that it was impossible for me to promise something like that until I had considered the detail and consulted others about it. Until then we would not change the DIS position.

A few days later I was called in by my boss, the director general of scientific and technical intelligence, who said the Assessments Staff was complaining that I was being uncooperative. Could I be more considerate of their needs in future? I was appalled that my boss did not even ask me about the detail of the issue. When I emerged from his office, his secretary told me she had never heard anyone shout at him like that before. However, it transpired that I had been right not to change my position and I heard no further complaints when I, or any of my staff, dug our heels in – not that we won every argument.

Intelligence was disseminated at various levels and in different forms. The JIC-approved assessments were sent to ministers, senior officials and to appropriate recipients throughout government. Really important papers were sent also to the Queen.

JIC assessments invariably offered a consensus view. As distinct from the practice for national-level assessments in the US,[2] minority or dissenting views were not recorded. If, at the end of its debate, the JIC was still uncertain, it could report agreed alternative interpretations of the available intelligence but did not attribute such views to individual members or organisations. However, there was always a great desire to avoid ambiguity and provide a unanimous assessment that constituted clear advice and this sometimes imposed a peculiar ritual on a JIC process which was designed to minimise, if not disguise, differences of view. What started out as a difference of assessment that required detailed explanation and argument with reference to the original intelligence reports often became distilled, as time went by, to a debate about wording so that an acceptable interpretation could be claimed by either side in an unresolved argument whilst maintaining a facade of unanimity. Thus a much more detailed debate might reduce to an argument about whether the intelligence 'shows' or 'indicates' a particular thing. If an analyst thought the evidence was not conclusive he or she would argue against the word 'shows' and in favour of the more equivocal 'indicates'.

One difficulty with a central intelligence process that provides papers for use across government is that the special interests and sensitivities of individual customer departments or organisations are not easily catered for in general assessments – one size does not always quite fit all requirements. It is important to remember that particular customer groups have specific requirements that do not necessarily match, and the focus of the assessment and the language used to describe it, ideally, should be tailored for its purpose. Unfortunately, the British system as it existed up to the time I retired did not have the capacity at the top (JIC) level to fine-tune assessments for individual customers. Even within the MoD, for which the DIS was able to provide assessments tailored to the needs of the individual customer, the existence of more ambiguous top-level assessments sometimes caused problems.

A good example of this, in WMD intelligence, is the differing requirements of the military commander and the arms controller. The operational requirement of the military commander is much less demanding than that of the arms controller (although his needs may be greater if he is concerned about the position of impending military action in international law). Once committed to a particular operational engagement he needs to know as much as possible about the likelihood of encountering WMD, its nature, quantity and means of delivery. He needs to consider if he has or does not have the capability to detect and protect against the threat to his forces and then he can decide what risks he might take and balance them against the possible consequences. He needs guidance on the probability of the threat arising but can accept and work around the uncertainty involved.

However, the arms controller demands a much greater degree of certainty, which implies a more comprehensive and detailed knowledge of the overall WMD programme, before he can make quasi-legalistic challenges about possession or capability in formal pursuit of those who renege on treaties or agreements. His accusations may ultimately be tested by independent weapons inspectors and voted on at the UN Security Council.

Politicians wanting to influence parliamentary or national or international public opinion about a particular policy must make judgements about the degree of certainty in the intelligence assessment that is required to carry their argument.

Chemical warfare

My hope that intelligence on chemical and biological warfare (CBW) would be a minor part of my responsibility was dashed within hours of taking up my post. Without any previous hint having been given, it was quickly revealed to me that my predecessor had been moved to a new job following a major disagreement over intelligence on chemical warfare. Furthermore, the chemical warfare desk officer would be moving to another job within a few months, for similar reasons. Although the details were sketchy, there had apparently been a breakdown in the relationship between the DIS and the Chemical Defence Establishment at Porton Down. In my first interview with the director general as a member of his staff with full clearances, he told me my highest priority was to rebuild a good working relationship with the CDE. I began to see that my main qualification for this job had been my near-complete ignorance of anything to do with CBW and the absence of any 'baggage' in relation to Porton Down. This worked because within weeks, by taking a very direct approach with the director general of the CDE, I was able to start the bridge-building process towards establishing an excellent working relationship that endured beyond my tenure. Dr Graham Pearson was the director general at the time, and I will be forever in his debt for the positive, considerate and enthusiastic contribution he made to this process. He made arrangements for me to visit Porton Down and any of his staff almost at will and I developed contacts with many of the CDE's leading scientists. It was about this time that I met David Kelly again and spoke with him from time to time on biological warfare issues. However, at this stage David did not become greatly involved with intelligence, not least because of his commitment to the decontamination of Gruinard Island.[3]

The dispute between the organisations had centred on the interpretation of intelligence gleaned from information on research and development in the field of chemistry in Russia that might be linked to military capability. In those days, in the depths of the cold war, there was little direct intelligence from well placed sources on our subjects. We had to work with scraps of secondary information about individuals and organisations which seemed to be related to military interests. In the chemical warfare field this had led to assessments of new chemical compounds that might be effective as weapons. Unfortunately, scientists can be very sceptical about the revolutionary new ideas of others and Porton Down rejected the DIS assessments as theoretically naive. Shortly before he died, I learned from Britain's long-retired first director of scientific and technical intelligence, Professor R. V. Jones, that the experts at Porton Down had rejected the notion of nerve agents, which was contained in intelligence brought back from Hitler's Germany during World War II.

A few months before I arrived in the job and unknown to me as one with no interest in such things at the time, President Gorbachev abruptly announced that the Soviet Union was ceasing the production of chemical weapons. Since it had not previously admitted to having such weapons, this was a very significant statement. It was enough to stimulate a thorough reassessment of the intelligence estimate and the process of producing a new JIC assessment was drawing to a close as I took up my new job. Because of the lack of expertise on the Assessments Staff, the DIS had been invited to write the first draft. The wrangling within the DIS and at the CIG in those first few weeks provided me with my first experience of both intelligence and chemical warfare. I was on a very steep learning curve.

Soon the UK was pitched into an exchange of 'confidence-building' visits between Soviet and British laboratories and although the main Soviet chemical warfare trials centre remained hidden from us at that time, what we learned from the exchange did nothing to increase our confidence in the old enemy.

I quickly learned about the very haphazard and unscientific process of intelligence assessment that was in place. It was quite often difficult to trace from the draft JIC assessments exactly what the base intelligence input was. Nonetheless we achieved what proved to be a groundbreaking assessment – chemical warfare was acknowledged as an existing Soviet offensive capability and a threat that had a new but poorly defined dimension. In its aftermath I insisted we would generate fully referenced papers in which the underlying intelligence was fully cited. It had some profound benefits but this approach to formulating assessments was something that never permanently penetrated to the Cabinet Office. Many years later I would reflect on what a problem that must have been for Lord Butler and his committee as they tried to review WMD intelligence in the aftermath of the 2003 Iraq War.

As time passed I learned about the complicated variety of chemical warfare agents that were possible and the wide range of scenarios in which they could be used. The technologies involved were complex: from synthetic chemistry through chemical engineering to aerosol technology; weapons engineering, storage and logistics to toxicology and medical counter-measures. I learned about British forces' poor state of preparedness at that time to deal with a chemical warfare threat and about arms control diplomacy and the control of the export of chemicals and equipment. I am struck now as I look back by the comment of the US presidential commission in 2005,[4] which, despite being very critical of the US community over Iraq and its WMD, said: 'We have been humbled by the difficult judgments that had to be made about . . . weapons [of mass destruction] programs. We are humbled too by the complexity of the management and technical challenges intelligence professionals face today.' It reminds me of what just a few of us had to cope with two decades earlier, in an environment that was reluctant to accept our assessments. The revelations accompanying the collapse of the Soviet Union, and the focus on the subject generated by the first Gulf conflict, would improve our credibility by demonstrating the existence of significant offensive chemical warfare and biological warfare capabilities which had previously been viewed with scepticism by many.

In 1987 and 1988, the threat from the Soviet Union was the dominant factor but we were also working on the problem of proliferation. Intelligence about a chemical warfare programme in Libya was accumulating, and Iraq was already employing chemical weapons in an otherwise primitive war with Iran that had raged for much of the decade. Iraq attacked the Kurdish town of Halabja close to the border with Iran in a region where Kurdish militants supported frequent Iranian incursions. It made the headlines because chemical weapons were used and caused many civilian casualties. There was no doubt chemical weapons had been used but it was never properly established exactly which chemical warfare agents or how many casualties they had produced.

Biological warfare

I neglected biological warfare for the first year or so that I ran my branch. The chemical warfare desk was very busy, there was not much intelligence coming through on biological warfare, the demands of export control were continuous, and I was so short of staff that I could afford to give it little attention. Luckily, there were no significant consequences of this and my appreciation of biological warfare was that much better for it being allowed to evolve in a more measured way. I could not have guessed at the time, and no one was able to warn me, what a major issue biological warfare would become.

When I think about the wider awareness of chemical and biological warfare in Whitehall in the 1980s, I am reminded of some words written in the aftermath of World War I. They were in an ancient report I came across by a military body called the Holland Committee. Its conclusion, reached in 1919, was of great significance in relation to weapon systems that the UK had abandoned thirty years earlier:

> It is impossible to divorce the study of defence against gas from the study of the use of gas as an offensive weapon, as the efficiency of the defence depends entirely on an accurate knowledge as to what progress is being or is likely to be made in the offensive use of the weapon.

Britain had opted out of offensive biological and chemical warfare in the mid-1950s. The Americans retained their programmes partly because they were just beginning to understand the additional dimension that scientific and technological developments were starting to offer, especially in the case of biological warfare. An appreciation of two factors combined to greatly enhance the impact that could be achieved with some biological weapons. The first was that only minute quantities of some biological warfare agent had to reach its target to infect a human being. The second was that the properties of aerosols (solid or liquid particles suspended in the air) provided a means by which amounts of biological agent could be spread over very wide areas in sufficient quantity to cause such infections. Although biological weapons had been available for decades or even centuries, it was not until there was a coincidence in the development of the understanding of micro-organisms and of aerosol technology that their potential to cause massive numbers of casualties – as weapons of mass destruction – was realised. It is noteworthy that this appreciation lagged the development of nuclear weapons by over a decade.

Through the 1960s, the Americans made great strides in their highly secret investigation and development of biological weapons. As well as exhaustive work in research and development laboratories, extensive aerobiology testing was undertaken, much of it in field trials covering vast areas of land and sea. Some land-based trials were conducted in which large numbers of American civilians were unwittingly exposed to notionally harmless micro-organisms. These experiments were designed to simulate the behaviour of real biological warfare agents. However, most testing was done at sea, mainly in the Pacific Ocean, where human exposure was minimal and, sometimes, real agents and animal targets could be used. The scale of the activity was so large that the fleet of ships the Americans devoted to this work would, on its own, have constituted the fifth largest navy in the world. In addition to the work done in the context of more traditional military scenarios, the Americans investigated the potential of biological warfare agents for covert delivery by individuals and small groups against both military and civilian targets. The vulnerability of the UK to attack from biological agents using aerosols and other delivery methods was confirmed by tests conducted as part of the British biological defence programme in the same period.

Towards the end of the 1960s the enormous success of the American biological warfare programme was, at the same time, the cause of great dismay in some influential circles which gained 'access' to the Nixon administration in its early months and years. That access was achieved mainly through Henry Kissinger, who was President Nixon's first National Security Advisor. The problem was that once the potential of biological weapons was understood, it became clear that, being so much easier and cheaper to acquire than nuclear weapons, they were within the reach of many countries that could never contemplate the nuclear option. Whilst the technical complexity and enormous cost of nuclear weapons was a challenge even to rich and advanced countries, here was a weapon of comparable, if slightly different, strategic potential that almost anyone could afford.

The American government considered the circumstances under which it, as a nuclear power, might wish to use biological weapons. It seemed there were very few. However, possession of them might stimulate other nations to investigate their potential. American intelligence assessments indicated that the Soviet Union's capabilities in the field of microbiology were lagging behind those of the West. Soviet biology had been severely retarded by the influence of deeply flawed political doctrine and, apparently, the Russians had not grasped the potential of biological weapons. The Nixon administration was persuaded that the dangers of continuing the US offensive biological warfare programme outweighed the advantages. On 25 November 1969 in Washington DC, the President, with frequent reference to his script, haltingly made the following announcement:

> Biological warfare, which is commonly called germ warfare . . . this has massive, unpredictable and potentially uncontrollable consequences. It may produce global epidemics and profoundly affect the health of future generations. Mankind already carries in its own hands too many of the seeds of its own destruction . . . Therefore, I have decided that the United States of America shall renounce the use of lethal biological agents and weapons and all other methods of biological warfare.

There was no hint in this statement of the success of the US programme. There was more than a hint that such weapons were uncontrollable, and this may have been playing on public perceptions of recent issues on which the US government was being widely criticised – the use of the defoliant agent orange in Vietnam, and a recent accident in a trial of nerve agent in the Rocky Mountains, which killed many free-grazing sheep. Whether or not Nixon's strategy amounted to a deliberate confidence trick from the outset – a clever double bluff as far as biological warfare was concerned – it soon became one. The administration may not have encouraged the view that Nixon's fine words concealed the disastrous failure of America's huge investment in biological warfare and that biological weapons were useless, but it chose never to challenge that perception as it grew over the ensuing years. On 14 February 1970 Nixon clarified that his decision encompassed toxin weapons as well as live biological agents. America now expressed strong support for British proposals for a biological weapons convention towards which it had previously been lukewarm.

Most appeared to swallow the idea that biological warfare was a waste of time but, unfortunately, the Soviet Union did not. It believed America's renunciation of biological weapons was a trick and that black programmes would continue in secret. Presumably, it was aware of some aspects of the huge US programme such as the vast field trials. They would have been difficult to hide. Moscow was unconvinced even by Washington's attempts to demonstrate its sincerity by sharing information on newly discovered micro-organisms such as that which causes Lassa fever. Even if Soviet science lagged significantly behind America's in the field of microbiology in the period around 1970, influential Soviet biologists understood what recent developments meant to the potential of biological weapons. Leonid Brezhnev, himself a scientist, was convinced and, as the convention was being negotiated, the Soviet Union embarked on a massive covert investment in biotechnology. Its aim was to exploit for military purposes the revolution in microbiology that was at last gaining momentum in the wake of Francis Crick and James Watson's discovery of the double-helix structure of DNA back in 1956.

Many in the American intelligence community urged caution over the complacent assumptions that were being made in Washington about the Soviet Union, but they did not have hard evidence and they were overruled by the politicians. Perhaps American policy makers were comforted by the sort of logic explained by the British Defence Secretary, Denis Healey, in July 1968, when he told the Commons Select Committee on Science and Technology: 'We have not felt it necessary, nor indeed did the previous [Conservative] government, to develop a retaliation capability here [with chemical or biological weapons] because we have nuclear weapons, and we might choose to retaliate in that way if there were a requirement.' Perhaps such logic was further attributed to the Soviet Union and this may have been a contributory factor in the eventual agreement in 1973 to a BWC 'without teeth' – that is, with no provision for the verification of compliance. This is exactly what the Soviet Foreign Minister, Andrei

Gromyko, had promised the worried Soviet military, whose investment in biological warfare was continuing to grow.

Unfortunately, a factor that most of the strategists in America and Britain failed to recognise was that the different political doctrines of the West and of the Warsaw Pact meant that the potential utility of the various weapon systems was also viewed differently. But that devil was in the scientific and technical detail of the subject. When that knowledge is married to a detailed understanding of modern warfare it quickly emerges that biological weapons have no easily definable place in a politico-military philosophy which is non-expansive, non-aggressive and based primarily on defence and deterrence. However, the expansionist communist thinkers had long appreciated and practised the subversion of capitalism by non-military means and aspects of biological warfare capability aligned closely with such an objective.

For the Americans the problem with what had become a confidence trick was that knowledge of the real truth had to be held close. In domestic democratic politics, the ratification of an international treaty relating to national security is a transparently sensible step to take. Thus after 1975, when the BWC entered force, the majority within government as well as outside it held the flawed perception that biological weapons were not particularly useful and that the BWC was proving effective. This left those concerned about the security risks of biological weapons with a mountain to climb in their attempts to warn their respective governments.

For the next fifteen years biological warfare defence was almost ignored in the West. Intelligence was neglected and research and development reduced. In Britain the Ministry of Defence cut back work so much that in 1979 it dispensed with its Microbiological Research Establishment at Porton Down.

Even as the Soviet Union, despite the huge investment, was experiencing difficulty with its biological warfare programme, clues about its activities did arise. However, intelligence assessments to this effect were fiercely resisted and undermined by poor political judgements. President Reagan's Secretary of State, Alexander Haig, reacted too hastily to incomplete evidence of the Soviet use of fungal toxins in remote areas of south-east Asia. US intelligence was put under unnecessary pressure to prove the claims and this led to their ridicule, especially by those responsible for ending the US biological warfare programme a decade earlier. Intelligence was said to have mistaken the 'yellow rain' caused by mass defecation from swarming bees for Soviet-inspired biological agent attacks on troublesome Hmong tribesmen close to the Chinese border with Vietnam and Laos. In the same period substantial evidence of an accident at a military facility in the closed city of Sverdlovsk in Siberia was rapidly dismissed by the same influential people as poisoning from the consumption of diseased meat sold on the black market, rather than the accidental aerosol release of anthrax spores from a biological warfare production plant. A decade later, after the collapse of the Soviet Union, the intelligence assessment of a military accident was revealed to be accurate.

As the evidence accumulated through the 1980s that the Soviet Union was engaged in a massive secret biological warfare programme, the prevailing 'wisdom' and entrenched attitude to biological warfare continued to exert an influence on the interpretation of what was being detected. To the West the tactical or operational utility of chemical warfare on the battlefield was easier to comprehend than the strategic value of biological weapons to a state that already had nuclear weapons. (America retained its 'more useful' chemical warfare capability beyond the Reagan administration into the Bush era of the early 1990s.) There was a tendency to explain the Soviet biological warfare programme as a drive to produce super-effective 'chemical warfare-type agents' for use on the battlefield. This conclusion represented the worst kind of mirror imaging – the reflection of Western value judgements in the assessment of Soviet thinking – and it was the prevailing view when I joined the intelligence community.

At that time, the Soviet Union was unnerved by the challenging 'Evil Empire' rhetoric of the Reagan administration. This was exacerbated by Reagan's investment in the ballistic missile defence programme, which became known as 'Star Wars' because the concept involved the interception and destruction of Soviet ballistic missiles outside the earth's atmosphere, thus negating their deterrence value. In December 1987, whilst accompanying President Gorbachev on a visit to the United States, Valentin Falin, who had been Soviet ambassador to West Germany at the height of the Cold War in the 1970s and was now the influential head of Moscow's Novosti Press Agency, attempted to get an important message across. With the benefit of hindsight we can reflect that he may have been acknowledging the impact of the surge in US defence spending on the Soviet economy by illustrating an alternative but dangerous response. He said in an interview on American TV:

> We won't copy [the US] any more, making planes to catch up with your planes, missiles to catch up with your missiles. We'll take asymmetrical means with new scientific principles available to us. Genetic engineering could be a hypothetical example. Things can be done for which neither side could find defences or counter-measures, with very dangerous results. If you develop something in space, we could develop something on earth. These are not just words. I know what I am saying.

Despite this brazen reference to biological warfare as a strategic factor in the superpower struggle, it took another three years and a significant intelligence breakthrough for the west to begin to grasp the strategic nature of the Soviet biological warfare programme.

Pasechnik

Vladimir Pasechnik defected to Britain late in 1989 from the institute he ran in Leningrad. His motives were unclear and probably complex but he told us his institute had been created specifically to support the Soviet offensive biological warfare programme and that he had been appointed in the early 1970s to lead it. The main surprise he had for us was that an important part of the Soviet programme was strategic in nature. It was aimed at selecting, improving and optimising lethal biological warfare agents and weapons based on micro-organisms. We had been fooling ourselves by believing the programme was about producing super-effective 'chemical' weapons. We suddenly had a wealth of scientific and technical information on the Soviet biological weapons effort that my branch did not have the capacity and, in some areas, the expertise to analyse. On advice from my biological warfare expert, I approached the CDE and asked if David Kelly could be nominated for additional security clearance and provide us with some assistance. Thus it was that he became involved with the intelligence community, and was eventually nominated to join the joint UK–US team that visited the USSR to conduct the first ever biological warfare inspections.

During the first half of 1990 we were busy analysing the huge amount of information Pasechnik was giving us. We were now sure that the Soviet Union had thought lethal biological warfare agents and weapons worth investing in even when it possessed a massive nuclear arsenal, and despite the existence of the BWC. Why did it need them and how did it plan to use them? There was a great deal of discussion. Most who heard about it displayed an initial scepticism, doubting that our source was telling the truth. Their subsequent reaction was to suppose the capability persisted through some irrational adherence to obsolete military concepts. But our intelligence was telling us otherwise.

The good relationship I had built with the CDE at Porton Down was invaluable at this stage. Key experts, in addition to David Kelly, were enlisted to help. The director general, Dr Graham Pearson, and I embarked on a programme of 'education' for anyone in Whitehall who would listen, from ministers to chiefs of staff and from select committee parliamentarians to Foreign Office diplomats. Graham, with the great advantage of rank, was able to gain access to more senior people and the message we carried seemed to be understood. We could not have anticipated how soon many of those we briefed would have to confront the problem of biological and chemical warfare – and, indeed, in 1991 the CDE became the Chemical *and Biological* Defence Establishment in recognition of the threat from both biological and chemical warfare.

MI6 rightly accumulated much kudos for having 'acquired' Pasechnik. JIC papers were written and the intelligence was shared with the Americans. The information quickly found its way to the highest levels and soon Prime Minister and President were involved. Diplomatic activity went into overdrive, Gorbachev was confronted, negotiations began. All this involved my branch in hectic amounts of work analysing what we had and writing papers and briefing to support top-level international discussions.

CHAPTER TWO

1990–2000: The First Gulf War and its consequences

Iraq invades Kuwait

My first awareness that something serious was at hand in the Middle East came one hot August evening in 1990 when I settled into a seat next to my boss on our homebound train from Waterloo. Travelling together was not routine but our journeys sometimes coincided. For obvious reasons of security we tended not to say much about work in these circumstances but he chose to on this occasion. He said quietly that I should be aware there had been much excitement all day in the upper realms of Whitehall because Iraqi forces were massing on the border with Kuwait. We discussed how this might influence our work but it did not seem a matter of primary importance to my branch.

Within days Saddam Hussein had occupied his country's tiny neighbour. He had not needed to call upon his arsenal of chemical weapons to do so. However, President George H. W. Bush, encouraged by Prime Minister Margaret Thatcher, resolved to evict him. In no time at all Britain was committed with the US to drive Iraq from Kuwait. In due course a broad coalition of countries was given United Nations approval to use military force to achieve this objective.

But at the highest level this decision seemed to have been taken without detailed consideration of the risks. Senior American and British politicians appeared to assume that nations prepared to meet the might of the Soviet Union could not be greatly troubled by Iraq. A 'can-do' military establishment, worried about having to offer up a 'peace dividend' from its budget, was not inclined to disagree. It seems that, although there was a general background awareness of Iraq's possession of chemical weapons and wider interest in WMD because of the Iraq–Iran war, this knowledge was not automatically linked to the military action that was being proposed.

It was, of course, immediately obvious to me and I quickly adjusted the main priority of my branch away from the Soviet Union's biological warfare capability and focused on the new and unexpected challenge our military had to face. However, the Soviet problem could not be ignored and it continued to compete for our attention. The intelligence we had on Iraq's WMD programmes had been generated and presented specifically for our arms control customers. Now we had to translate it into assessments of the risks to British forces and recast it in a form that would be useful to military commanders and those concerned with related diplomatic activity, rather than arms controllers.

We believed that the training of Iraqi military officers by the Soviet Union in the 1970s and 1980s would be a significant factor in their appreciation of how to use their chemical and biological weapons.[1] It was unlikely that the Soviets trained Iraqi officers formally in the acquisition or use of such weapons. Indeed, awareness of the Soviet offensive biological warfare programme was constrained even within its own military circles and the chemical warfare programme, although it offended no international agreements, was also a matter of great secrecy. Instead, visiting Iraqi officers were almost certainly given instruction in chemical and biological defence. But as a consequence they would have learned much about the weapons' offensive potential and concepts for their use in order to understand how to defend against them. The level of awareness achieved by the Iraqis would have been high since they were being trained by the most experienced CBW experts in the world. Through the 1980s they added to their knowledge by direct experience as they used a number of chemical weapons against invading Iranian forces and Kurdish populations in Iraq.

In the 1980s, some in the West had been keen to use Iraq to constrain the fundamentalist ayatollahs who gained power in Iran when the Shah was deposed. Presumably, Iraq's Western supporters were either unaware that Saddam Hussein was acquiring such high quality advice or did not consider there might be security issues that would affect the West in the short term. Early on in the war between Iraq and Iran it became clear that Iraq faced major problems due to the numerical superiority and fanaticism of Iranian forces. Something to even up the balance was desperately needed. Ignorance of the true potential of CBW may have contributed to the tolerance of, and possible assistance to, Iraq's programmes for such weapons from the US and other Western countries. Towards the end of the war with Iran, and perhaps contributing to the ceasefire, Iraq made extensive use of nerve agent weapons against massed Iranian forces which killed very large numbers. Now, a few years later, the resulting well-practised capabilities that Saddam had developed might be turned on the coalition.

The commitment to go to war to liberate Kuwait was made by a generation of politicians and senior military commanders in America and Britain who had not previously thought much about CBW. The major strategic military decisions relating to WMD had been taken in the late 1960s and early 1970s in America, even earlier in Britain – well before the current leaders were engaged at high levels of government or military service. They were suddenly confronted with a terrifying problem.

Graham Pearson and I rapidly developed an approach to help the British forces deal with the chemical and biological threat they might face from Iraq. My branch worked through the intelligence assessments and, together with the scientific and technical experts at Porton Down, we deduced what they implied in relation to military operations. Together, we generated and progressively updated detailed papers to provide guidance to military commanders. As part of the central intelligence community we were also contributing to the JIC papers which outlined Iraq's capabilities but, as part of our role within the MoD, we generated these more detailed descriptions of Iraq's capabilities. We explained what agents and weapons we knew the Iraqis definitely had, what we thought they probably had and described the additional possibilities that it would be wise for our forces to take account of, just in case. Our opposite numbers at the Defense Intelligence Agency in the United States seemed to be doing something similar and, as far as we could tell, our assessments did not differ greatly.

From a plethora of intelligence from multiple sources, we were sure that Iraq had certain identified chemical warfare agents, including nerve agents, and was capable of delivering them by a variety of well-known means. Although they could cause casualties and slow any military action down, these challenges should have been within the range that our forces could cope with from their Cold War training. But British and American forces were much more vulnerable to biological warfare agents. We could not be sure but our assessment was that Saddam probably had some biological weapons. It was judged credible that biological warfare agents might even be delivered covertly against British or American cities. Iraq probably had the capability to deliver them using its intelligence services, which had operatives in place. Unfortunately, Cold War preparations had largely neglected biological warfare since the BWC came into force in the mid-1970s. Our belated rediscovery from our Soviet sources of the USSR's wholesale but secret disregard of the convention was so recent that military preparedness in that field had not yet been regenerated to an appropriate level.

The small size and relative compactness of the British political and military system is a great advantage with regard to responding rapidly in a crisis such as this. Over the four months between the decision for military action and its commencement in 1991 many of the shortcomings in the preparedness of UK forces for the biological threat were rectified. Concern about the vulnerability of mainland Britain was recognised and, to reduce the threat, a number of Iraqis judged to be a potential threat to national security were detained and/or deported. But the comparative size and complexity of the American commitment to the Gulf conflict and of its homeland defence arrangements placed it in a more difficult position.

A problem for Washington

Lewis Libby, a deputy to the Pentagon's under-secretary for policy, Paul Wolfowitz, commissioned a study of the biological warfare threat from Iraq in the autumn of 1990.[2] It confirmed his worst fears: not only the US forces in theatre but the American homeland itself was vulnerable to a biological attack that Iraq appeared to be capable of making. Saddam did not need long-range missiles to deliver the agents to America. A surrogate terrorist group or a team of trained specialists using civil or public means of transport could mount a terrorist-style anthrax attack with very serious consequences. The Defence Secretary, Dick Cheney, was briefed and his department began its frantic action to improve biological defence. The chairman of the Joint Chiefs of Staff, General Colin Powell, was also soon involved. The National Security Advisor, Brent Scowcroft, led efforts to prepare for civil defence aided by a White House staffer called Condoleezza Rice.

The dawning realisation of the horrific possibilities must have led to a tortured few months for these individuals as they struggled with the problems of achieving rapid enhancements to America's defence against biological warfare attack. There were challenging dilemmas of whether to authorise the use of vaccines that were not yet licensed. Should civilian populations be inoculated? Should nuclear deterrence be activated? Almost overnight, the strategic potential and intractable nature of biological weapons were brought home to a generation which, until that point, had been blissfully unaware of the nightmare in store. Weeks before the US-led coalition began military action, Secretary of State James Baker, meeting with his Iraqi opposite number, Tariq Aziz, in Geneva, left him in no doubt of the personal consequences for Saddam and his government if Iraq resorted to such weapons. The unmentioned possibility of a nuclear response hovered over their exchanges.

Mercifully, the war came and went without the coalition having to face biological or chemical weapons. The question that remained for intelligence was: had Iraq possessed the capability we had assessed and for which the coalition had so urgently prepared itself?

Ceasefire conditions

The ejection of Iraq from Kuwait in 1991 led to a ceasefire that imposed certain conditions on Saddam Hussein. Coalition forces halted at or close to the Iraq border on condition that Saddam make a declaration of all Iraq's WMD capabilities and programmes, close them down, demonstrate to the United Nations that it had done so, and allow long-term monitoring to ensure they were not reconstituted. The exact requirements were defined in UN Security Council Resolution 687 of 3 April 1991. Responsibility for verifying Iraq's compliance with this resolution was given to the International Atomic Energy Agency (IAEA) in relation to the nuclear weapons programme and to a new, specially created United Nations Special Commission (UNSCOM) for chemical and biological weapons and ballistic missiles. All in all, this should have provided a rare opportunity for us in the intelligence community to compare our pre-war estimates to what Iraq actually had or was developing.

However, from the outset I was very concerned that in the two areas for which I had intelligence responsibility, biological and chemical weapons, it would never be possible to certify that Iraq had eliminated all capability. The problem was that a biological warfare capability was not necessarily represented by any unique, easily identifiable facility or any stockpile of agent or weapons. Small seed-stocks of micro-organisms could be hidden or acquired when needed. Significant quantities could be produced in equipment legitimately retained and operated for other reasonable, even necessary, purposes. The means to disseminate them against an enemy could be simple adaptations of spraying equipment for agriculture or modifications of ostensibly conventional munitions.

There was less of a problem for chemical weapons since large quantities and stockpiles were needed to be of military significance and these would take time to accumulate and were likely to become visible to intelligence in the process. But they could still be made from materials that were essential for a robust commercial chemical industry in plants that existed for legitimate purposes and which would require only slight modification to produce agents. In other words stockpiles could be generated from scratch in a few weeks or months. Because Iraq had already produced these things and used some of them in anger, it would retain the essential detailed know-how for many years. We tried hard to make sure the intelligence assessments of the time carried the right messages. However, although many understood it, it I believe it was not popular with politicians and diplomats to suggest they had signed up to something that fell short of a guarantee of totally disarming Saddam of his WMD capability. It also challenged the ultimate effectiveness of the existing BWC, for which Britain had been a prime mover, and, to a lesser extent, the Chemical Weapons Convention, which was being negotiated and for which the UK was pressing hard. Although we were not ignored completely, what we were trying to say was watered down and did not appear prominently in the JIC-level assessments. It was not our place to interfere with political decisions which were, anyway, dominated by American policy, but we succeeded in putting down a marker which reminded the reader that, even if Iraq did not retain actual weapon stockpiles it could probably produce significant quantities of biological warfare agents within days or weeks and chemical warfare agents within weeks or months. This form of words appeared in most assessments of Iraq's WMD capabilities for the next decade.

The WMD hunt begins

Despite the strict and intrusive ceasefire requirements accepted by Iraq, the environment in which verification of Saddam's compliance was attempted proved hostile from the start. It was made much more difficult by Saddam's decision, in contravention of Resolution 687, to commence dismantlement and destruction unilaterally. This obviously provided him with an opportunity to destroy evidence of activities or progress he wished to conceal. Iraq's initial disclosures about its pre-war programmes and capabilities were so far from our intelligence assessments they were not credible. Incontrovertible evidence that its nuclear facilities, equipment and materials were part of a programme to acquire nuclear weapons began to accumulate in the first few months of the IAEA investigation, but Iraq denied it all and continued to do so for several years. It tried to explain away some of the evidence by suggesting that it represented embryonic research that was being done to assist political decisions in the future should Iraq's security require its government to consider the development of a nuclear weapons capability. It acknowledged no more than a similar incipient interest in biological warfare. However, proof of the existence of a more advanced programme proved to be difficult for the UNSCOM inspectors to find. It was some years before significant progress was made on the biological warfare problem.

Iraq's possession of large numbers of chemical weapons and the prior use of some of them meant that it could not deny having an offensive chemical warfare capability. However, it soon became apparent that the regime was not willing to cooperate unreservedly even on chemical warfare.

'Supergun' and the Scott inquiry

Almost coincident with the ceasefire in the Gulf conflict, at the end of March 1991 a Canadian called Gerald Bull was murdered in Belgium. It turned out that he was an expert in ultra-long-range artillery who had links to the Saddam regime. Shortly afterwards the Iraq 'Supergun' affair erupted, which for the next five years was to prove a major distraction from what I considered to be my main job. As the matter broadened into wider aspects of arms-related sales to Iraq, several of my desks became involved. The atmosphere that pervaded Whitehall at the time was a disgraceful one in which the avoidance of blame was a guiding principle in a difficult policy area where the occasional mistake was inevitable.

There were three inquiries in all: one by the Cabinet Office, a second by the Trade and Industry Select Committee and finally, when it could not be avoided, a fuller inquiry by Sir Richard Scott which began in 1992, was conducted partly in public, and finally reported in 1996 in five massive volumes running to over 2,000 pages.[3] One of my staff became something of a scapegoat in all this and I was left frustrated that I was not able to help him escape the blame that was heaped upon him by those who bore the real responsibility. The whole experience was an education, particularly in some of the dark arts of MI5 and MI6. There were many reasons for the confusion which led to my colleague's victimisation. I believed a main cause was that he had been caught in a web of intelligence deception but Scott would not accept this and his report was critical of my desk officer.

I took two important lessons from the Scott inquiry. The first was to insist my staff committed every significant decision, disclosure or exchange to the record. The second was to be wary of the motives of others in a Whitehall environment that had a crueller and shabbier underbelly than I had previously understood.

Helping the inspectors

In parallel with the pressures of the Scott inquiry, there were the demands of Iraq. With Saddam Hussein still in power, Iraq remained a closed society ruled by terror. There were few useful secret informants and individuals feared being open with the inspectors. The inadequacy of Iraq's initial response in terms both of its declarations and of its cooperation with inspectors created suspicion. In order for progress to be made the verification authorities recognised that intelligence from national governments was necessary to assist with their investigations. Additionally, in the UK, as a result of our experiences in attempting to deal with the Soviet Union's CBW capabilities and programmes, we were beginning to understand more clearly the need for intelligence to work very closely with those involved in the verification of declarations.

For that reason we gave trusted inspectors, such as David Kelly, detailed intelligence briefings at very high levels of security. Arrangements were also made to provide appropriate lower-level, less comprehensive briefings for multinational teams about to embark on specific missions in Iraq. To deal with this the DIS set up a small cell of analysts to focus on the intelligence requirements of inspectors. The activity and the cell itself were given the codename Operation Rockingham.

Some have suggested that Rockingham was an organisation that additionally engaged in inappropriate activities, but I never had cause to suspect this. The initial claim of inappropriate activities came from former UN weapons inspector

Scott Ritter in an interview with the *Sunday Herald* in June 2003 in which he was quoted as saying that the role of Operation Rockingham was 'producing misleading intelligence on Iraq's weapons of mass destruction, which could be used as justification for action against Iraq'.[4]

Despite the low level of Iraqi cooperation, the inspectors dealing with nuclear and chemical weapons programmes made rapid progress. Our intelligence assessment of Iraq's chemical warfare turned out to have been reasonably accurate. We had identified most of the facilities and senior personnel involved in the programme, the type and quantity of agents produced, and the constitution and size of the weapons stockpile. Using some of this information and its own resources of inspection and interviewing, UNSCOM was able to press Iraq towards ever more credible declarations each of which was ludicrously named 'full, final and complete'. However, Iraq's reluctance to be any more forthcoming than it thought necessary to placate the Security Council created the impression, shared by intelligence and inspectors alike, that it was seeking to retain as great a chemical warfare capability as possible.

We had been less confident of the intelligence picture we had provided of Iraq's biological warfare capability. We were *certain* a programme had existed. We had thought that an offensive capability *probably* existed and that Iraq *possibly* possessed ballistic missile warheads filled with anthrax spores and botulinum toxin. Although no 'smoking gun' intelligence was available in the years before Iraq eventually admitted possession, our information together with suspicions arising from some tenacious investigations by a dedicated group of inspectors was sufficient to keep the process going long enough for the breakthrough to be made in 1995.

The key factor was the persistence of a series of inspectors: two Britons, Dr David Kelly, a microbiologist, and Lieutenant Colonel Hamish Killip, a chemical engineer, who had both developed experience of biological warfare inspections in Russia; an Australian microbiologist and intelligence analyst, Rod Barton; and a retired American senior defence scientist, Dr Richard Spertzel, a vet and former deputy commander of the United States Army Medical Research Institute of Infectious Diseases at Fort Detrick, Maryland. They pursued information about Iraq's purchase of 'growth media' that could be used to grow bacteria for biological warfare agents such as anthrax. That eventually forced Iraq to admit it had produced large quantities of the micro-organism that causes anthrax and of botulinum toxin. But Iraq continued to deny they had been put into weapons until

Lieutenant General Hussein Kamil, a son-in-law of Saddam, left Iraq for Jordan. There he was interviewed by the Americans and this appeared to prompt the discovery of a trove of incriminating documents on a chicken farm owned by Kamil.[5] It was suspected that the Iraqi authorities had placed the documents there to incriminate Kamil, who, it was claimed, had been conducting his own secret programme. However, they disclosed sufficient information so that Iraq could no longer deny biological warfare production. A series of progressive declarations between 1995 and 1997 indicated that our intelligence assessments had slightly under-estimated Iraq's biological warfare capability. Progress with a few biological warfare agents was more advanced than we had estimated and at least one agent in addition to anthrax and botulinum toxin was declared to have been loaded into bombs and ballistic missile warheads.

Kamil's apparent defection also pushed Iraq to finally acknowledge the existence of the extensive nuclear weapons programme that IAEA inspectors had uncovered. It transpired that the programme was considerably more advanced than intelligence had estimated before the war with respect to both the production of weapons-grade fissile material and the design and development of an implosion weapon.

The mismatch between the nuclear assessment and what was found in Iraq raised some interesting issues for intelligence and for arms control. It seems that intelligence analysts, whose experience was mainly in advanced Western nuclear technology, tended to focus on the sophisticated Soviet nuclear weapons programme and that meant they were not alert to the indicators of the more primitive programme that Iraq was pursuing. It may also have happened that, as a party to the Nuclear Non-proliferation Treaty (NPT) and subject to IAEA safeguards, Iraq was not monitored as closely by intelligence services as it might have been. Intelligence was stretched in the late 1980s and preoccupied with the much more urgent Soviet and Chinese programmes and with the activities of four non-NPT parties—India, Pakistan, Israel and South Africa. Perhaps there was a general presumption, false as it turned out, that the IAEA had Iraq covered. The question that follows from this is whether membership of the NPT, and the apparent verification of its compliance by the IAEA, which operated nuclear safeguards, provided some advantage for Iraq in the concealment of its illegal activities. The IAEA and its membership implicitly acknowledged this to be the case by identifying the need to strengthen safeguards after this episode.

During the period after the Gulf War up to at least 1995–6, there was a high degree of cooperation and collaboration between UNSCOM/IAEA and several national intelligence organisations. It was later, when the IAEA effectively closed the book on the nuclear programme but UNSCOM was unable to do the same with the biological and chemical programmes it was covering, that problems arose. The problem, especially in the biological warfare field, was that, although no 'smoking gun' could be found, UNSCOM did not feel confident that Iraq's declarations and future intentions were honourable. This uncertainty was shared by my branch and it became the official British position. It was a view shared by the other intelligence organisations that were closely involved, and it resulted in the UK and US governments insisting that the verification process be kept alive. Consequently, there was a demand on intelligence to justify the continuation of the process by providing leads for the inspectors to follow up. In the absence of tangible evidence, this led to UNSCOM being fed increasingly speculative information.

Opposing American and British policy, there were contradictory pressures for progress in returning Iraq to some semblance of normality from countries such as Russia, France and Germany. They appeared to believe that, in the absence of 'proof' of non-compliance, Iraq should be given the benefit of the doubt. This was despite the reservations of at least some of their intelligence agencies. At the same time, humanitarian organisations were highlighting the severe impact of economic sanctions on the long-suffering Iraqi population, whilst the Iraqi leadership benefited disproportionately from the UN's Oil for Food programme.

Iraq claimed in 1998 that it had discovered inappropriate intelligence activity by US participants and others on UNSCOM missions. I was not aware of any spying of this sort and I doubt that anyone in my branch thought such a thing was happening. I do not recall that we received any intelligence that was indicative of new access in Iraq, but my recollection of that period is not good because I spent a lot of time absent due to illness.

Another interruption

In the autumn of 1997 I developed acute angina and a medical investigation showed that I needed a heart by-pass. I was able to carry on working, at a reduced rate, whilst I awaited the operation and my boss was accommodating in allowing me to adopt a manageable schedule at the office and also work at home. My operation eventually took place towards the end of May 1998.

It coincided with an outbreak of underground nuclear tests on the Indian sub-continent. I am sure there was no connection. We had concerns that such tests might be in preparation during the early part of 1998 but did not have the evidence to predict them. The Indians had apparently found a means of avoiding satellite detection of their preparations whilst reassuring Western diplomats that no such tests were planned. I could not take a detailed interest in these events for several weeks and on my return to work I was faced with a mountainous backlog. One of the consequences of staff reductions is that there is little capacity to absorb unanticipated events and absences and little scope to take remedial action when they do arise.

This was a difficult time because the job really needed effort at a higher level than my health would reasonably allow. I discussed the problems at length with my director. He appeared to believe that my long experience and detailed background knowledge together with the support of an excellent staff compensated enough for the decreased effort I was able to offer. But because of the disruption I do not have a comprehensive recollection of a period that provided a vivid portent of what was to come beyond the millennium.

Terrorists and proliferators

1998 was a difficult year, particularly for the US.

With their underground nuclear weapon tests, India and Pakistan challenged the NPT although neither had signed up to it. They demonstrated what had long been understood and joined Israel and probably North Korea as countries outside the treaty that possessed nuclear weapons.[6]

It was proving impossible to be confident of eliminating Iraq's biological weapons despite the unprecedented access that the UN inspectors had, and this threatened counter-proliferation efforts generally. Arms control agreements would never provide as much access as was required of Iraq, casting doubt on whether they could ever work.

The Iraq problem may have seemed even worse to the US. Through the 1990s, the American focus in Iraq may not have been primarily on the elimination of WMD capabilities and potential.[7] It may have been that from the outset Washington saw the WMD issue as a means of achieving regime change. If so the US would have had an interest in delaying its resolution.[8] I do not know whether this objective was discussed between the UK and US governments. To most in Britain, within and outside government, the emphasis appeared to be simply on eliminating Iraq's WMD capabilities and I do not know anyone who thought otherwise.

The tacit US objective of regime change survived Washington's own change of regime from Republican to Democrat in 1993, when Bill Clinton replaced George H. W. Bush in the White House. But it remained undeclared. As time went by and Saddam continued to deny UNSCOM either proof that he had abandoned WMD or evidence that he had not, American efforts turned increasingly towards more direct action. Towards the end of Clinton's first term, in 1996, it appears that the CIA 'hijacked' a covert UNSCOM listening system. Its installation, by the CIA, had been approved by UNSCOM to assist weapons inspectors. America, as the initial recipient of the intercepts, used the intelligence it acquired from this source to underpin the organisation of a coup to overthrow Saddam in June of that year. Apparently, Iraqi intelligence detected, anticipated and confounded the plot.

The impact of such a clear demonstration of the American objective to depose Saddam is likely to have been an important factor in determining the Iraqi leader's subsequent attitude to WMD disarmament. Realising the Americans were so determined to remove him come what may meant that he had nothing to gain by demonstrating compliance and this would have markedly influenced the balance of the equation Saddam was looking at. The advantage for him in continuing to be seen as the hard man, possessing WMD and resisting the American pressure, would now be overwhelming. He might benefit from giving an impression of cooperation with UNSCOM to attract whatever diplomatic sympathy was available from France, Russia and Germany, but there would be no point in allowing any real progress.

This would explain why, after Iraq had acknowledged its biological and nuclear programmes in 1995, it did not take the obvious way out by cooperating fully with UNSCOM. It would have been a relatively simple matter for Saddam to ensure that the knowledge and experience of WMD gained up to 1991 was properly recorded, and all that was necessary for the restoration of a capability deeply hidden. With the endorsement by the UN Security Council that he had given up his WMD, sanctions would have been lifted and the international focus moved off Iraq. Within a few years Saddam could have discreetly reconstituted his programmes as circumstances allowed. 'Saving face' with his supporters might have been enough of an incentive to justify Saddam's decision not to do this. However, a knowledge of or belief in America's determination to be rid of him may well have been decisive. Saddam would have nothing to lose. But this was not something British intelligence analysts were aware of. If we had understood this, the possibility that he had no WMD or related active programmes might have loomed even larger in our analyses.

By 1998, deep into Clinton's second term, the Republicans were increasingly keen to attribute responsibility for the failing Iraq policy to their political opponents. The administration's need for progress was so acute that, in March of that year, Scott Ritter believes he became a pawn in an American plan, hatched and approved at Cabinet level, to precipitate a crisis.[9] This was to be achieved by forcing Iraq to deny access to a team of inspectors led by Ritter to a Defence Ministry building. The building in question was of genuine security concern to Iraq unrelated to WMD. Ritter claims that UNSCOM had no real interest in the building. But refusing access would be a breach of Iraq's commitment to the UN Security Council and could be used to justify direct military action by America. Their objective would be to oust Saddam. Ritter insists that the deputy head of UNSCOM at that time, Charles Duelfer, an employee of the US State Department, was deeply implicated in this plan. It failed because the Iraqis negotiated with Ritter and UNSCOM and eventually permitted access. However, the degree of complicity between UNSCOM and the US was becoming increasingly blatant, and what limited cooperation Iraq was prepared to offer deteriorated even further. To all intents and purposes inspections in Iraq were at an end.

Enter al-Qaida

Shortly after I returned to work in August 1998, another issue that had been simmering in the background for most of the 1990s suddenly came to the boil. On 7 August, terrorists inspired by the Saudi renegade Osama bin Laden attacked the American embassies in the Kenyan and Tanzanian capitals, Nairobi and Dar es Salaam respectively, and several hundred people, including US citizens, were killed. At the time this was of no particular professional significance for me since there was no suggestion that WMD were involved. The organisation al-Qaida was linked with the attacks. Bin Laden's concept of the al-Qaida network was original and inspired. Its loose association of a large number of dispersed and relatively independent terrorist cells connected through the internet and by mobile telephone meant al-Qaida was as virtual as it was substantial, and extremely difficult for nation states to deal with. It was becoming familiar to my branch because of hints and suggestions in intelligence of its interest in conducting attacks that caused huge numbers of casualties. It saw nuclear, chemical or biological weapons as a means of doing this.

My branch did not cover terrorism. Indeed it was not a significant concern of the MoD except in the case of Northern Ireland. However, we were consulted from time to time by MI5 when WMD issues were involved in their counter-terrorism work and we assisted them in the spirit of the MoD's responsibility to provide support to the civil power. I was interested in the terrorist-type concept of use of WMD, especially for biological warfare agents, because of the ideas that had emerged from the Soviet biological warfare programme about the covert delivery of agent. Biological warfare agents seemed an ideal 'terrorist' weapon. In 1993 the KGB, rebranded as the Foreign Intelligence Service, published a document which revealed that Russian analysts believed that covert delivery would be a significant element in any biological warfare programme.[10] This chimed with what Vladimir Pasechnik had told us. I had no doubt that the Russians were the most advanced thinkers on the subject.

In 1993, there had been an attempt to topple the World Trade Center in New York with a truck bomb in the basement car park. Although it did not quite succeed, and al-Qaida did not feature in any reports that I saw at the time, it was a clear indication of the intention by terrorists to cause mass casualties. There were unconfirmed suggestions that the explosive device was intended to produce hydrogen cyanide gas. I could see that the use of chemical or biological agents in similar scenarios would be a horrifying prospect. This prompted me to raise the issue at a secure international intelligence conference shortly afterwards.

I led British delegations to such secret meetings over many years. They were intended to exchange assessments and update and review the status of our knowledge on specific issues and to identify where future efforts should be directed. I used the opportunity to fish for more information on the rumours we had heard about the New York bombing. I did this by presenting a paper that also served to alert intelligence collectors and analysts to the future threat I anticipated of biological or chemical weapons used in the terrorist mode. Whether or not there had actually been a chemical warfare element in New York, we had now seen evidence of groups intent on causing mass casualties. My paper was speculative and some intelligence purists were critical of me for departing from our usual constraint of only dealing with matters on which intelligence actually existed. My own view was that there should be scope in our work to try and look beyond the horizon.

The following year, 1994, there were vague reports of terrorist attacks in Matsumoto in Japan in which a nerve gas might have been used. But details were sketchy and this was not our patch so we did not follow them up. Then in 1995, the whole world became aware of the 'apocalyptic' terrorist group Aum Shinrikyo when it made an attack on the Tokyo Metro using the nerve gas sarin. Fortunately, the method used to disperse the gas was crude and inefficient. Nonetheless a dozen died and there were thousands of casualties. The threat of mass casualty terrorism with WMD had arrived, much as I had anticipated. However, my prediction had been non-specific and could only have created general awareness and possible contingency planning. It was easy to ignore.

Although the embassy attacks in east Africa in 1998 used conventional explosives, President Clinton had to find a way to strike at the nebulous al-Qaida organisation. Three weeks after the attacks, on 20 August, he chose to go after elements of its loose infrastructure with cruise missiles. He targeted al-Qaida terrorist camps in Afghanistan in the vain hope of catching and killing Osama bin Laden at one of them.

Clinton also chose to link the atrocity with both WMD and Iraq. Previously, Sudan had welcomed the al-Qaida leader and hosted similar training camps. America struck a pharmaceutical factory called al-Shifa in the capital, Khartoum, which the US administration claimed had some involvement with the production of chemical weapons, facilitated by a tenuous link between al-Shifa and both al-Qaida and Iraq. It was reduced to rubble. Within hours I heard the British Prime Minister, Tony Blair, endorsing Clinton's action. However, we had no intelligence to support the American assertions and I informed my managers of this. Over several weeks we examined the evidence that became available. This included chemical analysis results of samples acquired from near the al-Shifa plant which purported to indicate the presence of a chemical compound unique for the production of a particular nerve agent. We found nothing to convince us of the links between al-Shifa and nerve agent production, or Iraq, but it was not long before Iraq was brought more strongly into focus again.

Operation Desert Fox

In December, President Clinton and Prime Minister Blair ordered the precision bombing of Iraq's 'WMD-related' infrastructure in a manoeuvre called Operation Desert Fox to demonstrate that its continued intransigence on WMD could not be tolerated. Since Blair, in office for little more than a year, first endorsed the attack on al-Shifa and, subsequently, was an enthusiastic participant in Desert Fox, it seems highly likely that Clinton had already shared his perceptions about strategic security, WMD and terrorism with the new British Prime Minister.

By now the direct involvement of my branch with Iraq and its WMD had been considerably reduced. The formation of Operation Rockingham separated us from the inspection process early in the 1990s, and a reorganisation of my branch at about this time meant that those non-technical analysts that kept a close eye on the detail in support of Rockingham were transferred to work under another director. We retained a responsibility for the assessment of the offensive WMD capability of Iraq but there was precious little intelligence on that. Our role on Iraq was reduced to the provision of technical support to others.

As Operation Desert Fox approached, the DIS came under pressure to provide suitable targets for the Allied bombardment of Iraq. Although those concerned with Iraq's ballistic missile programme were able to do so, we had no intelligence on the existence of any active biological or chemical warfare-related facilities. There was a strong suspicion that Saddam was concealing something and that he had plans to break out when sanctions and monitoring ceased but we had no real targets to offer. We did not see the target lists, which were the responsibility of the Americans, and so we had no idea whether our counterparts in the US were making any strong suggestions. I doubted it but we could not be sure whether they had additional intelligence they had not shared with us.

The operation lasted just four days, from 16 to 19 December 1998, and when the dust settled it transpired that our allies had offered no nuclear, biological or chemical weapons sites based on intelligence we had not seen. In the following months there was pressure on the Ministry of Defence to generate a public paper promised at the time of the 1998 Strategic Defence Review on defending against biological and chemical weapons. The MoD policy staffs, strongly influenced by those they were consulting in the Foreign and Cabinet Offices, tried to use it to suggest that Operation Desert Fox had been a great success in eliminating Iraq's chemical and biological weapons capability. I think they were genuinely surprised when the DIS responded that such a claim was not credible. They then tried to spin various forms of words to create the required impression. Strongly supported by the deputy chief of defence intelligence, John Morrison, we dug our heels in and eventually assented to a form of words that gave a good indication of the intelligence assessment at that time. We had no evidence of an existing biological or chemical weapons capability, nor any fear that such a capability could be of direct or immediate concern outside the region or within it. The following statements are from the published document:[11]

> Operation Desert Fox . . . was designed to degrade Saddam's ability to regenerate and deploy biological and chemical weapons and his ability to threaten his neighbours with these and other weapons.
>
> Saddam's ability to regenerate his biological and chemical weapons capability has been set back as a result [of Operation Desert Fox].

However, I feared that this might create the impression that the problem of Saddam's WMD had been resolved and I continued to warn people that intelligence was not all-seeing, that latent capabilities could be concealed relatively easily and that, because Iraq had done it all before, a capability, especially for biological warfare agents, could be regenerated quite quickly.

The intelligence on which Clinton and Blair acted in 1998, in relation to Sudan, Iraq, terrorism and WMD, was no better than that available to President Bush in 2002–3. The sequence of events, though, was similar – non-WMD terrorist attack followed by attacks in response against those who 'harboured' terrorists, and eventually military action against Saddam's Iraq. Bush's operations were on a scale magnified in all respects. Had Clinton's strikes produced the result he was seeking in 1998 things would almost certainly have unfolded differently. In the event, although Sudan further distanced itself from al-Qaida after 1998, the terrorist organisation continued to develop elsewhere, especially in Afghanistan, and Saddam had freed himself of UNSCOM inspectors without incurring the wrath of those inclined to support the removal of UN sanctions. Gradually he began to find more ways around those sanctions.

The creation of UNMOVIC

All IAEA and UNSCOM inspectors were withdrawn from Iraq before Operation Desert Fox. Early in 1999, a panel of the Security Council concluded that the bulk of Iraq's WMD programmes had been eliminated but thought the presence of inspectors in Iraq was necessary to ensure that Iraq did not retain, acquire or rebuild prohibited capabilities.[12] Iraq's refusal to contemplate the return of inspectors unless sanctions were lifted led ultimately to the demise of UNSCOM through 1999 and to the absence of inspectors from Iraq until late in 2002.

At the end of 1999 the UN Monitoring, Verification and Inspection Commission (UNMOVIC) was created with the adoption of UN Security Council Resolution 1284 and replaced an UNSCOM which was seen by many, even outside Iraq, as having been discredited by its association with intelligence. To preserve the separation between arms control and intelligence, its newly appointed executive chairman, Hans Blix, insisted that intelligence agencies would be kept at arm's length from UNMOVIC. He also appeared determined to ensure that some of the leading personalities in UNSCOM, who might be seen as tainted by intelligence connections, were not dominant players in the new organisation. As a result, some long-established links at the working level between individual UNMOVIC inspectors and intelligence analysts were lost and Blix apparently had no channel by which he might discover the views of the specialist intelligence analysts. It appears from his 2004 book *Disarming Iraq* that he was unduly swayed by high-level, politically inclined interpretations of the intelligence assessments available to them.[13] This was to prove important in relation to future developments and the war that followed in 2003.

Meanwhile, as the US presidential election of 2000 approached, the Foreign Office considered how the change of administration might affect British strategy on Iraq. It judged that sanctions would erode and recommended that attempts should be made to persuade the incoming US administration to support efforts to get UNMOVIC inspectors back into Iraq, if necessary by the removal of sanctions.[14]

CHAPTER THREE

2001: 11 September

The world changes

After eight years in opposition, several Republicans who had served President George H. W. Bush at the time of the Gulf War in 1991 returned to office in January 2001 as part of the administration of his son, President George W. Bush. They had watched with frustration as the Clinton administration wrestled with a small war in the Balkans, hesitated on WMD proliferation and floundered in the face of the Iraq problem and the growing new threat from global terrorism. In the mid-1990s they claimed, with a good deal of spin that relied heavily on fading public recollection, that President Reagan's Republicans of the 1980s had engineered the end of communism. It was convenient to forget how surprised the first Bush administration had been by events at the time. But, in the wake of that 'victory', they now believed America had not grasped the reward it deserved. Had the Republicans remained in power, they would surely have claimed it.

Amongst those who found themselves inhabiting familiar territory before 2001 was out, Vice President Dick Cheney and his chief of staff and national security assistant, Lewis Libby, Secretary of State Colin Powell, National Security Advisor Condoleezza Rice and deputy Secretary of Defence Paul Wolfowitz were the more significant players. Iraq and its WMD rose towards the top of the political agenda again in the wake of the 9/11 attacks, apparently propelled there at the deliberate instigation of some of that number.

When Bush the son became President he was warned by the departing administration that the greatest threat to the security of US citizens was from terrorism and from the proliferation of WMD. President Clinton had come to understand the special security challenge of unconventional weapons. He had read with great interest Richard

Preston's book *The Cobra Event*[1] – a strange concoction of near truth and fiction that imagined a potent mix of national and terrorist biological warfare capabilities launched against the continental United States. Clinton consulted with his experts in and out of government and had become convinced that biological weapons were a special concern because of the relative ease with which a capability could be developed without detection, and the problems of verifying compliance with arms control agreements.

Bush's White House was initially more focused on the WMD issue, and the implications of their possession by 'rogue' states, especially Iraq, than on terrorism. Diplomatic means for containing both WMD and terrorism were failing because many of the nation states of concern were beyond influence and too many other states, especially on the Security Council of the UN, lacked the inclination to address the problem.

There was no great inconsistency between the Bush administration's attitude to these problems and its immediate predecessor's, but one important difference was that the newcomers had less patience. They felt that the most powerful nation in the world should not passively endure potential strategic threats which could inhibit the pursuit of America's global objectives.

Throughout 2001 there had been a steady stream of non-specific intelligence about al-Qaida's determination to achieve mass casualty attacks against the West and its interest in WMD as a means of achieving this. Without knowledge of where, when and how such attacks were planned to take place it was difficult for the officials concerned to react. Politicians do not take kindly to the receipt of warnings that are not accompanied by suggested solutions. But even vague warnings should at least generate an alertness in those concerned with security. Despite this, and a few significant straws in the wind, the Bush administration was caught totally off guard by the terrorist attacks of 11 September 2001 on New York City and Washington DC. The nature of what happened, the use of commercial airliners as weapons of mass destruction, may have been a bolt from the blue to senior politicians, but there was to be a subsequent demonstration that the administration would have been equally wrongfooted by a mass-casualty attack using a more familiar form of WMD. It appears that Bush and his cabinet were not good on detail.

In the crisp morning light of 11 September, vivid television pictures captured not only the monumental events of that fateful day, but also images of individual terror and a multitude of personal tragedies. The images that were transmitted almost instantaneously across the globe fixed the whole world in those moments and burned deep into the minds of billions. For a great many, national boundaries were blurred and cultural barriers lowered, and *Le Monde* was even to declare 'We are all Americans'.

The palls of horror and grief that hung first over Manhattan spread steadily over city, state, nation and beyond, signalling that the whole world was to be changed, as much by a collective imagining of the implications of what had happened as by the immediate consequences of the incident itself. To the south, in Washington DC, a smaller impact on the Pentagon that produced fewer victims also lacked the vivid images of the event in New York.

The attacks demonstrated, beyond the previous reservations of many senior politicians and officials, that some terrorists saw their grievances as global in nature. They sought to produce casualties at the level normally associated with WMD and were organised, imaginative, ruthless and, above all, suicidal enough to achieve this even in the American homeland. Here was the fanaticism of the Japanese suicide pilots that devastated the US Pacific fleet at Pearl Harbor, visited on the mainland more than half a century later. America's lack of experience of atrocities by large groups of well-organised terrorists was an important factor in its ensuing response. Countries such as Britain, Spain, France and Israel, which have lived for decades with terrorism, loss and frustration at the absence of any meaningful way of hitting back that would eradicate the threat, understood the need for patience in addressing the problem. Islamic fundamentalists were displaying a growing propensity to link their lives to their cause and offer themselves as suicide bombers to produce small numbers of casualties, but most people had not, up to this point, translated this to a global terrorist threat on a scale that could project itself so far and produce thousands of deaths. That shocked realisation conditioned the world to America's impatient response and drew sympathy from many quarters for their action in Afghanistan.

Two American intelligence analysts on a liaison visit to my branch huddled with the small crowd of my own staff around one of the few television sets in our part of the Old War Office Building on that fateful Tuesday. Together we watched as the terrible event unfolded. We all turned a shade paler when the second aircraft hit and confirmed that the first strike was no accident. Our visitors were, understandably, even more shocked than the rest of us. It was many days before they managed to get home to their loved ones and their much-altered country.

Anthrax letters

The scale of the tragedy in New York evoked the threat of WMD and, as if to underscore that message, before September was out the US authorities were further challenged with a 'weapon' they could more readily associate with the acronym. Small quantities of anthrax arrived unannounced at a number of media organisations in the eastern United States – one in Boca Raton, Florida and four more in or near New York City. Letters and possibly a package appear to have been posted on 18 September from Trenton, New Jersey to news media offices in Florida, Washington DC and New York City. They contained small quantities of anthrax spores as a white powder. A rudimentary handwritten note made a link to 9/11. Fortunately, the powder was not in a form that readily found its way into the lungs of those exposed when the letters were opened. The main effect was infection of the skin where abrasions already existed rather than respiratory infection, which would have been much more serious.

But a few days later, into October, government buildings and a postal sorting office in Washington DC were contaminated, this time with a much finer powder that more readily formed an aerosol which entered the atmosphere and was easily inhaled. This second batch of letters was posted in Trenton on 9 October. In all twenty-eight people are known to have contracted the disease and five of them died. The deaths occurred as far apart as Florida, Washington DC, New York City and Connecticut. Whether the perpetrator understood that the envelopes would leak a few anthrax spores, or that the robust action of a mechanised envelope sorting system would contaminate postal buildings, or that the cross-contamination to other envelopes would occur, is not known. It may never be known whether the targeting was specific to the addressees or intended to have a more random element, and in fact it could all have been much worse than it was. Although the casualties were few, the panic and disruption that ensued brought the US mail to a halt and was very costly.

The anthrax attacks will have resonated strongly in the minds of those members of the Bush administration who had wrestled with biological warfare issues and Iraq a decade earlier. It is more informative than surprising that several amongst this group of politicians leaped immediately to a presumption that there was a link to Iraq, or *international* terrorists, or both. The inability of the security agencies to identify the perpetrator of the anthrax attacks or to establish such links in the following months and years served only to emphasise the intractable nature of the security problem America faced.[2]

It may well be that this is the factor that cemented together a number of arguments that already existed for regime change in Iraq. Vice President Cheney seemed already to have formed the view that the standard of proof of malign capability and intent required to trigger an American security response would have to be lowered.[3] The anthrax letter incident illustrated clearly that irrefutable evidence to identify the perpetrators of a covert biological warfare attack would be hard to obtain and so the United States would have to act to defend itself without it. The previous administration had already taken tentative steps in this direction following the east African embassy bombs, with the attacks on al-Qaida in Sudan and Afghanistan and with Operation Desert Fox. But President Clinton's limited response had not worked. There must have seemed only one option now at the end of 2001. President Bush had to demonstrate even more clearly the limit of America's tolerance.

But the diffuse network of terrorist groups and individuals to which al-Qaida gave financial, practical or notional support could not be deterred in the way a nation could. It did not offer a target that could be isolated and subjected to a retaliatory military strike. No 'regime change' option, as it were. So what was the President to do?

It was recognised that al-Qaida needed at least semi-permanent bases to establish and train their franchisees, acquire weapons and plan and practise attacks. It was clearly necessary for America to concentrate on denying them the opportunity to organise, plot and prepare. Having been kept out of Sudan in the only obviously successful element of Clinton's 1998 action, intelligence showed that Osama bin Laden was now relying mainly on the Taliban regime in Afghanistan to provide an environment in which preparations could be made for a wave of global terror. This furnished Bush with the opportunity to demonstrate beyond doubt that any regime that offered this sort of support to international terrorists would be forcibly removed and replaced.

The British perspective

There is no doubt that Tony Blair grasped immediately, in general terms, the American perception of where the greatest security threat would lie in future. He articulated that view rather more eloquently than President Bush. Blair stated often after 9/11 that he believed terrorism and WMD to be *the* security threat of the twenty-first century. Despite the earlier availability of ample evidence on terrorism, and his personal engagement with Desert Fox in 1988, he gave no indication that this realisation had dawned on him before 9/11. For example, in 1999 he rather hurriedly invented a foreign policy 'vision' to explain to the world when he had a global stage on which to perform during a visit to America.[4] In April, before going on to meet President Clinton, he gave a set-piece speech in Chicago that conveniently embraced the pre-existing policy of engagement in the Balkans into his broader if somewhat shallow new thinking which has been labelled 'liberal interventionism'. His grand idea was that, in the absence of any significant 'threat', countries like Britain and America could choose to intervene whenever they judged they could be a 'force for good' in the world.

I cringed when I heard this. Blair's imaginary 'threat-free' environment was apparently not cluttered with concerns about either the WMD or the terrorists that would loom so large once they were illuminated by the events of that single day some 2½ years later. My somewhat parochial interpretation of the Prime Minister's Chicago speech was that he was trying to charm both his own party and the wider British establishment by being all things to all people. He needed an excuse to maintain defence spending and the armed forces to retain the support of a still quite conservative Middle England at a time when New Labour's more traditional supporters had expected the government to divert more funds away from defence in search of a Cold War peace dividend. However, 'old Labour' already had a penchant for involving itself in support of the under-privileged beyond Britain's shores so the new doctrine was a neat political shuffle. It was already in my mind, though, that piecemeal military interventions could stimulate new threats to Britain which would replace the one that had supposedly disappeared with the Warsaw Pact and Soviet Union.

During 1998, I had tried hard to introduce a note of caution in papers on the WMD threat being prepared by the JIC to inform a Strategic Defence Review that was in progress. I had much time to contemplate this matter as I spent a good deal of that year away from the office as I awaited and recovered from heart surgery. 'Asymmetrical' warfare, in which poorer nations, including 'rogue states', might be able to use unconventional weapons to punch above their military and economic weight, had been much discussed in defence circles through the 1990s. I added to this my belief in the potential of biological weapons. We had convinced Whitehall in the run-up to the first Gulf War in 1991 that the country was vulnerable to covert attack with biological warfare by special forces or intelligence agents and some precautions had been taken. But seven years on, that underlying vulnerability was no longer widely understood. This despite the first terrorist attack on the World Trade Center in New York in 1993, which had provided early evidence of the global reach and mass casualty objective of some terrorists. The sarin attack on the Tokyo Metro in 1995 added to the picture by demonstrating that some terrorists would pursue WMD. The growing indications in intelligence of Osama bin Laden's interest in chemical, biological and nuclear weapons, which had been mentioned in JIC assessments, emphasised the point. Whilst terrorists might initially struggle to produce weapons capable of causing massive casualties, I was especially concerned in the short term that a nation state with biological warfare capabilities would have the potential to use such a weapon employing the tactics and guise of terrorist groups to avoid attribution and retaliation.

I summarised my thoughts for colleagues in Whitehall, identifying ten key points in an unclassified note I prepared during my period of sick leave. It provides a good indication of perceptions at that time – before our participation in Operation Desert Fox against Iraq and before there was any clear understanding of the nature and objectives of al-Qaida. I judged that risks to the UK were low and likely to become significant only if they were stimulated by government policy. I also thought that the civilian population would be at greater risk than deployed forces. Although there was an acknowledgement of some elements of my argument in the resulting JIC paper, the cautionary advice achieved no prominence and apparently no penetration to No. 10.

Despite the further accumulation of background intelligence, by the end of the millennium the potential threat of mass casualty terrorist-type attacks using WMD had apparently not been accepted by the government department responsible – the Home Office. There was no reason why they should not have been better informed but I believe a blinkered mindset about terrorism persisted for too long in Whitehall. The narrow attitude was a misleading product of many bitter years' experience of the Provisional IRA – a terrorist group with the focused political objective of achieving a united Ireland. Attacks causing large numbers of casualties were understood by these terrorists to be counter-productive to their aim and would lose them the support of the community they relied upon for shelter, finance and foot-soldiers. There was a failure at the higher levels of Whitehall to realise that other terrorists would not necessarily be similarly constrained.

After 9/11, Blair proclaimed Britain's vital interest in the benefits to be gained from the progress of globalisation. Further progress depended on 'order'. The danger was 'disorder' as threatened by the 'new' breed of terrorist that had emerged. Avoiding any reference to Islam, he suggested that the terrorists and the states that support them did not have conventional military means to pursue their aims and that their weapon was 'chaos'. They saw WMD as the means of precipitating that chaos. Blair believed that where UK security was under direct threat, there would have to be recourse to arms. He identified the risk as being that terrorism and states developing WMD would come together, and he noted that, although it had not happened up to then, there were clear pointers that it was likely.

I am not aware that there had ever been a detailed discussion involving Whitehall intelligence specialists about the issue of states supplying or 'enabling' terrorists with WMD. I cannot recall the matter being addressed by the JIC in any overarching way. If there was ever such a debate, the WMD experts in my branch were not involved. The link the Prime Minister made between national capabilities and terrorism was rather simplistic. It is likely to be an important factor with regard to nuclear weapons. However, it is much less significant for biological or chemical weapons, where the scientific and technical concepts involved are simpler and the means of production and deployment much less challenging. Of course, the assistance of experienced personnel or the provision of equipment and methods would speed progress to the acquisition of a useable capability, but the evidence is that independent terrorist groups could eventually succeed without such help.

Blair's declaration that he *suddenly* understood in September 2001 the implications of the potential threat from terrorism and WMD is not easy to explain. It suggests he did not fully understand the background to President Clinton's military strikes in Sudan and Afghanistan in 1998, which he enthusiastically supported. Although he did not articulate it, I assumed such thinking was his justification for the destruction of the al-Shifa pharmaceutical factory. That rationale was underlined by the simultaneous attacks on al-Qaida terrorist training camps in Afghanistan, and direct British military participation in the attacks later in the year on Saddam's Iraq that were designed to force cooperation on the elimination of WMD. Even if Blair's prime motives were to cement his relationship with the President and bolster support for action in the Balkans, the relationship between chemical weapons and terrorism implicit in the American reaction was impossible to overlook.

It is difficult to gauge to what extent the British Prime Minister really understood the detail of the potential threat from WMD in general and biological warfare agents in particular. Rather than request briefings, Blair's Downing Street preferred to establish studies by its own 'appointees'. Their remit – to cut through the complexity and relative insularity of Whitehall's departmental approach – and their confident all-knowing personalities led to somewhat blinkered reviews because the contributions of experts were curtailed. We were invited to comment on at least some of the draft papers on WMD, invariably at short notice. The ones I saw were not very good. I was not confident that the comment we made on these drafts ever penetrated the filters that existed between our lowly altitudes and the more stratospheric climes. First, DIS-wide inputs were 'coordinated'. They were fed into the MoD-wide view where they were further rationalised before the departmental response was sent across Whitehall to the Cabinet Office to be combined with inputs from other departments. Each stage was one step further removed from the main focus of knowledge or 'centre of excellence' on the subject. Short-circuiting the careful but inevitably slow consultation mechanism of a traditional civil service process in this way was an extension of attempts to streamline the way government worked that had been going on for over a decade. The quest for improved efficiency appears to have had the unfortunate consequence of confusing status or rank with knowledge. An overview to take account of the 'bigger picture' is an essential part of the process but the art is not to undermine the quality or influence of the detailed individual contribution of the experts. Unfortunately, the inadequate distillations that resulted under Blair were partly a consequence of the omission of some of the vital ingredients.

Following 9/11 the Prime Minister argued that if Britain and America walked away from the issue of al-Qaida in Afghanistan, and Iraq and weapons of mass destruction, the West would have been completely powerless to deal with other threats to do with terrorism and WMD in the future. However, to gain the respect of those you are dealing with and to move them in the right direction, it is essential that your decisions are firmly based and that your purpose is transparent.

Afghanistan

In the second half of September 2001 a dossier for public consumption was commissioned by Downing Street to explain that al-Qaida was responsible for 9/11 and, we presumed, to help justify British participation in the invasion of Afghanistan. My branch was called upon to provide draft contributions to this document. We had few problems with it and were happy with the final product although the intelligence agencies seemed concerned about public access to information synthesised from the information they had collected. The Afghanistan/al-Qaida dossier was never advertised as the product of the intelligence community.

As the operation to remove the Taliban from power was in progress, any reservations that may have existed about the terrorists' WMD ambitions were quickly eliminated by the discovery of documents and facilities belonging to al-Qaida which showed its interest in nuclear, chemical and biological weapons and the means to use them against their declared enemies in the West. In particular, the discovery of a laboratory near Kandahar in a remote area of southern Afghanistan indicated a determination to develop biological warfare agents such as anthrax. It appeared to have been close to success, or may even have already succeeded.

To develop WMD the terrorists had sought the help of expert scientists and technologists. The experts most able, if they had been willing, to help terrorists would have learned about WMD in the weapons programmes of 'rogue' states or the Soviet Union. President Bush believed that a rogue state might work covertly with a terrorist group to attack the US with WMD, hoping it could avoid retaliation by denying involvement. That risk had to be reduced. Nations that actively opposed the US could not be allowed to develop weapons that they could use, directly or indirectly, to exert influence on the US disproportionate to their economic or conventional military capacity. This led to the policy of pre-emptive military intervention mainly as a deterrent to the development of WMD. Such a policy had been mooted in Pentagon circles a decade earlier, before George H. W. Bush lost the presidency. As soon as his son's administration was in office the idea was resurrected and it was eventually declared as policy in June 2002. By then, Vice President Cheney had already understood that it meant action might be necessary on the basis of probability rather than 'smoking-gun' proof.

There was a need now for a clearer, more impressive lesson to be given to proliferators than the partial warning that President Clinton had given in 1998. After the liberation of Kuwait in 1991, Saddam Hussein had been demonised as a threat to the region and for his treatment of his own citizens for over a decade. There was no disputing that Iraq had developed and used chemical weapons, completed development of some biological weapons and sought nuclear weapons. It was widely held that the reason for Saddam's prevarication with the weapons inspectors was because he retained his ambition to possess WMD and probably still had some capabilities, despite long ago agreeing to eliminate them. He had refused to obey related Security Council resolutions for over a decade. He was implicated in an attempt to assassinate the current President's father. He was a source of instability in a region of strategic importance to the US and its energy demands. Consequently Saddam's Iraq was a target few Americans would argue about. Iraq represented the clearest opportunity for Bush to demonstrate America's determination to eliminate all potential WMD threats, especially if its action could be linked to the highly emotive 'war on terror', which already had huge domestic and wide international support.

Insiders probably realised that regime change in Iraq would not eliminate the threat completely, but judged that it would make a major contribution. Nations wondering whether they should join the WMD 'club' would understand what it might cost them to do so. Nations that were already on that road would be given cause to think again and turn back. Nations that thought terrorism was a way to undermine US global hegemony, whilst avoiding retribution, would learn that mere suspicion of an association with terrorists could cost them dearly. All of the countries and organisations involved would know that the United States would err on the side of caution (from *America's* point of view) – the US would get its retaliation in first, in the interest of the safety of its own citizens and national security.

So the stage was set for US action against Iraq. Bush was prepared for America to go it alone, but a partner in the enterprise was highly desirable. The quest to identify exactly when Tony Blair determined that he was prepared to commit British forces directly to an invasion of Iraq has prompted an unwarranted degree of interest and speculation in the wake of the event. Britain's commitment over a decade to the enforcement of the Iraq no-fly zone, its token participation in Operation Desert Fox, its eagerness to play an active role in the military operation in Afghanistan, together with the Prime Minister's declaration of solidarity with America after 9/11 were all tangible indicators that such an undertaking was possible, if not likely. However, no leader would, or could, make an absolute commitment to such a venture when any one of a number of domestic or international developments could have intervened before it commenced. The suggestions from within the Bush administration that Iraq was implicated in the 9/11 attacks and in the subsequent anthrax letter attacks set the alarms ringing around Whitehall. It is reported that as Blair swept through the Middle East in October, garnering support for America's Afghanistan strike, he was concerned that any overt threat of the invasion of Iraq from Washington would undermine his objective. The corollary of that is that he must have been well aware of the possibility. What is clear from a retrospective analysis of subsequent developments is that he fully understood that those in the administration who were openly advocating it might well gain presidential approval for military action. After all the policy was in place. President Clinton had already established that the American objective was regime change in Iraq.

PART II

DECEPTION

CHAPTER 4

January–July 2002: Iraq ascendant

Iraq, WMD and the State of the Union

On Tuesday 29 January 2002, on Capitol Hill in Washington DC, President Bush gave the annual State of the Union address. He began by celebrating regime change in Afghanistan, where the Islamic Taliban government had so recently and efficiently been removed from power. He made the link between terrorists and the nations that shelter and supply them, blurred the difference between them and then won applause when he introduced WMD into the equation by saying: 'We must prevent the terrorists and regimes who seek chemical, biological or nuclear weapons from threatening the United States and the world.' He singled out Iran and North Korea and then said: 'Iraq continues to flaunt its hostility toward America and to support terror. The Iraqi regime has plotted to develop anthrax, and nerve gas, and nuclear weapons for over a decade.' He conjured images from Halabja in 1987 of 'the bodies of mothers huddled over their dead children'. The President claimed that Iraq had 'kicked out' UNSCOM inspectors.

Bush asserted that those three countries – Iraq, Iran and North Korea – constituted an aggressive 'axis of evil' that posed 'a grave and growing danger' to the world. He drew further applause by saying: 'I will not wait on events while dangers gather. I will not stand by as peril draws closer and closer. The United States of America will not permit the world's most dangerous regimes to threaten us with the world's most destructive weapons.' It did not take a lot of imagination to appreciate that Iraq was firmly in his sights.

A frantic reaction in Whitehall

It is doubtful that anything the President said was new to the British Prime Minister. What may have surprised him was that the President was prepared to say these things publicly and in the State of the Union address, which has such a prominent place in America's political calendar.

The realisation of Bush's determination to act on Iraq seems to have spurred No. 10 to undertake an assessment of the implications of such a development for Britain. But few in Whitehall were aware it was taking place. The Foreign Office was not asked to do it, but it was undertaken by the group of Cabinet Office foreign policy advisers in the Overseas and Defence Secretariat. The secretariat was overseen by Sir David Manning, a very senior Foreign Office diplomat, about six months into a secondment to Downing Street. His job combined two distinct, previously well-established, posts – the Prime Minister's personal adviser on foreign affairs and the separate head of the secretariat. These two ostensibly similar jobs had reflected subtle but important differences in responsibility. One reported to the Prime Minister as part of No. 10. The other was part of the adjacent Cabinet Office and reported to the Cabinet Secretary. I assume this change was an 'efficiency measure'.

Under the old system the Cabinet Secretary and the Cabinet at large would automatically have had visibility of the secretariat's assessment, called the 'Iraq Options Paper'. The evidence suggests that this key document, classified 'Secret UK Eyes Only', was not seen by many ministers. Apart from the Prime Minister perhaps only the Foreign and Defence Secretaries were shown it. The copy that was leaked and published in the *Daily Telegraph* in September 2004[1] contained no indication of who read it. The Butler review of July 2004 refers to what is clearly this same paper as important 'inter-departmental advice' to ministers, but does not clarify who saw it. A supporting paper of legal advice from the Foreign Office was attached to the options paper. I was not aware of either paper until they were leaked in 2004. A policy paper that referred to an intelligence assessment would normally have been circulated to the DIS if it came to the MoD.

The 'Iraq Options Paper' was issued on Friday 8 March 2002, the day *after* a Cabinet meeting at which there was a detailed discussion about Iraq. Robin Cook, leader of the House, and the Home Secretary, David Blunkett, had asked for a discussion at the previous Cabinet.[2] An unusual 'real discussion' took place on 7 March but there is no indication that it reflected on a paper provided by Manning's secretariat. It surprises me that, with a week's notice of a planned Cabinet discussion on Iraq, a version of the 'Iraq Options Paper' was not rushed through to form the centrepiece of the discussion. There is little in normal Whitehall practice that is more important to officials than providing papers for Cabinet. However, it seems that Blair's Cabinet contained members he could not trust with all aspects of government policy.[3]

There is no evidence that there was a substantive Cabinet discussion of the analysis contained in the 'Iraq Options Paper' despite it being of the greatest relevance to the historic events that were about to unfold.

The 'Iraq Options Paper' noted that the Bush administration had 'lost confidence in containment' and that some wanted Saddam removed. The success of the intervention in Afghanistan, distrust of the UN, and 'unfinished business from 1991' were additional factors which persuaded Washington towards a military attack on Iraq which it believed would be legal. The paper explained the contrary legal advice contained in the attachment provided by the Foreign Office. The analysis concluded that although the policy of containment which had been pursued since 1991 had been at least partially successful, military action was the only sure way to remove Saddam Hussein. This was seen as a necessary precursor to the achievement of a long-standing British objective[4] – 'to re-integrate a law-abiding Iraq which does not possess WMD or threaten its neighbours into the international community'. The emergence of a 'democratic' Iraq was not mentioned as a factor.

Although there had not been a recent JIC assessment on Iraq's WMD status there was one in preparation and Overseas and Defence Secretariat appears to have had a preview. The 'Iraq Options Paper' said that intelligence was poor but Iraq continued with its biological and chemical warfare programmes. If it had not already done so, it could produce significant quantities of biological warfare agents within days and chemical warfare agent within weeks of a decision to do so. It was believed it could deliver chemical and biological warfare by a variety of means, including ballistic missile warheads. There were also some indications of a continuing nuclear programme. Saddam had used WMD in the past and could do so again if his regime were threatened.

The 'Iraq Options Paper' went so far as to recommend the steps that would be necessary as a precursor to military action against Iraq. It would be necessary to wind up the pressure on Saddam including a military build-up to frighten him. Justification for military action could come from a refusal by Saddam to admit UN inspectors, or the likelihood that inspectors would be frustrated if they were allowed back in. Intensive diplomatic activity would be necessary to build Security Council and wider international support. It would help if the Middle East peace plan was re-energised. It would be necessary to conduct a media campaign to warn the public of the dangers posed by Saddam and to prepare public opinion in the UK and abroad. The strategy recommended was to be the template for the government's approach to Iraq in the weeks and months ahead.

If the 'Iraq Options Paper' was not produced for Cabinet, what was its purpose? It was almost certainly to ensure the Prime Minister and his policy adviser gave a coordinated message to the Americans when Blair met US Vice President Cheney in Downing Street the following Monday and Manning attended important meetings in Washington at about the same time.

Whether or not Blair was primarily involved in developing the policy, he appears to have accepted the advice of the 'Iraq Options Paper' very quickly and immediately started to 'wind up the pressure on Saddam'. At the press conference which followed the Blair–Cheney meeting the two men were asked about the second phase of the war against terrorism and were challenged to produce evidence for the WMD threat from Iraq.

Blair responded:

> Let's be under no doubt whatever, Saddam Hussein has acquired weapons of mass destruction over a long period of time. He is the only leader in the world that has actually used chemical weapons against his own people. He is in breach of at least nine UN Security Council resolutions about weapons of mass destruction. He has not allowed weapons inspectors to do the job that the UN wanted them to do in order to make sure that he can't develop them. Now we have said right from the very outset, you will have heard me say on many, many occasions, no decisions have been taken on how we deal with this threat, but that there is a threat from Saddam Hussein and the weapons of mass destruction that he has acquired is not in doubt at all.

An important tactical element of the government's case was signalled in this statement. Two parallel strands would be evident in the argument for years to come. One strand was that Saddam had WMD and was a threat. This was needed to convince the British public that the war would be worth fighting. The second strand – that Saddam had not met his obligations under UN resolutions – was more subtle but offered the legal basis on which Blair could claim that participation in a war was justified if the threat could not be established. The two things are not necessarily the same. Saddam did not have to possess WMD and represent a threat to be in breach of UN resolutions. The nature of the threat to which Blair referred was never explained in any practical terms. That was left to a public imagination already sensitised by its well-developed terror of nuclear weapons.

Letters from America

On 14 March, three days after the Blair–Cheney press conference, Sir David Manning sent a 'Secret – Strictly Personal' memorandum to Blair describing talks he had held in Washington with 'Condi' Rice, the US National Security Advisor.[5] It was copied only to the Prime Minister's chief of staff, Jonathan Powell – further evidence that the strategy was being held close in No. 10. Manning had spoken privately with Rice, and also in meetings with her team of advisers.

There is little doubt that Manning was relaying messages to Bush's advisers in preparation for Blair's visit to the US President at his ranch at Crawford, Texas early in April. The ground being prepared was apparently too important or too secret to be left to the British ambassador, Sir Christopher Meyer. The messages relayed were entirely consistent with the recommendations of the 'Iraq Options Paper' and with Blair's statement at the press conference with Cheney a few days earlier. The Prime Minister wanted to tell Bush that, despite the flak it would create for him, he was supportive of the President's desire to progress US policy for regime change in Iraq. Manning says he reassured Rice that Blair's support was solid and, although there were conditions, there was a plan to work them through.

The tone of the memo suggests that no option to achieve regime change other than by military action was mentioned by either side. If Britain were to actively participate, Rice was told, the US must display concern for international opinion and the United Nations dimension, and acknowledge the paramount importance of tackling the Israel–Palestine problem.

According to Rice, Bush did not yet know how to persuade international opinion that military action against Iraq was necessary and justified, nor whether there would be useful support from Iraqis within and outside Iraq. There were no clear post-conflict plans; Rice told Manning there were no preparations for 'what happens on the morning after'. Manning judged that Bush was offended by the remarks of other European leaders and wanted Blair's support, and this gave Britain 'real influence'. He outlined for Blair the areas of potential influence and said the Prime Minister's upcoming talks at the ranch gave him a chance to push Bush on the Middle East. Manning, a former ambassador to Israel, felt there would never be a better chance to get this administration to give sustained attention to reviving the Middle East peace plan.

A second memorandum, classified 'Confidential and Personal', was written on the same subject on 18 March, four days after Manning's note.[6] It was to Manning from Meyer and focused on a discussion that Meyer had had with the US Deputy Defence Secretary and arch-neoconservative, Paul Wolfowitz, over Sunday lunch in the few days since Manning had returned to London. Meyer made it clear in 2005 that this leaked memorandum was genuine.[7] Having been briefed by Manning, Meyer was now in a position to advance the Downing Street strategy himself.

It is interesting that Wolfowitz was selected to be given privileged access to the inner thoughts of Downing Street. He was the leading advocate for an invasion of Iraq. Clearly, No. 10 was taking deliberate steps to ensure the neocons were 'on side' when the President considered the British proposals. It suggests there was a good appreciation in London of how the Bush administration worked.

Meyer's memorandum made it clear that Manning had been speaking the previous week from a 'script' and that he had also used it with Wolfowitz. Meyer reveals a little more about the content and the nature of the suggested plan, which the Americans were told 'had to be clever'. The British approach began by accepting regime change was the only option – a view that neither Wolfowitz, nor Rice previously, seemed to have contested – pointing out that a coalition of the willing could be built through a skilful strategy. At the centre of this strategy was a plan to 'wrongfoot' Saddam on the inspectors and UN Security Council resolutions. Meyer clarified later that the 'clever plan' needed to convince people there was a legal basis for toppling Saddam:

> The UN had to be at the heart of such a strategy. One way was to demand the readmission of UN weapons inspectors into Iraq. If Saddam refused, this would not only put him in the wrong but also turn the searchlight onto the security council resolutions of which he remained in breach.

Through the summer of 2002, the British government continued to argue in public that it was attempting to resolve the Iraq WMD problem peacefully through the United Nations and, up until the eve of the invasion of Iraq a year later, the Prime Minister protested that all that was required to stop it was for Saddam to demonstrate he was relinquishing his WMD. But it seems that the real policy was to devise a trap for Saddam in order to justify the military action he wanted Britain to take should Bush decide to invade Iraq. No. 10 thought it just possible that an ultimatum on the readmittance of inspectors could be cast in terms which Saddam would reject because he was unwilling to accept unfettered access but which would not be regarded as unreasonable by the international community. Failing that, the Prime Minister's Office acknowledged, 'we would be most unlikely to achieve a legal base for military action by January 2003'.[8] Blair thought it would make a big difference politically and legally if Saddam refused to allow the UN inspectors in.[9]

However, the Iraqi leader was unpredictable and intelligence offered no clear indication that he would be fearful of the return of inspectors. Iraq had denied inspectors any 'smoking guns' over many years and there was nothing in intelligence on the existence of any weapon stockpiles, current production facilities or evidence of plans that Saddam thought inspectors might find. Saddam might be confident of a return to the fruitless stand-off experienced by UNSCOM in the 1990s.

Meyer linked the 'clever plan' to a UK dossier that was in gestation. He made the nature of the paper clear to Wolfowitz. Its purpose would be to make the case well enough to create a critical mass of parliamentary and public opinion that would support British participation with the US 'in any operation against Saddam'. Thus the plan seems to have been to make such a strong case against Saddam, real or otherwise, that he was trapped. This would account for the strength of the statements Cheney and Blair had already made, and would make again, to the effect that they knew Saddam had WMD, despite the absence of intelligence to support that contention.

The British ambassador, on behalf of No. 10, was anticipating in March 2002 the need to make political preparations for military action. A comment he made about the tendency of many to overlook Saddam's crimes seemed to trigger a response from Wolfowitz that relegated the importance of WMD in the justification for regime change. Meyer does not say that he disputed this.

The ambassador drew out from Wolfowitz his belief in the value of information from Iraq opposition groups in exile, especially the INC and its head, Ahmed Chalabi. Wolfowitz said they had a 'good record in bringing high-grade defectors out of Iraq' and he was critical of the CIA for refusing to recognise this. This suggests that, at least before pressure was brought to bear on it, the CIA was exercising sensible caution with the intelligence available to it. However, it was also telling Meyer there was a way in which the WMD case could be made.

More advice from Whitehall

On 15 March 2002, in parallel with the Washington memoranda of Manning and Meyer, the JIC approved and issued JIC(02)059 on 'The Status of Iraqi WMD Programmes'.[10] It must have been a great disappointment to No. 10. It reflected, like all other assessments since 1991, the difficulty intelligence analysts had to deal with because of the UN Security Council's flawed Resolution 687.[11] The resolution demanded the eventual certification of the absence of WMD in Iraq, generating a political requirement that such a thing was achievable. Now, over a decade later, the JIC made clear in the most prominent part of the assessment that the intelligence was 'sporadic and patchy' and that a complete picture of the various programmes was difficult to assess. This was a note of caution that should have prompted any reader to raise questions about exactly how much was known. It said specifically that although there was little intelligence relating to it, Iraq 'may have hidden small quantities of [chemical warfare] agents and weapons' but noted that anomalies in Iraqi declarations to UNSCOM suggested stocks could be much larger. The JIC went on to reiterate a point we had been making to Whitehall for many years: stockpiles were not a definitive indicator of capability. Because it had the experience (up to 1991), an active chemical industry and the necessary chemical precursors, Iraq could generate chemical weapons in weeks or months if it wanted to do so.

The situation on biological weapons was similar and they could be generated even more quickly in facilities that could easily be concealed. From our perspective the uncertain intelligence on mobile production facilities, which were to attract so much excitement, was not hugely relevant. Small static facilities would probably represent a better investment for Iraq. We were trying to warn that, if we attacked Iraq, a possible chemical or biological threat could not be ignored and that absolute certainty of the absence of capability was impossible to achieve.

The assessment did not support the Prime Minister's assertion of four days earlier that there was no doubt that Saddam was a threat. But perhaps he understood that anyway and this is why there is no evidence that the chairman of the JIC or any other high official warned the Prime Minister that his statements were at variance with JIC assessments.

On 22 March, a week after the JIC issued its assessment, the political director at the Foreign Office, Peter Ricketts, wrote to the Foreign Secretary, Jack Straw. His paper[12] was marked 'Confidential and Personal' and copied to his civil service boss, the permanent secretary, and headed 'Iraq: Advice for the Prime Minister'. It offered views on what Straw might include in a personal note he intended to send to Tony Blair. Ricketts was a previous chairman of the JIC and still a member of the committee which had approved the assessment a few days earlier.

Ricketts recognised the opportunity for the Prime Minister to help shape the definition of Bush's objective and the mechanics of achieving it, but drew attention to two 'real problems'. The first concerned 'the threat', which he said was in reality unchanged from recent times. He was pleased that publication of 'the unclassified document' (or dossier) which the Foreign Office had been trying to write had been postponed, suggesting it did not meet the policy requirement, but noted 'even the best survey of Iraq's WMD will not show much advance on the nuclear, missile or CW/BW fronts'. Having argued that the WMD case was unpersuasive, he then wrote that 'to get public and parliamentary support for military operations we have to be convincing' that the threat from Iraq is 'significant enough for troops to die for and greater than that posed by other WMD proliferators'. He raised doubts about persuading the public of the imminence of a threat from Iraq. Although Ricketts seemed to begin by assuming the US was bent on military action, he subsequently hinted that Bush might be persuaded to accept something less than regime change.

The Foreign Secretary sent 'Secret and Personal' advice to the Prime Minister in a document dated 25 March and headed simply 'Crawford/Iraq'.[13] It reflected most of the advice from Ricketts. Straw's memo was downbeat, especially about the attitude of the Parliamentary Labour Party. The Foreign Secretary was very clear that the intelligence assessments up to that time did not identify enough of a threat from Iraq to justify military action but appears to offer a personal view that Saddam's regime 'plainly poses a most serious threat to its neighbours and therefore to international security'. In fact, Saddam's neighbours, who will have been very alert to such a threat, did not perceive it to be as destabilising as American military action to bring about regime change might be.

So the 'clever plan' that Britain was offering Washington seems to have included the requirement for Washington to offer Saddam no hope of survival regardless of whether or not he had WMD. If the impression could be created powerfully and widely enough that he had developed a major stockpile of WMD whilst inspectors had been absent, then Saddam would lose, whatever the real situation was. If he really had stockpiles he would either refuse admission to inspectors or deny them the freedom to uncover his new capability, thus openly defying the UN and incurring its wrath. If he had no stockpiles to declare he could not meet the expectations of the Security Council and would be held in breach. Military action could legitimately follow. After all, intelligence could not say with any clarity that no WMD would be found. Although there was some risk involved, it was likely that the discovery of at least a few WMD could be spun big enough to satisfy public expectation. Given that No. 10 clearly was aware of the lack of evidence of WMD in Iraq, the really 'clever' part of the plan is likely to have been the witting exaggeration of Iraq's WMD capability, to ensure Saddam could never satisfy the challenge to prove that he had disarmed. The way would then be open for regime change under the guise of forced disarmament sanctioned by the Security Council of the UN.

Visiting Crawford

On his way to Crawford on 3 April 2002, Tony Blair gave an interview to NBC News.[14] He was asked why he was so concerned about Iraq in terms of its chemical, biological and nuclear weapons. The following unqualified statement was included in his reply:

> We know that he [Saddam] has stockpiles of major amounts of chemical and biological weapons. . .

The JIC had stated unequivocally on 15 March in an assessment that went to the Prime Minister that it did not have a clear picture of

Iraq's WMD and that any stocks it did have were likely to be small. The Foreign Secretary had written to Blair on 25 March warning that intelligence did not identify a threat that would justify the invasion of Iraq. However, the statement was compatible with the strategy of talking up Saddam's capability and the threat it posed. Given on the day before Blair met President Bush in Crawford, the interview will have left the President in no doubt of the Prime Minister's determination to commit Britain to America's support. Perhaps Blair also wanted to demonstrate his seriousness about the 'clever plan' he believed the President should have been told about by now.

Blair was not to stretch the truth quite so far in future. Although he gave a similarly strong impression time and time again, his subsequent statements left him just enough room for manoeuvre. He was more careful at the press conference following the Crawford summit, where he seemed to have had some success in pressing the Israel–Palestine question. Bush said:

> We also had extensive conversations about the situation in the Middle East. Both our nations are strongly committed to finding a just settlement. Both of us agree on the fundamental elements that a just settlement must include. We share a vision of two states, Israel and Palestine, living side by side in peace and in security. We agree that this vision will never be realised through terrorism and that it can only be realised through a political process. We agree that the Palestinian leadership must order an immediate and effective ceasefire and crackdown on terrorist networks. And we agree that Israel should halt incursions in the Palestinian-controlled areas and begin to withdraw without delay from those cities it has recently occupied. The Prime Minister and I agreed to work closely in the weeks and months ahead on these difficult issues.

When asked about military action against Iraq, Bush emphasised the WMD aspect and the United Nations, but he was adamant about regime change. He spoke at some length about Saddam's WMD past and his ambitions but he concluded with this sentence: 'I explained to the Prime Minister that the policy of my government is the removal of Saddam and that all options are on the table.'

At first, Blair tried to avoid the regime change aspect but when pressed to say whether the President's policy to directly remove Saddam was now also British policy, his reply was clumsy, evasive and ambiguous:

> You know it has always been our policy that Iraq would be a better place without Saddam Hussein. I don't think anyone should be in any doubt about that for all the reasons I gave earlier. And you know reasons to do with weapons of mass destruction, also [to] do with the appalling brutality and repression of his own people. But how we now proceed in this situation, how we make sure that this threat that is posed by weapons of mass destruction is dealt with, that is a matter that is open. And when the time comes for taking those decisions we will tell people about those decisions. But you cannot have a situation in which he carries on being in breach of the UN resolutions and refusing to allow us the capability of assessing how that weapons of mass destruction capability is being advanced, even though the international community has made it absolutely clear that he should do so. Now, as I say, how we then proceed from there, that is a matter that is open for us.

Over the next few days I made clear in several routine briefings to DIS directors that the intelligence did not support the Prime Minister's claim about the existence of major stockpiles of chemical or biological weapons. I am not sure how far up the chain they were transmitted, if at all. Without any knowledge of the discussions and decisions that had taken place on the other side of Whitehall, I judged that if I pushed the point I would be told I was making a fuss over nothing because no consequential action had been identified. However, the uncomfortable feeling grew that military action was much more likely than our leaders would admit.

At the next Cabinet meeting, after his visit to Crawford, on 11 April, Blair reported back on his discussions with Bush. Robin Cook, the leader of the Commons, considered that Blair's message was encapsulated in his statement 'I do believe in this country's relations with the US'.[15] Cook thought Patricia Hewitt, the Trade and Industry Secretary, brave when she raised the issue of the domestic implications of military action. She said:

> There will be a lot of tension among the Muslim communities in Britain if an attack on Iraq is seen as a unilateralist action. They would find it much

easier to understand and we would find it much easier to sell if there was a specific agreement at the UN on the need for military action.

Blair said he regarded the UN process as important but that 'we should not tie ourselves down to doing nothing unless the UN authorised it'.

I had met Hans Blix, the head of UNMOVIC, for the first and only time on 26 March when he visited the DIS. I was one of a group of officials asked to talk with him. His organisation had been in a state of limbo ever since its creation, preparing to do a job that had not materialised in two years. He arrived late, seemed tired and his manner and movement struck me as those of a man who should be enjoying a well-earned retirement. But he was affable and the few things he said suggested he had an encouraging grasp of the situation. He said he intended to make clear to Iraq that the ball was in its court and that it had to demonstrate its compliance with the UN resolutions. None of us realised then that the exaggerated claims of Washington and London about Iraq's WMD capabilities would shift the onus of proof back onto the inspectors. For various reasons, including its brevity, the briefing Blix received from the DIS was not a good one. It focused mainly on ballistic missiles.

Iraq receding?

As strange as it may seem, most of what had been happening on Iraq was invisible to me. Media coverage spiked now and again but things were quiet for most of the summer. Staff moves and recruitment issues occupied much of my time. Out of the blue in May, the chief of defence intelligence decided a major reorganisation of work on WMD was needed and there was a proposal for reform on the table. Although I thought the idea was a good one, my staff was very unsettled by it and a detailed response was necessary. Then my boss, the director of scientific and technical intelligence, told me he was to retire early. He and I had forged an effective working relationship based on mutual respect. He was replaced by a man of very different character with no previous experience in intelligence. Dealing with intelligence on a difficult, politically charged and sensitive subject such as mine required subtle engagements with all involved, not least my bosses. The required relationships cannot be established overnight and I found myself increasingly remote from a management chain which did not have any meaningful experience of WMD intelligence.

Although preparation of a dossier on the main proliferators of WMD, which included Iraq, had started early in 2002, it was led by the Foreign Office and was never greatly in my focus. I first heard about a requirement for something for No. 10 specifically on Iraq as I left a meeting in the Cabinet Office, sometime in the early summer. The deputy chief of the Assessments Staff who covered WMD told me a request for it had come from Downing Street. I immediately made a link with the public dossier on al-Qaida we had contributed to the previous autumn. The al-Qaida dossier had been used to underpin the case for joining America in the invasion of Afghanistan. The ongoing sabre-rattling about Iraq fed my suspicion, and I thought this dossier would serve a similar purpose. We agreed that there was no significant new intelligence to report and the deputy thought that would not be well received in Downing Street.

Background work proceeded on the new dossier through the summer, but I cannot recall having seen any drafts, presumably because there was little to add to existing papers. By the end of July, things seemed to have gone quiet again, but appearances were deceptive. At the top level in Whitehall very serious processes were secretly in motion.

The secret Downing Street meeting

The Prime Minister held a meeting on Tuesday 23 July 2002. A briefing paper prepared for the meeting was dated two days previously, 21 July.[16] The new urgency seems to have been generated by the imminence of two matters. First, it was reported that on 4 August President Bush would receive a briefing from US military commanders on plans for the invasion of Iraq.[17] The origin of this information is unclear. It may have come from the embassy in Washington, from military sources or from Sir Richard Dearlove, the head of MI6, who had been in Washington at about this time. However, it raised fears that an invasion might take place sooner rather than later. There was much that still needed to be done to facilitate Britain's participation and there was a need to press Washington on this. The second factor was that, at the end of the week, Whitehall would 'break up' for the summer recess and it would become more difficult to coordinate decisions and actions. The important requirement seemed to be for those involved to engage with their opposite numbers in Washington to press for progress on issues relating to the British interest.

The briefing paper and the advice from the Foreign Office legal department which had been prepared earlier in 2002 were circulated to the few senior people invited to attend. The main briefing paper was a 'note by officials' called 'Iraq: Conditions for Military Action'. It was classified 'Personal Secret UK Eyes Only' and is said to have been produced by the Cabinet Office, presumably by Sir David Manning's team that had written the 'Iraq Options Paper' in March. Views from other departments were apparently canvassed and are reflected in the paper.

The paper was quite formal in nature and, at the outset, requested ministers to note certain statements or endorse specific actions. This was followed by a review of the background to the requests. There was a high degree of frustration amongst those concerned in Whitehall that US military planning for action against Iraq was proceeding in a political vacuum. No effort was being made to create favourable political conditions for an invasion nor was there planning to deal with its aftermath. The paper confirmed that the Prime Minister had taken forward the plans developed in March as described in the options paper and the Manning and Meyer memoranda, and that he had explained the conditions for British involvement to President Bush in April. However, it made no mention of the intention to wrongfoot Saddam, suggesting that this detail may not have been known to all its recipients or all the attendees at the meeting. It noted that, despite Bush's generally positive reaction to British suggestions in the spring, no significant movement had taken place by July. Surprisingly, the demands on Israel and Palestine that were part of the original No. 10 'script' appear to have been downgraded: by now, no more than a 'quiescent' condition was needed. There had originally been a requirement for more significant progress in the peace process.

The briefing paper identified the desirability of British participation in any military action and the necessity to 'create the conditions' in which Britain could legally support it. The possibility of the US embarking prematurely on a course of action that the government would find very difficult to support was seen as a danger. This might have arisen in reaction to an incident such as the downing of an American aircraft patrolling the Iraqi no-fly zone.

Apparently, No. 10 now realised that the Americans cared little about meeting Britain's conditions, despite the earlier optimism at being able to influence Bush's approach, and despite the belief that Bush wanted Britain 'on board'. Nonetheless, the paper appears to reflect a desire, presumably on the part of Tony Blair, for direct British participation in any military action. My recollection is that the mood of those military officers I was working with reflected a keenness on the part of the senior military establishment to be involved, not least for fear of otherwise being marginalised at home and abroad. However, there was a problem on which the MoD was pressing: that British forces would not be adequately prepared for action unless decisions that were likely to attract public attention were taken well in advance of any possible operation. Such visibility was presumably judged to be undesirable in the summer of 2002, and the failure to obtain the release of funds for fear of the reaction of an 'unprepared' public most likely cost lives later in Iraq because some service personnel were inadequately equipped or trained.[18]

The need to 'prepare public opinion in the UK that it was necessary to take military action against Saddam Hussein' was identified again. An 'information campaign' would be needed and it would have to be 'closely associated with a similar campaign to influence Saddam, the Islamic world and the wider international community' including the threat posed by Saddam and WMD. Interestingly, at this stage it was not France but Russia that was seen as the potentially difficult country, especially with regard to agreeing a UN Security Council ultimatum to Iraq on the readmission of inspectors. It also seems that UK officials were still uncertain towards the end of July 2002 that the removal of Saddam's regime would lead to the elimination of Iraq's WMD. It is not clear whether the Cabinet was ever advised of this judgement, but Parliament and the public were given no hint of it.

Two days later, on 23 July, the meeting for which the briefing paper was prepared took place. A record of it was circulated by the Prime Minister's private secretary, Matthew Rycroft, later the same day.[19] This memo was addressed to Sir David Manning and copied to the others present, except the Prime Minister personally because he was, in effect, its originator. The document was titled 'Iraq: Prime Minister's Meeting, 23 July' and classified 'Secret and Strictly Personal – UK Eyes Only'. It contained a further warning about its extreme sensitivity, an instruction that it should not be copied and that it should not shown to anyone else unless there was a genuine need for them to know its contents.

In addition to Blair, Manning and Rycroft, those present at the meeting were (in the order and form cited)[20] Defence Secretary [Geoff Hoon], Foreign Secretary [Jack Straw], Attorney General [Lord Goldsmith],

[Cabinet Secretary] Sir Richard Wilson, [chairman of the JIC] John Scarlett, [head of GCHQ] Francis Richards, CDS [chief of the Defence Staff, Admiral Sir Michael Boyce], 'C' [head of MI6, Sir Richard Dearlove], [No. 10 chief of staff] Jonathan Powell, [No. 10 political director] Sally Morgan and [No. 10 head of communications] Alastair Campbell.

As well as Scarlett, both Richards and Dearlove were members of the JIC and, therefore, guardians of the intelligence position. No politicians or officials were present who had a direct responsibility for the security of Britain against covert action by foreign countries or terrorists.[21] The homeland security of Britain does not appear to have been discussed at the meeting despite the Prime Minister having described elsewhere his nightmare of the nexus of rogue states such as Iraq, WMD and terrorism. Despite the absence of key players directly concerned with domestic security, others who attended had related responsibilities and experience.[22] There appears to have been an unrecorded, perhaps unspoken, consensus that the country's continued good relations with the US were of greater importance than the increased risk of a terrorist attack – presumably even one that involved WMD.

Rycroft's record of the meeting creates the impression of a strangely disjointed, stilted and uncoordinated session. In my experience note takers or record makers generally do their best to represent meetings in the most cogent and constructive light possible. The apparent lack of structure may reflect Blair's informal approach to decision-making and a reluctance to press for firm commitments from ministers. Or it may be that some, perhaps a majority, of those present were not aware of the full game plan. Although it has been since been described as involving an 'inner circle' of informed players, the impression is of a meeting forced on the Prime Minister by the perception of the key Whitehall department of Defence, and perhaps the Foreign Office or even the Cabinet Office itself, that they were being required to operate without adequately defined parameters. The Prime Minister's response appears to have been relatively unsympathetic.

Scarlett is reported to have started with a summary covering intelligence on Iraq's military and strategic reckoning, but not on WMD. Dearlove, recently back from Washington, reported his unequivocal view that the intelligence and facts were being fixed around President Bush's policy for regime change through military action, justified by the conjunction of terrorism and WMD. His insight may have come from a meeting he is said to have had a few days earlier at CIA headquarters with George Tenet, the US director of central intelligence.[23] It has been widely interpreted as a criticism of what was happening in America but that is not necessarily the case. It may have been a suggestion that London would have to do the same.

Straw warned that despite its inevitability, the case for military action was thin because Iraq was not threatening its neighbours and had less WMD capability than Libya, North Korea or Iran [he might also have added Syria to the list]. Blair thought there were different strategies for dealing with Libya and Iran.

Straw pressed the need to 'work up a plan for an ultimatum to allow the UN inspectors' back in, suggesting, 'This would also help with the legal justification for the use of force.' Presumably, he was anticipating either that Saddam would refuse to allow them in or that he would fail to cooperate with them if he did. Goldsmith said that, although regime change was not a legal basis for military action, there were three possible legal bases: self-defence, humanitarian intervention and UN Security Council authorisation. Neither of the first two could be the basis in this case. The last might be a possibility but relying on Resolution 1205 of three years previously would be difficult.

Boyce confirmed that the minimum required of the UK would be to provide basing for US forces in Diego Garcia and Cyprus and there appears to have been no question that this would be made available. Hoon thought military action would begin in January and wanted immediate decisions to enable him to make preparations for this; Rycroft reports him as saying that 'if the Prime Minister wanted UK military involvement, he would need to decide this early'.

There is no indication that Blair was greatly concerned about this plethora of problems. Although no reference to a plan to 'wrongfoot' Saddam is recorded, one sentence stands out from Rycroft's record: 'The Prime Minister said that it would make a big difference politically and legally if Saddam refused to allow in the UN inspectors.' This echoes a comment made in Manning's memo to Blair of 14 March in which he appears to say, despite a typographical error, that 'renwed refused [renewed refusal] by Saddam to accept unfettered inspections would be a powerful argument' to establish a legal basis for military action in an international framework.

The meeting concluded that attendees should work on the assumption that the UK would take part in any military action but that decision was not firm. The Prime Minister did not authorise the expenditure of funds in preparation for the military operation, despite the MoD's obvious desire for a commitment to be made early. Various pieces of follow-up work on the possible UK military contribution, UN and other regional political aspects, intelligence and legal issues were commissioned. The need for an 'information campaign', which was a major feature of the briefing paper, is not mentioned in Rycroft's record of the meeting although Blair observed the need for the right political context to win support for regime change.

There can be little doubt about the authenticity of this document. Looking back in 2005, Sir Christopher Meyer believed it to be genuine. We also know that the Prime Minister chaired a meeting on Iraq that day because it is referred to in the report of the Butler review.

CHAPTER 5

August–September 2002: The road to the dossier

Summer recess

August is usually a quieter time in Whitehall, with Parliament in recess and many ministers and civil servants on holiday. For a lot of us it was a time for catching up on the more routine tasks whilst crises were at a minimum, telephones remained quiet and in-boxes light. This August was not very different. Although I did not know at the time, I can see now there were indications of a reaction to the Prime Minister's July meeting because two unusual JIC studies were set in process during that period. I formed the impression then that they represented sensible low-key contingency planning by the JIC and, because they were so speculative, I interpreted them as betraying a degree of frustration with the paucity of available intelligence, not least because their commission coincided with a call for everyone to trawl their data banks to ensure nothing was being overlooked. One of the papers, issued on 21 August, was titled 'Iraq: Saddam's Diplomatic and Military Options'.[1] We were not greatly involved in this paper since it was about much more than WMD. However, it noted that there was little intelligence on Iraq's 'CBW doctrine' and judged that the most likely time Saddam Hussein would order the use of any chemical and biological weapons he had against coalition forces would be after coalition attacks had begun.

The second paper was still in preparation when I went on leave on 29 August for a holiday in Greece.

A dossier ordered

By the beginning of September Tony Blair had further confirmation that America's march to war was virtually unstoppable. President Bush may well have told him so when they spoke on the phone on 25 August, before the Prime Minister had concluded his summer break. If not, he would have found out by the end of the month, after Vice President Cheney made two aggressive speeches saying that war was inevitable because there was no doubt that Saddam now had weapons of mass destruction.[2] Cheney was not contradicted. Within days, more American troops began arriving in Kuwait. Some believe the Defense Secretary, Donald Rumsfeld, authorised attacks on Iraqi targets at about that time, changing the rules of engagement beyond those that were already in place.[3] American and British military aircraft enforcing the no-fly zone had regularly responded to Iraqi attacks on them from the ground. My former boss as chief of defence intelligence, who was by now retired, says he detected a switch from containment to preparation of the battlefield for war at this time.[4]

Blair obviously wanted to press on urgently with the preparation of an appropriate 'political context' to enable Britain's participation in the war. As soon as he returned from his holiday he asked for a dossier on Iraq's WMD to be produced. Sir David Manning immediately informed the heads of the JIC and the SIS of the decision. At a press conference at his Sedgefield constituency on 3 September, Blair announced that the dossier would be published 'within the next few weeks' and said if there were any developments in the situation 'the fullest possible debate will take place, not just in the country but obviously in Parliament and elsewhere'.[5] Over the next few days a number of MPs, concerned that developments might occur rapidly, wrote to the Prime Minister asking for Parliament to be recalled quickly, as it was not scheduled to sit again until 15 October. He refused to do so.

New intelligence

Late on Friday 30 August MI6 had issued several new top secret intelligence reports on Iraqi chemical and biological weapons. With a weekend intervening most of those to whom they were distributed would not have seen them until Monday 2 September. The second of the JIC assessments that had been commissioned in August was scheduled to go to the committee for approval on Wednesday 4 September. This was too late for the information in them to be properly digested and included in the draft paper which the JIC would consider. During discussion of that draft, 'C' drew the attention of his JIC colleagues to the new intelligence reports and suggested there was new information in them that should be incorporated in the assessment. The Assessments Staff was asked to deal with this before the paper was issued.

On the basis of the new intelligence an addition to the main text of the paper was drafted. A single item from one of the new reports was judged to be significant enough for inclusion. It was a rather vague assertion from an apparently new sub-source informing an established source that 'chemical and biological munitions' were available and could be with military units within a certain range of time the upper limit of which was forty-five minutes. The Assessments Staff drafter judged that the intelligence probably referred to the time taken to deliver the munitions from conveniently located storage facilities to selected military units which had the means of firing them. He sent his revised draft to those who had been involved in the assessment.

On Friday 6 September, a member of my staff who had looked at the revision responded by email with some advice on a slight modification to the wording. On receiving this the Assessments Staff drafter telephoned back to clarify some points. Such an exchange was typical because my branch was recognised as having the greatest experience and knowledge on WMD matters. However, when the drafter asked for confirmation of his assumption about forward deployed storage facilities my analyst referred him to another branch in the DIS that dealt with military matters including doctrine and tactics in Iraq. As the earlier assessment[6] had noted, there was little recent intelligence on this. The advice was that the report was not clear enough for reference to 'forward deployed storage sites' and that detail was removed from the assessment. The sentence that appeared in the assessment finally issued on Monday 9 September was: 'Intelligence also indicates that biological and chemical munitions could be with military units and ready for firing within 20–45 minutes.' It was not considered strong or important enough to be given any prominence in the assessment. It was buried deep in the report, suggesting to me that the Assessments Staff had concluded the new reports added little but felt obliged to respond to the instruction from the JIC by including something from the new intelligence.

An unusual paper

The assessment, entitled 'Iraqi Use of Chemical and Biological Weapons: Possible Scenarios',[7] was an unusual JIC product. It did not assess, as a primary requirement, Iraq's capabilities. When it was commissioned by the JIC in August, no new intelligence had arrived which changed the existing assessment of the status of Iraq's WMD programmes.[8] There was no suggestion that a paper to update the March assessment should or could have been written. Nor was there significant up-to-date intelligence available to make an assessment of how Iraq might use such weapons. Analysts were, in effect, asked to assume Iraq did have such weapons and to make their 'best guess' assumptions about how Saddam would use them.

I presumed that the JIC had requested the paper because it judged that war with Iraq was a strong possibility and wished to provide additional background to inform the final decision and to advise military commanders. To help military planning and preparations it seemed appropriate to make 'worst but reasonable'-case assumptions about Iraq's capabilities. I knew from my discussions within the MoD that the military wanted such guidance.[9] To do this analysts drew on their general knowledge of WMD and the dated intelligence of Iraq's past capability and experience.

As the DIS representative on the Nuclear, Biological and Chemical Defence Committee, which met every few months, I was required to give an intelligence update at each meeting. After what they had been hearing from senior UK and US politicians, they could not understand why my briefings suggested the intelligence on Iraq was so vague and non-specific. A JIC paper on possible scenarios seemed to be a good idea because, in the absence of hard intelligence, approved 'best guesses' would be better than nothing for them to get their teeth into. It did not occur to me before I went on leave that for those with inside knowledge the paper might take on a different purpose before it was completed.

It was not until much later that I learned of the Prime Minister's inner circle meeting of 23 July. Several members of the JIC, including its chairman, John Scarlett, had been present and it had been noted that current intelligence assessments would not support a war. With that knowledge, I am now suspicious that the 'Scenarios' assessment, which was not finalised when the dossier was commissioned, might have assumed a purpose that was hidden from most of those involved in its production. There was now a political need for a more positive statement about Iraq's WMD capability. The existence of a JIC paper that made more positive statements, albeit speculative ones, would better serve the Prime Minister's need to justify the likely military course ahead.

I saw only an early draft of this JIC paper before I went on holiday. I returned to work a week or so after it had been approved. Due to the urgency of dealing with the final stages of the preparation of the dossier, it was not until later that I gave the final assessment any detailed attention. When I did, I was surprised at its first key judgement, which said: 'Iraq has a chemical and biological warfare capability and Saddam is prepared to use it.' Although the word 'capability' was suitably qualified in the body of the paper to make clear it did not necessarily mean Saddam had 'weapons', that possibility coupled with the bold phrase 'and Saddam is prepared to use it' created an impression that would stick in the mind of the reader who did not delve more deeply. The detail of the paper emphasised that much of it was 'necessarily based on judgement and assessment'. It made it clear that it was not certain that Iraq had any chemical or biological weapons whilst recognising the possibility it did or that it could produce some quite quickly if it decided to do so. I was glad to see reference to the fact that availability of stocks of agent and weapons was an important factor, that the political costs of using such weapons militated against their use pre-emptively, and the acknowledgement that there was no intelligence on specific plans for how chemical and biological weapons would be used in a conflict. The relationship between the JIC assessment and the dossier which was being drafted was less obvious to me when the dossier was being completed in mid-September than it became later.

Political moves

Following a meeting with President Bush at Camp David on 7 September, Blair, paying scant regard to the detail of the previous day's JIC assessment, stoked things up. On 10 September in a televised speech to the annual Trades Union Congress,[10] he claimed that when the weapons inspectors were evicted from Iraq in 1998 there were still enough chemical and biological weapons remaining to devastate the entire Gulf region. However, following Operation Desert Fox in 1998, the government had clearly stated that the military action had been taken to degrade Saddam's ability to *regenerate* his biological and chemical weapons capability. It was judged at the time to be unlikely that Iraq retained significant quantities of any such weapons. Without quite saying so, Blair was creating an impression of Iraq bursting at the seams with a huge stockpile of chemical and biological weapons that had been added to in the years since 1998. No such assessment had ever been made by the JIC.

This will have added to the frustration of the MPs who wanted Parliament recalled. A number of them, led by Graham Allen, considered the possibility of calling an unofficial assembly of members to discuss the matter.[11] Canvassing the entire membership of the Commons, they found a huge majority in favour of an official recall of Parliament, and 65 per cent who declared they would attend an unofficial debate. Arrangements were made and the date for the debate fixed for 19 September. By 10 September it was clear there would be overwhelming attendance and wide coverage by the media. As far as the leader of the House, Robin Cook, was concerned, Allen was pushing at an open door and on 11 September Blair bowed to the pressure and agreed to a recall of Parliament.[12] The date was set for 24 September 2002 and this became the deadline for the publication of the dossier which had to be available for the debate.

President Bush addressed the General Assembly of the United Nations on 12 September, indicating a willingness to work with the UN Security Council to resolve the Iraq issue but warning that action must be taken if it failed. If the clever part of the British plan had been to have Saddam refuse to readmit inspectors, a major flaw was already beginning to show. The aggressive words of Blair and the US administrations together with the accelerated build-up of forces in the region made the readmission of inspectors more, rather than less, likely. On 16 September Iraq said it would allow the return of UN weapons inspectors 'without conditions' as an indispensable first step towards an assurance that it no longer possessed WMD.[13] Towards the end of September the drafting of what was to become UN Security Council Resolution 1441 began.

Holiday over

I was unaware of any of these events when I returned to work on Wednesday 18 September 2002. I was surprised to be told that work on the Prime Minister's dossier had dominated my staff's activities in my absence. 'All hell' had broken loose at the beginning of the month with the requirement for the dossier to be written and published within three weeks. The Assessments Staff had written several drafts in quick succession. There had not been enough time for the analysts to consider and respond to one draft before the next appeared. Many important comments and suggestions that had been made were not being incorporated. The Assessments Staff drafters were telling my analysts that No. 10 was taking a close interest in the process and that 'Alastair Campbell's hands were all over it'. The latest draft had arrived that morning for further comment. I needed to look at it and read the new intelligence that had arrived at the beginning of the month.

My nuclear analysts seemed to have resolved their issues, the biological warfare part 'wasn't too bad', but my chemical warfare expert had major problems. Several other hot intelligence issues had been in play before I had gone on holiday. I had to decide on my priorities.

Top of the list had been the work on al-Qaida's efforts to obtain WMD. We knew that they already had a limited capability with chemical warfare. We had also played an important role in identifying a Pakistani biotechnologist who was apparently offering to help Osama bin Laden. American specialists in Afghanistan had uncovered evidence of strategic thinking about biological warfare agents and they eventually discovered a laboratory near Kandahar.[14] They found evidence of significant progress. There was also intelligence on nuclear weapons to be considered and a struggle to wrestle apart information that might be about the real thing from material on a radiological weapon or 'dirty bomb'.

Iran's nuclear, biological and chemical warfare plans and capabilities were of major concern. There was intelligence to consider on what was happening in North Korea, in India and in Pakistan. And my analysts had done a superb assessment job in pulling together a large amount of disparate intelligence on the Pakistani scientist A. Q. Khan, who had played a central part in Pakistan's nuclear weapons programme before apparently being sidelined.

However, I had just two days to deal with the dossier problem before it went to press to meet the 24 September deadline, so I had to give it priority. I decided I did not have time to go through the whole document in detail so, unsatisfactory as it was, I focused on those issues that were causing my staff concern. I hated having to work without the full picture in my head, but there was no alternative.

The process of producing an intelligence assessment for the JIC to endorse is iterative and often involves compromise. This exercise for the dossier, although not quite the same as for a typical JIC product, had many similarities. Experience tells you that once a draft has been generated there is a barrier to changing it. With each successive draft, as the deadline shortens, that barrier grows higher.

Although they were relatively inexperienced and neither of the Assessments Staff drafters for WMD at the time of the dossier was a scientist or an engineer, they had gained our respect for dealing in a straightforward manner with the assessments they coordinated and listening critically to our advice. Because the usual deputy chief of the Assessments Staff was not available to oversee the work for the dossier, the drafters were being supervised by the chief, Julian Miller, who was less familiar with the subject.

The dossier, in different forms and being written by different groups, had been in gestation for months and the urgent timescale now set by the Prime Minister caused my section heads to avoid suggesting major redrafts. They tried to concentrate only on changes essential to reflect or at least not contradict our assessments, influencing the balance towards our position. This might look like minor quibbling over a few words but it had a deep significance. Arguing about replacing 'shows' with 'indicates' carries important messages about the degree of doubt or confidence in an assessment.

There had been difficulties surrounding the estimate of how quickly Iraq could acquire a nuclear weapon. We had been under pressure to estimate shorter times than our analysis suggested, but a satisfactory form of words had eventually been agreed. My experts were satisfied with the dossier from a nuclear perspective.

My chemical warfare expert insisted I study the new intelligence reports that had been received at the beginning of September. He was not happy with the way they were being used to justify stronger assessments of the availability of chemical weapons than had previously been made and wanted my opinion. The report that was to promote most interest, because of the way it was highlighted in the dossier, is the only one I can discuss in detail because its coverage in subsequent inquiries has not only released the normal constraints but has kept the memory of it reasonably fresh in my mind. It has become known as the 45-minutes intelligence. My recall of the detail of the others is not good.

For a variety of reasons none of the reports was convincing. They contained no specific information or detail to qualify them as reliable. The 45-minutes report was probably the easiest to reach a conclusion about. The information came from a new source, apparently untried, but was passed through another source who was said to have been reliable on other matters. The new source clearly knew little about chemical or biological weapons. The report amounted to assertions that were credible, but anyone with a passing knowledge of published information on Iraq's WMD could have made them up. The 45-minutes report used the terms 'weapons of mass destruction', 'chemical warfare' and 'biological warfare' in an ambiguous manner. It referred to 'chemical and biological' as a single entity. Some of what was being said might be credible for biological but not chemical warfare and vice versa. When I had digested the reports, I discussed them with my chemical warfare expert.

'The trouble is,' said my colleague, 'I have absolutely no reliable intelligence that Iraq has produced significant quantities of any chemical warfare agent or weapon since the Gulf conflict of 1991.' He thought it likely that Iraq had produced small quantities. But it would be difficult to detect something like that. If large quantities of agent had been produced and filled into weapons there was a higher chance that some part of the process would have been detected in intelligence.

'I have been making this point in comments on every draft of the dossier,' he said, 'but we are just being ignored. The same thing comes back time after time. There was a drafting meeting yesterday and our two representatives on the drafting committee were going to raise the points again. I have not heard the outcome but they were not hopeful.' To his mind the certainty implied by the draft dossier was unreasonable, especially in the foreword. We understood the foreword would ultimately be signed by the Prime Minister. It painted a picture of significant stockpiles of agent and weapons ready for use. We were not clear who had drafted it.

Since the 45-minutes report did not differentiate between biological and chemical weapons I discussed the same issue with my biological warfare experts. They felt that some specific intelligence on mobile biological warfare agent production facilities meant that they could with confidence substantiate an assessment that judged that biological warfare agent had been produced by Iraq. The significance of much smaller quantities of biological warfare agent compared to chemical meant they were not as concerned that they had not seen physical evidence of production or deployment in intelligence.

'And we have this from two sources?' I asked.

They said we did.

'And we are confident that the two sources are independent?' I was asking them to confirm they had made a check I had asked for earlier in the year.

'We checked and were told they were unrelated sources,' said one.

'And in any case, Brian,' said the other, 'You know as well as me that we are sure Iraq has the knowledge from the last war to make at least anthrax, and that we assess it could produce significant quantities in a few days, whereas it would take weeks or months to produce CW. We are not entirely happy but I think we can live with what the dossier is saying on BW.'

I needed to look again at the draft dossier and the new intelligence reports. As I walked back to my office along the broad, bright corridor on the top floor of the Old War Office Building, I spotted David Kelly absorbed in a report. I stopped to have a brief word. He explained he was going through the latest draft of the dossier and said my staff had been letting him look at the DIS drafts otherwise he would have a much longer walk to the Foreign Office, on whose behalf he was contributing, from his own office, which was in a building adjacent to ours. Although ultimately destined for public release these interim drafts were considered by the Assessments Staff to be very sensitive, and the few copies made available had to be read in a secure environment.

I asked him what he thought of the dossier and he said he thought it was good. I decided not to pursue the discussion further because I wanted to consider what I would do next, so I excused myself and returned to my office to put my thinking cap on.

I heard then what had happened at the final drafting meeting on the previous day. Our representatives had returned with some startling new information. They had continued to raise the DIS objections about the intelligence being stretched too far and over-generalised. They repeated that we had no firm evidence of chemical warfare agent production or the availability of either chemical or biological weapons, and the sourcing of and information in the 45-minutes intelligence report was not specific enough for us to be confident about it. They could not endorse the draft on behalf of the DIS. Only then were they told that there was additional intelligence they had not seen that allowed the stronger statements to be made with confidence. Unfortunately this intelligence was highly sensitive and could not be distributed beyond a few key people. For convenience, I shall refer to this intelligence as Report X.

Our DIS colleagues took the only line they could. The DIS position could not be changed on the basis of something that its analysts had not seen and assessed. Faced with this impasse the chief of the Assessments Staff, who was chairing the meeting, turned to the MI6 representative present and gained his agreement that the sensitive intelligence contained in Report X could be made available to the chief and deputy chief of defence intelligence, who could then decide on the DIS position.

A few hours after their return they reported on the status of the draft dossier to a meeting called by the deputy chief, Tony Cragg. The two directors most concerned, one being my new boss and the other the director of our DIS colleagues, were in attendance. The continuing DIS problems with the draft dossier were explained. Cragg told them that reassurance had been received from MI6 that Report X removed the doubts of the analysts and that the DIS would desist from further objection. When this news reached me my worries multiplied. I did not think Cragg knew enough about our subject to make such a judgement and I thought him inclined to make decisions without offering explanation. I suspected he was keen to provide uncritical support to the policy community. There is an important line between intelligence and policy and I was worried that it was becoming blurred under his influence.

I had plenty to think about through the rest of the day and to sleep on that night. My conviction was growing that my staff had sound reason to be so concerned. In the previous months I had been amazed by the brazen exaggerated assertions made about Iraq's WMD capabilities and its links with terrorists, first by the Bush administration and subsequently by the Prime Minister. Now it seemed that intelligence might be caving in to the demands of policy rather than guiding it. My mind went back to 1998 and the US strike on the al-Shifa pharmaceutical plant in Khartoum that reduced it to rubble. Operation Desert Fox against Iraq followed despite the lack of a good intelligence case. I remembered our part in the Scott inquiry into the arms-to-Iraq scandal, as a result of which I was careful to ensure we kept meticulous records of our assessments and advice on all potentially controversial issues.

I was in no doubt that there were dangers for us in what was happening with the dossier. At the heart of it was our duty to strive to ensure it accurately represented our assessment of the intelligence. The suggestions my staff had been making for modification of the successive dossier drafts were entirely reasonable, would normally have been accepted and were not at a level of conceptual technical difficulty that should have been a challenge to the Assessments Staff. Under normal circumstances, the ever-sceptical JIC would have welcomed our reservations. The JIC usually erred on the side of caution, not least because of the grilling to be expected from the politicians on difficult issues. Most of my battles in the past had concerned the reluctance of the Assessments Staff and others to push the intelligence as far as we wished they would. They did not expect us to be cautious. Suddenly, the tables were turned and it was they who seemed to be throwing caution to the wind. We were not used to arguing from this position.

But I thought the battle was lost. The existence of Report X was the critical problem. Although I suspected it might be a device to circumvent our objections, it is impossible to mount an argument against evidence that is invisible to you. I wondered whether I was seeing shadows where there were none, in danger of making a fuss over nothing. I felt very uncomfortable. I decided that, as a minimum, we probably needed to be sure the record showed clearly we had done all we reasonably could to put our concerns to our line managers.

A meeting with David Kelly

The next day, I told those members of my staff involved in the affair that my views were consolidating in support of their concerns, even in the face of the deputy chief's instruction to desist from argument. But I was worried that David Kelly had told me he thought the draft dossier was 'good'. I said it would be difficult if his view was quoted against us if our argument escalated.

Then I was told that Kelly was visiting my branch later in the morning. It was suggested I might like to chat with him about the situation. I agreed and said we would have an informal meeting in my office at 11.30. Before that I had another long discussion with my chemical warfare expert. We looked closely again at the 45-minutes intelligence report. The description of the source of the information was not straightforward, and it was not as clear as we would normally have expected. My staff had asked MI6 about it but their response was unusually vague and unhelpful. We decided we had to be cautious with this information and could not dismiss the possibility that the sub-source might have ulterior motives and be giving false information.

The report was unclear and imprecise. It did not differentiate whether it was biological weapons, chemical weapons or both that could be ready for firing so quickly. There were no clues for analysts as to which agents were involved or how deadly they might be. The report did not even explain whether the source was talking about long-range missiles or battlefield weapons – rocket launchers or artillery shells. We discussed the term 'munitions', which was the only clue given to the type of delivery method. Was there such a word in the sources' language? How did it translate? What was being deployed? We knew Iraq had previously developed air-dropped bombs, shells, rockets and ballistic missile warheads for some known chemical agents, and ballistic missile warheads and bombs for two known biological agents. I was inclined to dismiss bombs because Iraq stood little chance of putting aircraft up and I questioned whether you would call a ballistic missile warhead a munition.

'No, I don't think you can dismiss that possibility,' said my colleague.

There was also uncertainty about the word 'deployment'. We decided there was really no clue about the scenario in which these undefined weapons would be used. This then was a very tenuous piece of intelligence, especially considering the absence of any other recent information indicating that Iraq had produced agent and filled it into weapons, or that either agent or weapons had been moved around the country. Our inclination was to treat this report with caution until some collateral appeared to support it or otherwise. But it was not inconceivable that the other signatures we always looked out for had been missed. It was important for military commanders to keep the possibility that they might have to deal with chemical or biological weapons at the back of their minds and this reduced any inclination to argue that the intelligence should not be mentioned at all.

'I think there should be mention of this,' I said. 'But it should be that there is an unlikely possibility – no more.'

My colleague surprised me when he suddenly asked, 'Look, no one is going to move on this but I think it is wrong. What should I do?'

I thought for a moment and replied, 'What you need to do is write to me explaining your position. That will protect you. If I still agree with your position after I have heard what David Kelly has to say, and I am pretty sure I will, I'll pass your minute on up the line, making it clear that I support you. It probably won't have any effect, but at least our position will be on the record. But we need to get this done today. I'm not around tomorrow. Could you work on it immediately?'

When Kelly arrived he brought someone with him and asked if it would be alright for him to attend. I will call him Mr A because a year later this is how he would be referred to when he gave evidence to Lord Hutton. Mr A worked in an arms control job for the MoD and had been an UNSCOM inspector in Iraq specialising in chemical warfare. Although my staff had worked with him and I was familiar with his name, I had never met him. This was to prove significant later. Mr A did not have the professional stature and authority of David Kelly and had not worked with us in the same way. I was hesitant because I knew that Kelly understood intelligence well enough for me to push the boundaries of our relationship if I needed to. I wondered if the presence of Mr A might inhibit our discussion but I decided it would be too complicated to refuse and that, if necessary, I could always find a way to have a private word with Kelly.

So my intelligence experts joined us, and we had a short meeting. My office was just large enough to seat the six or seven of us in reasonable comfort. I made it clear that the meeting was informal and there would be no record. I was uncomfortable about discussing the difficulties we were experiencing with outsiders but I had little option. I explained that we had problems with the way some of the intelligence was being used in the dossier and had reached the point where it looked as though we might have to take exceptional action to ensure people understood the strength of our views. I said that Kelly had told me he thought the dossier was good and I was worried that there might be something we were missing. The last thing I wanted was for the few people in Whitehall who understood WMD to be having an argument amongst themselves on such an important document if a row broke out.

Kelly confirmed what I suspected – that he had not even seen the recent intelligence and could not make much sense of what the draft was saying about forty-five minutes. He said that he thought the draft dossier was generally good, especially in relation to the history of the weapons inspections with which he had been so closely involved. He made it clear that he considered the intelligence aspects our responsibility and assured me he would not join any debate on them. He had told me all I needed to know.

Mr A commented on the statements in the draft dossier with respect to the 45-minutes issue. He said he also could make no sense of what was being said. Neither Mr A nor Kelly had come across any Iraqi weapon system about which they felt such a statement could be made without further qualification. Although we could not discuss the intelligence with them because of the restrictions on it, I told them the issue was included in the concerns we had and that we would be taking the matter further with our bosses. A few other details of the draft dossier were discussed, but I was keen to draw the meeting to a close. I wound it up as soon as I could with a brief summary of what we had covered and agreed.

As he left, I told my chemical warfare expert that I would have no hesitation in supporting the minute he was drafting, and asked him when it would be ready.

There was a problem. 'I've just been called to an urgent meeting at the Foreign Office,' he said. 'It is planning the strategy for the visit to the Middle East I have to make with them next week. I can't afford to miss it and it could go on a bit.' I knew there was an important negotiation involved here and he would need his wits about him.

'OK,' I said. 'But remember I am out tomorrow so I may need to take the initiative on this if we are to make sure Cragg knows how serious we are before the dossier is published. If you're not back before I leave I will write something and copy it to you. You can write separately to him tomorrow if you need to.'

Early in the afternoon, before I wrote the minute, I managed to speak with a colleague who I knew had seen the sensitive intelligence in Report X. 'Don't answer this if you don't want to,' I said, 'but you have seen this new intelligence on Iraq's chemical and biological weapons and we haven't. I don't want to ask you about the actual information, I know you couldn't tell me, but I could do with some advice. We have no convincing evidence that Iraq has produced any chemical or biological warfare agent or weapons since 1991 – nothing about the background or infrastructure. The strongest evidence would be this 45-minute stuff. We have serious doubts about it. We think that the dossier is about to push it too far and we have been arguing about it all along but have been ignored. DCDI says he will hear no more argument because of this new intelligence [Report X]. I cannot imagine what intelligence could have come in that would fill in all the gaps in the picture without my experts examining and cross-checking it in detail. It would have to be a huge amount of complicated new information and would take a lot of analysis and cross-checking. But without having seen it I can't be absolutely sure. I am about to write to DCDI, to put it on the record that we have these problems. However, if you told me the new stuff really was magic and comprehensive and credible I would not embarrass him by doing that.'

'You should send the minute.' The advice was firm.

I sat down to write it but before I had got far the phone rang. It was my boss asking me to pop along to his office. I strolled the 30 metres or so, knocked on the door and, responding to his shout, went in. He looked very small behind his large desk, and he waved me to sit down at an adjacent table where he joined me.

I felt a pang of sympathy for the man across the table from me. He had only been with us for a few weeks and had never worked in the intelligence world before. He had a huge amount of new information and unfamiliar practices to absorb and understand. He had arrived in the middle of a significant reorganisation of part of his directorate and was trying to understand the implications of that. But he had a prickly manner and had not made many friends so far. His challenging attitude saw my sympathy rapidly evaporate.

'This dossier business,' he began. 'DCDI wants me to tell you that there is some new intelligence, very sensitive, can't be shown to many, that clears up this business your chaps have been worrying about. OK?'

'Sorry,' I said, 'I'm not sure what you're telling me.'

'Cragg has decided the dossier is going through as it is in this latest draft. So no more comments are needed.'

'I'm afraid that's not acceptable,' I responded.

'Why not?'

'We cannot endorse an assessment on the basis of information we haven't seen. And keeping quiet about it is tantamount to doing just that.'

'But an officer from MI6 [he mentioned the name of an MI6 man who was well known to me] has reassured me that it is OK.'

'Has DCDI seen this new intelligence, then?'

'I suppose so.'

'Have you seen it?'

It was like pulling teeth. I now realise that, despite his inexperience, he had personally accepted MI6's reassurance and passed it on as advice to the deputy chief of defence intelligence, who had not been contacted directly. Neither of them had actually seen, let alone studied, the report – assuming that it existed at this stage.

'No. But MI6 have told me it was good stuff.'

'Look, it may be that I am missing something, but Cragg doesn't know much about this subject and I can't imagine what he could have seen that was so convincing he could reach that conclusion in less than twenty-four hours. This will have to be on his shoulders. I shall write to put on record that our assessment, based on what we have seen, cannot be that firm.'

'But that's not the way things are done.'

'It's the way I do things.'

'He won't like it.'

'I don't like it, either.'

CHAPTER SIX

September 2002–March 2003: Concern and departure

Recording concerns

My course of action was now clear. I had to ensure Tony Cragg knew of our continuing concern and to place it on the record before the dossier was published, despite him having already issued a firm instruction that we should cease our argument. If I sought a discussion with him I thought he might try to persuade or even instruct me not to write anything so I would give him no opportunity to do so. I was determined that no one would have grounds for blaming the analysts for a flawed assessment. Clearly, I lacked faith that, if things went wrong, the system and the senior individuals involved would acknowledge that we had warned them.

There was no way in which I could argue with Cragg about something I had not seen. Over the years, I had come to know most of the other senior officers and officials in the DIS quite well and was able to discuss or argue issues with them, sometimes in a heated manner. But I hardly knew Cragg, the deputy chief, or the current chief. They seemed to me to be remote figures more inclined than their predecessors to make autocratic decisions. Perhaps circumstances had made it difficult for them to establish the mutual trust and respect that are essential elements in intelligence. Whatever the reason, I had no confidence that they or my new boss would do the right thing. Even if my previous boss had not supported me to the hilt, he would have honestly recounted my position after the event. My reservations about my present management chain seem to have proven well founded.

I resolved to send a minute on our secure email system to my boss and to Cragg's military assistant, asking the latter to bring it to Cragg's immediate attention. I would also copy the minute to a few others in the DIS who were involved in this business and print off a hard copy to be put in the appropriate file in the branch registry. This way there was little chance that the minute could be made to 'disappear'.

There was some urgency now and the classification level of the 45-minutes intelligence was such that the handling procedures of my note would slow it down unless I wrote something at a lower classification. This requirement accounts for the oblique references and clumsy style of my memorandum, which is reproduced below.[1]

19 Sep 02
<u>DIST</u>
MA/DCDI [+others]

IRAQ DOSSIER
Reference: Iraq Dossier Draft issued on 19 Sep 02

1. [My branch] has been involved in the generation of the Iraq dossier which, in the last two weeks involved a number of iterations which have incorporated new intelligence. It is my understanding that some of the intelligence [Report X] has not been made available to my branch. Because of this they have had to express their reservations on several aspects of the dossier. Most of these have been resolved. However, a number remain in the document at reference and it is important that I note for you at this stage the remaining areas where we are unable to confirm the statements made on the basis of the information available to my branch.

2. Although we have no problem with a *judgement* based on intelligence that Saddam attaches great importance to possessing WMD we have not seen the intelligence that 'shows' this to be the case. Nor have we seen intelligence that 'shows' he does not regard them only as a weapon of last resort, although our judgement is that it would be sensible to assume he might use them in a number of other scenarios. The intelligence we have seen *indicates* rather than 'shows' that Iraq has been planning to conceal its WMD capabilities, and it would be reasonable to assume that he would do this.

3. We have a number of questions in our minds relating to the intelligence on the military plans for the use of chemical and biological weapons, particularly about the times mentioned and the failure to differentiate between the two types of weapon.

4. We have not seen intelligence which we believe 'shows' that Iraq has continued to produce CW agent in 1998–2002, although our judgement is that it has probably done so. Whilst we are even more convinced that Iraq has continued to produce BW agent (on the basis of mobile production intelligence) we would not go so far as to say we 'know' this to be the case.

(Signed) Brian Jones
ADI NBC ST

As soon as I had clicked 'send' I telephoned Cragg's military assistant and told him the message would be in his email in-tray and that it should be brought to his boss's attention as soon as possible. Then I closed up my office and left for a long weekend.

In my absence on Friday 20 September yet another draft of the dossier was circulated. It has since become clear that this was necessary, at least in part, because No. 10, through Alastair Campbell, had produced the sort of substantive comments on 19 September that others had been told were not allowable at this late stage. The resulting alterations had to be given some sort of notional clearance, but this gave my chemical warfare expert, who had a copy of my minute, a good reason to add his views. Having argued the important expert points throughout the previous drafts he was able to be much more specific than I had been. Because my note was already on the record he could also afford not to worry that his, more highly classified, minute might not be read before the deadline. The higher classification allowed him to be more expansive. I was glad also that he chose to tackle the Prime Minister's foreword head on and that he was able to deal with the points we had discussed the previous day. My minute was to be released into the public domain much earlier than his and was given a thorough 'airing' in the media. His was released much later, is not easy to locate amongst the evidence of the Hutton inquiry, and received virtually no attention. In fact, well beyond Lord Hutton's final report, my colleague remained unaware that his contribution was in the public domain. His minute was much more important than mine. It said:

20 September 02
<u>DIST</u>
MA/DCDI, ADI NBC ST

IRAQ DOSSIER
Reference:
A. ADI NBC ST Minute dated 19 September 02
B. Iraq Dossier Draft issued on 20 September 02

1. At Reference A. Brian Jones recorded concerns of his Branch about some of the statements made in the draft of the Iraq Dossier issued on the 19 September. I have now seen the draft issued today (Ref B) and although one of the points referred to in Ref A has been addressed, others remain. The 20th September draft still includes a number of statements which are not supported by the evidence available to me. I have set out below my concerns about the CW aspects of the paper since this is my area of responsibility. Some of these statements have also been included in earlier drafts which I have commented on but my comments on those aspects have largely not been reflected in the later drafts.

2a. Prime Minister's Foreword, 5th paragraph, states: 'What I believe the assessed intelligence has established beyond doubt is that Saddam has continued to produce chemical and biological weapons. . .' I acknowledge that in this statement the Prime Minister will be expressing his own 'belief' about what the assessed intelligence has established. What I wish to record is that based on the intelligence available to me it has NOT established beyond doubt that Saddam has continued to produce chemical [and biological] weapons.

2b. Prime Minister's Foreword, 8th paragraph, states: 'And the document discloses that his military planning allows for some of the WMD to be ready within 45 minutes of an order to use them.' A similar statement appears in the Dossier. This is reported as fact whereas the intelligence comes from a single source. In my view the intelligence warrants no stronger a statement than 'intelligence suggests that military planning allows. . .'

2c. Executive Summary, paragraph 6, first bullet, states: 'As a result of the intelligence we judge that Iraq has . . . continued to produce chemical and biological agents.' I have seen intelligence that suggests that production of chemical agents has continued but in my judgement this warrants no stronger statement than 'Iraq has . . . probably continued to produce chemical [and biological] agents'.

2d. Executive Summary, paragraph 6, second bullet states: 'As a result of the intelligence we judge that Iraq has . . . military plans for the use of chemical . . . weapons. Some of these weapons are deployable within 45 minutes of an order to use them.' This is based on a single source. It is not clear what is meant by 'weapons are deployable within 45 minutes'. The judgement is too strong considering the intelligence on which it is based.

2e. Chapter 3, paragraph 1, first bullet. This contains a statement about 'recent production of chemical [and biological] agents' which cannot be supported by intelligence available to me.

2f. Chapter 3, paragraph 5, first bullet states that: 'Intelligence shows that Saddam attaches great importance to the possession of chemical [and biological] weapons. . .' I believe that the use of the term 'shows that' is far too strong . This is in contrast to other statements in this paragraph which use the term 'intelligence indicates that' which is more balanced.

2g. Chapter 3, paragraph 8, first bullet states that: 'Intelligence shows that Iraq has continued to produce chemical agent.' Based on the intelligence available to me it warrants no stronger a statement than 'Iraq has probably continued to produce chemical agent'.

(Signed by the originator)

An unwanted liaison

When I arrived at work after the weekend, my colleague was abroad on duty. I found his minute amongst my emails and read it with satisfaction. There was also a message from my boss thanking me for sending him the minute I had written on the dossier on 19 September, but making no other comment. There was no response from Tony Cragg. He said later that he did not see my colleague's minute until well after the dossier had been published.

I was quickly overwhelmed with normal business. During the day I was called to the director's office, where he told me there was to be a meeting later in the week in the Cabinet Office with representatives of the intelligence community of a foreign country.[2] The meeting had been arranged on the instruction of the Prime Minister in an effort to convince the country in question that the case made in the dossier was well founded and that Iraq had WMD. My boss had been told to represent the DIS because the deputy chief of defence intelligence would be away. 'I told Cragg I would need you there,' said my boss. 'He said he didn't want you to go but I insisted. He is absolutely livid about the minute you wrote, by the way.'

'Then why doesn't he tell me?' I said. 'I would be more than happy to discuss it with him.'

My intervention was ignored.

I said that because I could not endorse what the dossier said there would be potential embarrassment for all concerned if I was there.

'Now listen, Brian,' my boss lectured, 'I don't know what it is but you really seem to have a problem with authority, don't you? Decisions have been made, a position has been established and it is our responsibility as good civil servants to accept that and support the line as best we can.'

'I don't entirely accept that,' I replied. 'I have been in jobs where I respected that necessity, but you cannot apply it to our responsibilities in intelligence analysis. It would be sacrificing our credibility to argue something we didn't believe and our credibility is everything. When I joined the DIS I was told a JIC assessment is binding, and the whole of government must proceed according to what that dictates or implies, but it is quite reasonable for any one of us to hold an alternate view and to express it as long as we remind people of what the JIC says when we do so. It would not be appropriate to express an alternate view at this meeting with foreign representatives, and so I would rather not attend.'

'I want you there,' he said firmly, 'and I would like you to prepare a brief for me to make the best case possible.'

Publication day

The dossier was duly published on Tuesday 24 September. It was a major event. Parliament had been recalled especially to discuss it, and indeed this is what had dictated the rush to publication. It provided the Prime

Minister with a set piece to make a powerful statement condemning Iraq for retaining chemical and biological weapons, seeking nuclear weapons and being a threat to world peace.[3] It is important to remember that the irrevocable decision to write the dossier and recall Parliament to hear about it was made before the arrival of the intelligence contained in Report X that we had been told clinched the case that was being made.

It was not until its *second* edition of the day that the *Evening Standard* was 'on message'. '45 Minutes from Attack' was the black headline that set the tone for several of the dailies the following morning. I had thought the mention of the 45-minutes intelligence would easily be spotted as extravagantly inflammatory and quite meaningless when anyone tried to understand exactly what it implied. We had been concerned that the emphasis on 'forty-five minutes' might undermine not only the credibility of the dossier but of intelligence in general. Although some parts of the media were unimpressed by the dossier, none saw it for what it was. But the newspapers that reached the greater proportion of the population supported the dossier and it was swallowed by enough of the public (and Parliament) for the Prime Minister's purpose. I commented to a colleague that whatever we might think of him, Alastair Campbell was bloody good at his job – my assumption being that he had masterminded the intricate fabrication of a case to support an invasion of Iraq, and understood the potential of the 45-minutes issue to engage the public imagination.

After the dossier

For us, there was no 'comeback' from the dossier and for most some semblance of a return to normality. As my anger with my boss subsided, I put together a short speaking note for him to use at the meeting with foreign intelligence representatives. Although I did not agree with the general message the UK side would be trying to project, my suggested brief said nothing I could not live with or defend. It might even have seemed quite powerful to the non-expert, and was a case that the government could legitimately have made had it decided not to go overboard, but I was pretty sure the visiting foreign team would not be novices. In the event, the meeting was postponed for a week, but when it did happen I was still instructed to attend.

In the intervening period there was an interesting development. The original plan intended that MI6 would present the intelligence to convince the foreign visitors of the assessment. It was, after all, based on MI6 reporting and they had championed it despite the reservations of the analysts. Now it transpired that the senior officer who was to represent MI6 was not prepared to speak to the visitors. There may have been other reasons but I knew the man concerned and suspect he was not prepared to defend something he knew to be indefensible.

My boss told me that he might be called on to make a statement and I enjoyed telling him how outrageous it was that MI6 were not prepared to speak up for their own material. He ignored my dig but looked sheepish.

The meeting was held in the Cabinet Office conference room used by the JIC. Half a dozen visitors were there and perhaps twice as many represented the home side. My boss sat at the large circular table with the senior attendees whilst I sat with a number of other middle-rankers behind them so that advice and support could be offered if necessary. John Scarlett, with the chief of the Assessments Staff, Julian Miller, at his elbow, made all the running. In the event my boss was not required to make a major opening statement. Scarlett and Miller droned on, summarising the dossier and handing out copies of secret documents and assessments that they insisted supported it, in a gesture that was described as unprecedented in relations between the two countries. However, the whole process was conducted in a most low-key way, lacking totally any degree of animation or enthusiasm. It was as if their hearts were not in it.

I was struck by the silence of our visitors. They listened intently without speaking for over an hour. Then, at long last, their senior representatives made a few general comments, before handing the floor to a man described as their chemical warfare expert. I was both excruciatingly embarrassed by and exquisitely pleased with what he said. Embarrassed because he exposed the paucity of the case Scarlett and Miller had been trying to present, but pleased because here was someone who knew what he was talking about, responding directly to the flawed logic. His audience should not have needed the lesson in intelligence assessment he felt he had to give.

'We have listened very carefully to what you have said. But you have not provided us with any information that convinces us beyond doubt that Iraq actually has chemical or biological weapons. The sort of information we would look for and that you have not given us would be: what are the actual agents; what are the weapons; how were the agents made, where, how much? How, where and when were the weapons filled; where are they stored; where are they deployed; how will they be used? You have told us none of these things.

'Listen, we do not disagree with what you have told us. We also think that Saddam *probably* has weapons of mass destruction. But we do not know for sure and we could not support military action unless we were sure.'

I had to contain the temptation to applaud. This man's reservations would be shared by any sensible intelligence analyst from any country in the world. It was hard for me to gauge whether Scarlett and Miller understood what they were being told but they offered no counter-argument. After this the meeting stuttered to an end. It had failed in its objective. Our visitors were unconvinced. I was smiling as I crossed Whitehall back to my office, having found such a strong endorsement of our position from a most unlikely quarter.

After that the dossier faded quickly into a background that, for me, was filled with the hectic activity required to bring a new branch into being. The chief of defence intelligence decided he wanted to press on with reform before a new head of branch was selected. There was a whole new area of non-scientific activity that had to be melded into the work of the new branch. Within days I was told that I would be offered the early retirement I had requested and, although I was delighted, it brought with it even heavier demands on the time I had left.

With my focus on other things I could not concentrate on the detail of other business that was in hand and delegated increasingly to my section heads. I remained aware of significant new intelligence and paid some attention to various JIC assessments that were written but nothing of significance arose to challenge the position we had taken on the dossier. I spoke to Tony Cragg a number of times in the following weeks. Neither of us raised the matter of the dossier.

In October we were passed a NOFORN copy of a US National Intelligence Estimate on the status of Iraq's WMD capability and programmes.[4] It provided no indication that the US community held any intelligence that gave them significantly greater confidence than we had that Iraq held stockpiles of chemical or biological weapons. A JIC paper at the end of October contained the odd statement that 'confirmed intelligence reveals that transportable BW production facilities have been constructed'. Reflecting the reassurance we had been given earlier of the independence of a new source, it provided no detail of when the production facilities had been made, whether they still existed or what they had produced.[5]

On 8 November the UN Security Council adopted Resolution 1441. Sir Jeremy Greenstock, British ambassador to the UN, viewed it as a considerable achievement because of the ambiguity it established over whether further Security Council approval was necessary before military action could be taken.[6] Iraq was required to provide immediate, unconditional and active cooperation to UNMOVIC and IAEA inspectors and any 'material breach' would lead the council 'to consider the situation and the need for compliance'. This left open the exact definition of what would constitute a 'material breach', who would certify that one had occurred and whether a council decision was an essential precursor to military action. Ten days later Hans Blix was in Baghdad and discussed the mechanics of the inspection process with Dr Amin al-Sa'adi.[7] Inspections began towards the end of the month.

Resolution 1441 also required complete disclosure of all aspects of the WMD programme and related matters. It was delivered on 8 December and ran to 12,000 pages, mainly in Arabic. The sheer volume and requirement for translation generated a logistical nightmare for UNMOVIC because timescales were short. When copies arrived in London a few days later, my visibility was minimal because by now I had delegated most activities that would run beyond my impending retirement. Some of my staff, David Kelly and others worked long hours over several days to help provide early guidance on whether it was satisfactory. Although the detail of analysis which could be done was by no means ideal, they were able to establish that significant outstanding questions were not answered.[8] This was the view of the experts in my branch even though they had no expectation that weapon stockpiles or current production facilities would or necessarily should feature in the declaration. Unfortunately the document and the final analysis of it have never been made widely available because of fears about its potential to aid proliferators. The five permanent members of the Security Council also agreed that copies for the other member countries should be truncated.[9]

In December 2002, a JIC assessment noted that Iraq's ability to use chemical and biological weapons might be constrained by its available stocks of agent and the difficulty of producing more whilst UN inspectors were present. The JIC acknowledged that it did not know the extent of Iraq's stocks of chemical and biological weapons.[10] Neither the JIC assessment of late October nor the one in December reflected the degree of confidence about Iraq's possession of WMD that Report X was earlier alleged to have provided. This left me slightly happier that the analysts were regaining balance in the assessments.

I retired in January 2003, two months before the invasion of Iraq. In the closing conversation with my boss a few days before I left, he reminded me of how angry the deputy chief had been about 'that minute' I had written and said that he was still annoyed three months later.

'Pity he never mentioned it to me,' I said.

On the outside

The first weeks of my retirement were very busy with domestic matters but the approaching war with Iraq was always in the background and I found I had more time to organise my thoughts on what was happening.

I was sure inspections would find no smoking gun. The main question was whether an incident which clearly showed the inspectors were being obstructed would spark the conflict. I could not know for sure then that this is what Tony Blair and George W. Bush were hoping for, but I had my suspicions.

During the nine or ten weeks before the Iraq War started I was disturbed by much that was being said and written about the situation. I was constrained in what I could say publicly about the intelligence and policy background but I thought I had scope to write about it in general military and technical terms. When I came to do so, I faced the difficulty of explaining what could easily be taken for a contradiction in my logic. On the one hand, some commentators suggested that the dangers posed by chemical and biological weapons generally were being exaggerated by the government. I wanted to explain that, although the specific threat said to be posed by Iraq was 'overspun', these weapons did have the potential to be very dangerous.

On the other hand, the government was suggesting that the possession of WMD by a state such as Iraq presented a special danger in the form of leakage of capability to terrorists. This was a way of establishing a link between the threatened invasion of Iraq and Bush's 'war on terror'. There was a much clearer foundation of support to deal with the potential terror threat than there was for a war with Iraq. A point that I thought people should understand was that the link between state CBW programmes and terrorists was being much exaggerated. Terrorists could make such chemical and biological weapons as would suit their purpose on their own without enormous difficulty. The same was not the case with weapons capable of generating a nuclear explosion.[11] But the politicians were conflating nuclear, chemical and biological weapons as 'WMD' so that the blackest of pictures could be painted and the public's ready recognition of the devastating power of nuclear weapons exploited.[12] Iraq had never had nuclear weapons, nor was it particularly close to having them in 2003.

I thought it was important that the public should understand these differences and I drafted an article that explained them. I was surprised that my request to Whitehall for clearance for me to submit it for publication was promptly approved. Unfortunately, no one wanted to publish it.[13]

There were interesting differences between the cases for war that were being made in Washington and in London, although both insisted that Saddam possessed WMD and that the problem was acute. The British case was mainly about chemical weapons, blurred around the edges to encompass biological weapons. Much less was made of the nuclear programme – aluminium tubes for the enrichment of uranium from Africa were not a major part of the British case. And when Bush mentioned British intelligence on Iraq's attempting to obtain uranium from Africa, London remained silent, probably because the intelligence was not quite as incriminating as Washington made it sound. However, the fact that nuclear weapons were major elements in the American argument, if not the smoking guns that might never be found before a mushroom cloud revealed the threat, meant that they played well in a British media that hung on Washington's every word. Mobile biological weapon production trailers were a major part of the US argument, plucked out by the much-admired Secretary of State, Colin Powell, in a speech to the UN Security Council on 5 February. He showed the UN and the world drawings of the units which were probably imagined guesses of what they might look like, rather than accurate representations of the real thing.[14] Powell's well-known opposition to the war up to this point meant that the case he now made for Saddam's possession of WMD seemed all the more credible. American analysts appear to have seen much more from the source they called 'Curveball' than their British counterparts. We remained less sure of the current existence of biological warfare trailers. Of course, national intelligence authorities never share everything with their foreign counterparts and if the thrust of the US message was slightly different, it was all the more powerful in Britain because of that. Similarly although the US did not latch on to the 45-minute warning and recent chemical production, George Tenet, director of central intelligence, was to make it clear after the war that the reports from intelligence allies influenced him.

However, by now the lack of return from inspections was causing problems. As it became increasingly clear that the inspectors would not be obstructed nor find any WMD, No. 10 was desperate not to let any propaganda advantage it had slip too far. It contrived to invent yet another dossier purporting to show how efficient and effective Saddam's campaign for concealment and deception was. This was passed off as being underpinned by recent intelligence and endorsed by the JIC, but it was not.[15]

During February, as the struggle towards a second resolution continued, the idea of setting specific benchmarks for Iraq to meet was developed. They would provide the Security Council with a means of deciding whether Iraq was meeting its obligations. Jeremy Greenstock put down six tests on 13 March which were immediately rejected by the French as its opposition to a second resolution hardened. The British government accused the French of unreasonable obstruction, but it is extremely difficult to recognise at least three of the benchmarks as serious given the quality of the intelligence on which they were apparently based. It was by no means certain from the intelligence held by Britain that Saddam had the WMD he was required to admit to concealing, or that he had the anthrax he was supposed to surrender or prove he had destroyed, or that he had any mobile chemical and biological production facilities he could surrender. He was being asked to turn suspicions into certainties.

The first of two ministerial resignations immediately preceding the war was that of Robin Cook on 17 March, the day before the debate in which Parliament gave its approval for British participation in the Iraq war. It is the better remembered, not least for the emotional reception that greeted Cook's statement in the House. On that day the Cabinet met without him and heard advice on the legality of a war from the Attorney General, Lord Goldsmith. A few weeks earlier Goldsmith had been equivocal on the matter but with the chief of the Defence Staff requiring a clear decision he now told the Cabinet that if Iraq was in 'material breach' of Resolution 1441, British participation in military action would be legal.[16] Tony Blair decided Iraq was in material breach of the resolution, probably basing his decision on the written advice John Scarlett had provided to Sir David Manning that day. That advice recorded: 'The JIC view is clear: Iraq possesses chemical and biological weapons, the means to deliver them and the capacity to re-establish production. The scale of the holdings is hard to quantify. It is undoubtedly much less than in 1991. Evidence points to a capability that is already militarily significant.'[17]

The second, less publicised, resignation was that of John Denham during the Iraq war debate on 18 March. Denham was the Home Office minister whose brief included responsibility for civil defence and preparations for chemical and biological attacks against Britain. This would have made him acutely aware of the risks to the country from terrorism. The reason he gave for standing down was that he felt that in attempting to deal with the various causes of insecurity the government was, in fact, creating new ones.[18] He thought our resulting isolation was a real danger. Denham's resignation and comment suggested a significant dislocation in policy and did not inspire confidence that the government had invested enough to offset the increased risk of a terror attack at home as part of its contingency planning for Britain's participation in the invasion of an Islamic country.

By now it was clear that, as Greenstock would put it later,[19] an invasion of Iraq would not have the backing of a great majority of the states on the Security Council or perhaps even a majority of people inside the United Kingdom, and, even if Resolution 1441 made it legal, its legitimacy was therefore questionable. This much was clear to the House of Commons when it supported the government's motion which included an endorsement of the decision 'that the United Kingdom should use all means necessary to ensure the disarmament of Iraq's weapons of mass destruction'. Although the motion was passed comfortably, 139 of Blair's own backbenchers rebelled and voted against the war.

On 19 March a JIC assessment drew attention to a report from 'a reliable source' which indicated that, at that time, Iraq's chemical weapons remained disassembled and that Saddam had not yet ordered their assembly.[20] I cannot envisage a chemical weapon of the type Iraq was capable of producing that would be amenable to dismantling in this way.

Hans Blix had a long telephone conversation with Blair on 20 March.[21] From Blix's account it is difficult to afford either participant significant credibility. Although their line was secure, the discussion appears to have been conducted in the abstract. Despite guidance from UK and US intelligence, nothing to match the claims of Blair and Bush had been found. But Blix appears not to have asked challenging questions about types or quantities of agent or weapons or alternative locations. For his part Blair seemed to limply justify his certainty on the belief of the French, German and Egyptian intelligence agencies, without providing any detail.

Even without the leaks that came later, it was clear to me that some in Washington believed that diplomacy offered no solution to once-distant fears about America's security that had crystallised into a current crisis by dint of the direct assaults of 9/11. There is no doubt that America was prepared to pursue military action on its own. Faced with this Blair had recognised early not only the possibility of a split between Europe and the US, but also the potential for Britain to influence the Bush approach by persuading him to seek the support of the United Nations for any action that he was planning. But to do this from a position of strength against a hard core of the administration that was frustrated with the indecisiveness of the UN, Blair had adopted a public approach in support of the need for military action. He had been successful but failed at the final hurdle – there would be no unequivocal UN support for action.

Britain had worked hard to bring the Security Council on board. During this period Mexico held one of the rotational seats on the council, and Adolfo Zinser was its ambassador in New York. In February 2003, Greenstock had arranged for Zinser to be briefed by a team the Mexican believed to be from MI6.[22] This was during the period when a second, unambiguous Security Council resolution was being sought to give authority for military action against Iraq. The assessment on Iraq's WMD that Zinser received was more equivocal than the statements that were being made by members of the British and American governments. If, as seems likely, Zinser's briefers were indeed from MI6, it illustrates a sphere of MI6 activity that is rarely visible – promotion of policy on the government's behalf. Although it appears to have been undertaken with integrity, there is obviously risk that such action carries with it a temptation to compromise accuracy to achieve a favourable outcome.

I thought that in the long term British national security needs probably justified the support that Blair was offering Bush. Although the US was the main 'enemy' of rogue states and international terrorists, it would always be a difficult target for them to attack because of its vast intelligence and security machine. Hence other Western countries, like Britain, would become more attractive. Attacks on them would remind America that it was vulnerable to follow-up attacks after 9/11, and would keep it on edge, consume resources and foment instability. Such attacks would be good propaganda for the terrorists, boosting morale, aiding recruitment and increasing the US's inclination to isolate itself. If the US was not wrapped into the international community, making elements of its security machine available to its allies, the UK and the rest of Europe would be much more vulnerable.

I believed there were also other strategic security reasons for the UK and Europe to ensure the United States remained a close and involved ally because, although the inter-state security environment was relatively benign, it could change quickly in the most unexpected ways. For half a century, that environment was frozen with the hugely powerful Soviet Union threatening the West. Suddenly, Soviet communism collapsed and, throughout the 1990s and beyond 2000, the Russian rump which had claimed all of the former Soviet strategic military power edged only slowly towards the stable democracy that could make her a full partner of the West. By 2002, President Putin's determination to continue to strive for that goal appeared to be waning. Dark forces were visiting growing chaos on a country which had yet to experience anything like a universal benefit from its evolving 'democratic' politico-economic system. And whilst Russia had enormous problems to solve, it had huge economic potential and retained very real military power which, if only by virtue of its WMD, hugely outweighed that of its European neighbours. Perhaps fearful of her economic vulnerability, Russia appeared reluctant to drop her military guard. Russia's power in the military sphere was still matched only by that of the US. I thought it would have been an extreme folly to risk the exclusion of America from the wider security equation when it was less than certain that future Russian leaderships would adopt a benign attitude to the West in general, and the rest of Europe, its greatest economic competitor, in particular.

I thought it was vital for Britain and Europe that the US remain an active part of the democratic international community and that every effort be made to ensure this. It had been a dominant British policy during the Cold War and its validity had not diminished with the demise of the Soviet Union. I could see that such an objective was compatible with Blair's party political, and perhaps even his personal, aspirations. His successful election strategy had been based on the occupation of policy ground previously held by the Conservative Party. The Tories' traditional closeness to America and especially the Republican Party was a factor. Staying close to the Bush administration would have appeared a worthwhile objective for New Labour and would further underpin the personal popularity that Blair enjoyed in the States.

Given all that, and despite feeling that the case that was being made to the public leaned unreasonably on WMD, I was inclined to believe it was in Britain's national interest to join with America in the assault on Saddam's Iraq, even without full UN support. It was not a matter of supporting President Bush, but it was the danger of losing the American people as allies that worried me. For, as I have explained, America's friendship is of vital importance to us. But this is not just because of its wealth and power, or even because it is a democracy founded on principles of the greatest integrity. I felt it was the enduring good nature of its people and their values and humanity as reflected in their culture, their art and literature that should guide our actions, rather than the faults of a fleeting and unrepresentative administration.

But even more pragmatically, there was no easy choice for us. Our European partners could sit relatively quietly on the sidelines neither overtly helping or actually hindering the Americans. But we were already long-term military partners in Iraq, enforcing the no-fly zone. We also had assets in the region that the Americans would wish to use. If we withdrew from one and refused the other, that would be a betrayal of such magnitude and impact as would only be possible between close friends and allies. And ironically, if we did not join in, the failure of the invasion would spell greater danger for the UK than its success. A defeated America would become more isolated and insular than a successful one. The wedge between us would be driven harder and deeper by failure and the sense that our betrayal had contributed to it. Regardless of any later appreciation by a growing majority in the US that we were right and the terrible fault lay with President Bush, the desertion by an ally would weigh heavy in determining their future attitude to Britain.

But, even if he had wanted to, Tony Blair could not say to George W. Bush, 'You are wrong, but we are going to help you anyway.' And, given the political style he had adopted, there was little scope for him to explain himself to his party, let alone the British people. I felt a little sorry for him struggling with the dilemma that fate had presented him. Of course, I did not know in March 2003 about the 'clever plans' that Sir David Manning and Sir Christopher Meyer had trailed in Washington before

Blair's April 2002 visit to Bush, or of the 23 July 2002 Downing Street meeting that I now believe to have been the true genesis of the fudge in the September dossier. I thought Blair was taking a risk for which he would pay dearly if it failed. I was worried that he might try to slide away from the personal responsibility by projecting too much of the blame towards the intelligence community. However, I could not have anticipated how things would develop, nor Blair's powers of survival or the extent of my own involvement in what was to follow.

PART III

COVER-UP

CHAPTER SEVEN

March–July 2003:
The war and immediately after

Invasion

I watched the war unfold from an armchair. The experience brought home to me how different things were now I had retired and lost access to Whitehall, its frantic atmosphere and its secrets. Although I thought it unlikely there were large quantities of chemical or biological weapons in Iraq, I could not be sure there were none and I waited anxiously for news of a chemical or biological attack. If there was one, I was sure we would take casualties.

Early covert use of non-lethal agents could cause confusion and hamper our forces. An agent that caused a disease that incapacitated but did not kill Allied forces might disrupt the invasion enough to cause President Bush to think again without provoking a backlash against Iraq from the Security Council members that opposed military action. It did not happen. The next point of danger would probably be when the fall of the Baghdad regime was imminent.[1]

Hostilities began suddenly on 20 March without prior incident. Neither chemical nor biological weapons were used in the conflict that ensued. By the time the fall of Saddam Hussein's statue in Baghdad's Firdaus Square was choreographed for the world's media on 9 April, I was convinced that, as we had suspected might be the case, none had existed. On 1 May President Bush announced that major fighting in the war was over. As the triumph was celebrated, it was in the looming shadow of questions about what had happened to the WMD.

Kelly starts talking

In the first half of May, the science reporter for BBC Television's *Newsnight*, Susan Watts, spoke on the telephone with David Kelly. Kelly told her of the intelligence community's misgivings about weapons of mass destruction before the war and Alastair Campbell's influence on the dossier. In discussions with journalists over the next few weeks, Kelly associated himself with those misgivings. At first, Watts took this aspect of their conversation to be incidental 'gossip' and did not use the information. Kelly, who had been excluded from Hans Blix's UNMOVIC inspections in the early part of the year, was by now eagerly anticipating his return to work in Iraq with the Iraq Survey Group.

The eventual formation of a group to deal with WMD in Iraq after the war had been discussed in Whitehall for several months before the invasion. One of my staff was involved in anticipating the group's requirements. However, neither the advancing coalition forces nor the advance guard of the Survey Group, the 75th Exploitation Task Force, had uncovered any evidence of WMD. I am sure that did not surprise Kelly. Perhaps his words to Watts were intended to reduce the expectations of the media about what was to come when he got back to Iraq.

The Iraq Survey Group shapes up

By now the Iraq Survey Group was being assembled. The nature of the group – who had ultimate authority and whether it was led by the military, by intelligence or by civilian inspectors – remains something of an enigma.[2] Overall control was in the hands of the Pentagon and Major General Keith Dayton, of the US Defence Intelligence Agency. However, he was a military commander, not a WMD expert. The input of intelligence would be essential.

At the political level, it was hoped that the Survey Group would be seen as an independent and authoritative body when it found WMD in Iraq. To establish distance between government and the Survey Group, Dr David Kay was appointed as the CIA's special adviser to the group. Kay is a political scientist and had been an International Atomic Energy Agency employee and a chief inspector in Iraq in the 1990s. Now he was a senior corporate vice president with a company called Science Applications International Corporation and based just outside Washington, DC in McLean, Virginia, suitably close to the CIA at Langley and to the Pentagon. He was not a member of the intelligence community nor a direct employee of the US government. Neither was he a scientist or a technical expert on any type of

WMD. He had, however, played an important part in the IAEA effort that gained solid evidence in 1991 about Iraq's nuclear weapon programme. Kay knew about the subsequent UNSCOM experience and the nuclear weapon development programme that Iraq eventually acknowledged after the strange 'excursion' of Saddam's son-in-law Hussein Kamil to Jordan in 1995.

On 10 September 2002, Kay had provided a statement to the House (of Representatives) Armed Services Committee in Washington which appears to summarise his position before the invasion of Iraq. Not surprisingly it had a 'nuclear' bias. He told them he thought the capability to produce weapons of mass destruction arising from a national programme on the scale of Iraq's could not be eliminated by simply destroying 'weapons' facilities. The UN inspection process should be credited with destroying the physical aspects of a substantial nuclear weapons establishment in Iraq, but the secrets of nuclear weapons were now well understood by Iraq's technical elite, and the production capabilities necessary to turn these 'secrets' into weapons would survive even the most draconian of sanctions regimes. Kay thought that as long as a government committed to acquiring WMD remained in Baghdad, that capability could be expected to become – and without much warning – a reality.

Kay thought the four-year absence of inspectors from Iraq meant that it was impossible to be sure of the status of their nuclear programme. If inspectors started work tomorrow, it would take a very long, sustained period of unfettered inspections to establish the present position. He thought national intelligence efforts would offer only limited clarity on this. WMD programmes were the hardest targets for intelligence service to unravel, even when very large. Kay cited the extensive Soviet-era biological programme, which went undiscovered until after the end of the Cold War. He noted that the size of the Soviet uranium enrichment programme had been seriously under-estimated and that major nuclear production facilities had remained unidentified until after the fall of the Soviet Union.

Kay concluded that unless immediate steps were taken to address the issue of removing Saddam's regime from power, it was clear that the US would soon face a nuclear-armed and emboldened Iraq. Kay thought that given time, Saddam would be able to intimidate his neighbours with nuclear weapons and find the means to use them against the United States. This rhetoric will have endeared him to the White House and the Pentagon.

In May 2003, Kay was in Iraq as a consultant for NBC News observing the activities of the 75th Exploitation Task Force. He managed to gain access to the second of two suspicious trailers that the US forces had discovered. Unqualified himself to make a judgement about it, he is said to have sought the views of someone present who he believed to be knowledgeable. On 11 May, he reflected on what he had been told on *NBC Nightly News*, expressing certainty that the trailer was for biological warfare agent production.[3]

When he returned to Washington Kay was critical of the search for WMD that was in process and of the previous efforts of UNMOVIC. On 30 May the creation of the Iraq Survey Group was announced. A few days later Kay was selected by George Tenet and appointed as, effectively, the group's chief surveyor. President Bush endorsed the move. Kay appears to have had responsibilities to both Dayton and Tenet. His job was to run the search for Iraq's weapons as the senior civilian in the Iraq Survey Group.

Given all that he had experienced and observed, much of it encapsulated in his statement to the House Armed Services Committee the previous September, it is difficult to understand why, when the Iraq Survey Group commenced its work, Kay said he had expected to find large stocks of chemical and biological agents, weaponised ready for use on the battlefield, as well as a fairly substantial nuclear programme. He can have seen no intelligence as comprehensive as that available in 1990, when UNSCOM had still been unable to find any smoking guns, other than for chemical warfare. There was a possibility in 2003 of the existence of real weapons, but there would definitely *not* be the vast chemical stockpiles that had been found so quickly in 1991.

I suspect Kay's judgement may have been affected by his previous experience in Iraq of many obstructive and hostile inspections. In the period after UNSCOM left Iraq in 1998, I formed the opinion that Kay developed a tendency to make unsubstantiated assertions and adopted a hawkish tone with respect to Iraq. Tenet confirmed in his 2007 memoir that this is why he was selected, and the American administration approved Kay as the 'expert' most likely to find weapons.

British involvement in the Iraq Survey Group was established with the appointment of Brigadier John Deverill as Dayton's deputy. Some on the British side expected David Kelly to be appointed as the senior British civilian, working to Deverill alongside Kay. With his vast experience of inspections in Iraq he would have been an ideal choice. But that was not to be. However, it was still on the cards in mid-May, when Kelly travelled to Iraq.

Dayton, Kay and Deverill were to go together to Baghdad to assess and plan their task, prior to starting work the following month.[4] Kelly appears to have persuaded his manager at the MoD that he should accompany Deverill in order to better advise the British contingent what to expect and how to organise. He would have been a valuable member of that senior team, bringing authority, experience and technical expertise as the only scientist in the quartet. At last, Iraq beckoned and promised to provide a return to something like the status that he had enjoyed at the UN in his UNSCOM days.

Kelly got as far as Kuwait before it was discovered there was a problem with the required transit documentation. On 19 May, embarrassed and annoyed, he had to return to Britain. He must have wondered if his chance to return to Iraq had been lost. Would he be excluded from the Iraq Survey Group in the same way he had missed out on UNMOVIC? He may have been aware of the reluctance of some in Whitehall to involve him.

Kelly talks some more

On Thursday 22 May David Kelly met Andrew Gilligan at the Charing Cross Hotel in central London. Gilligan was a journalist who worked on BBC Radio 4's *Today* programme. He had experience of defence and security matters and possessed an investigative frame of mind. Perhaps Kelly, disappointed by failing to get into Iraq, was more forceful in what he told Gilligan than he had been with Susan Watts. Before a week had passed Kelly had spoken in similar terms both to Gavin Hewitt, another BBC reporter, and again to Watts. Gilligan appears to have taken him more seriously than his BBC colleagues.

By now, a storm was brewing in Whitehall at the failure of the WMD to materialise. The Prime Minister had convinced a clear majority in Parliament and enough of the country that the weapons were there – he had no doubt they existed. The government called for patience. It would take time for the experts of the Iraq Survey Group to uncover the incriminating evidence. We must wait for their report. The government's tactics were becoming clear: it was their intention not to admit the likelihood that there were no WMD until such an admission could be lost in the good news of a stable and improving Iraq, free from Saddam's chains.

Rumours and inquiries

But the press reported rumours from unnamed sources that the 'intelligence services' were growing increasingly angry about what had been done in their name. From the comfort and isolation of my retirement, I guessed that such reports were inspired mainly by MI6, an organisation that excelled at giving off-the-record briefings to selected journalists to ensure it was always seen in the best possible light. I knew it would be keen to avoid the blame for its mistakes. Stimulated by these leaks, the calls for an independent inquiry into the background to the Iraq War continued to rise. The government responded with an announcement that the Intelligence and Security Committee would investigate the matter. Few were satisfied with this, because of the unusual status of the ISC compared to parliamentary committees.

The select committee system of parliamentary oversight, borrowed from Washington and imperfectly applied in London, does not extend to the darker recesses of the world of intelligence. Only when forced by circumstances in the early 1990s did our executive devise a system for the oversight of intelligence. The ordinary inhabitants of Westminster had to be kept at arm's length from the subject of secrets. And so the ISC was invented.

The ISC meets in secret, is sworn not to discuss the most important matters outside its meetings, and is advised by the agencies, with the backing of No. 10, on what it would be unwise to make public. It has no responsibility to Parliament other than through the Prime Minister, who is the minister responsible for intelligence. It is the equivalent of allowing secretaries of state to choose which MPs should sit on the select committees that oversee their departments on behalf of Parliament. Not only does this fail to inspire confidence but it stifles wider parliamentary debate by preserving a high level of unmentionable ignorance of intelligence matters in the House. This is probably why the Foreign Affairs Committee decided, to the considerable consternation of No. 10, that it would hold a more public inquiry of its own.

Gilligan's broadcasts

It was not until 29 May 2003, a week after he spoke to David Kelly, that Andrew Gilligan made a number of broadcasts on BBC radio which were to inspire a national convulsion. Gilligan reported that a senior government official, who had been in charge of drafting parts of the Prime Minister's September dossier, had said the intelligence services were unhappy about the dossier. The intelligence about Iraq's capability to deploy and use chemical and biological weapons within forty-five minutes was one of the issues that concerned them. It was unreliable because it came from a single source but it had been seized on by No. 10 as something to support their case.

The first broadcast of this information, a little after six o'clock in the morning, reported that the '45-minute' item had been included against the wishes of intelligence and the government had probably known it was wrong. Gilligan continued, 'Downing Street, our source says, a week before publication, ordered it to be sexed up, to be made more exciting and ordered more facts to be, er, to be discovered.' He finished the piece with the words, 'Clearly, you know, if, erm, if it was wrong – things do, things are, got wrong in good faith – but if they knew it was wrong before they actually made the claim, that's perhaps a bit more serious.' Although he raised the question, Gilligan was equivocal about whether the government really had behaved in a disingenuous manner.

Gilligan was more fluent in a later contribution and stressed again the uncertainty of what his source had told him:

> But you know, it could have been an honest mistake, but what I have been told is that the government knew that claim was questionable, even before the war, even before they wrote it in their dossier . . . Now I want to stress that this official and others I've spoken to do still believe that Iraq did have some sort of weapons of mass destruction programme.

Immediately after Gilligan's second report, the *Today* anchor, John Humphrys, interviewed defence minister Adam Ingram. Ingram had been lined up to answer questions on other matters but Humphrys could hardly not raise Gilligan's report with him. During the course of a fractious discussion Humphrys was again careful to stress that *Today* was not suggesting any dishonesty on the part of Downing Street but simply reporting what a seemingly good source had said: 'The allegation was not that it was concocted by No. 10, the allegation was that a report was produced, it went to No. 10, it was then sent back to be "sexed up" a little. I'm using not my own words, but the words of our source.'

Ingram suggested the source was from within the security services. Humphrys echoed this shortly afterwards – 'What we have here is a source within the intelligence service' – appearing to confirm the minister's assumption. But Gilligan had not said the source was a member of the intelligence service. The suggestion that the source was from within intelligence was given further credibility when John Reid, a Cabinet minister, spoke rather hysterically in the House of Commons about a faction within the security service that was out of control.

It was to be some time before I made any connection between Gilligan's report and my discussions with Kelly back in September 2002. Kelly was not part of the intelligence community and had never expressed any reservations about the dossier to me. In fact he had only stressed its positive value in assisting the return of inspectors to Iraq. I assumed that Gilligan's source was probably someone from MI6 although I had never heard any member of that service voice concern about the 45-minutes intelligence or the dossier.

I was surprised at Alastair Campbell's later insistence that Gilligan had said the 45-minutes intelligence was included in the knowledge that it was wrong. Gilligan had clearly identified a degree of uncertainty about the information, but that counted for nothing in the fierce media battle that followed.

Probably more by design than accident, the timing of Gilligan's broadcast was exquisite. It coincided with the Prime Minister's triumphant visit to UK forces in Iraq to celebrate their achievements and bask in the reflected glory of a 'victory' swiftly won and with minimal casualties. Tony Blair's head of communications must have been angered when Gilligan's revelations undermined what should have been a public relations masterpiece. Campbell was already having a running battle with Gilligan over his reporting of the war. This was a victory for the BBC journalist.

Gilligan went on to claim that the source said it was Alastair Campbell who had driven the production of a flawed dossier[5] and, at first, this seemed to account for Campbell's vitriolic reaction. Looking back, it seems likely that there was a more complicated rationale for Campbell's angry attacks on Gilligan and the BBC.

Campbell's public explosion was not immediate. A few days later, on 2 and 4 June, Susan Watts gave reports on *Newsnight* that appeared to support Gilligan's case. They were little remarked upon in the press. The heat seemed to have gone out of the story. But they will have been noticed by Campbell's press office and it was Campbell who brought the matter back to the boil despite the obvious risk that it would 'damage' the Prime Minister. A more sensible course would have been to agree with the BBC that no such accusation had been made nor was intended by the corporation.

Campbell's game was a dangerous one, but a blazing row between No. 10 and the BBC was what he needed to provide a diversion from the growing arguments over the absence of WMD in Iraq. It was the greatest threat to the Prime Minister's reputation – and the House of Commons Foreign Affairs Committee was about to turn a spotlight onto the issue.

Mobile biological laboratories found?

Meanwhile, David Kelly managed to get to Iraq. During a short visit in early June, he managed to take a look at one of the suspected 'mobile biological laboratories' that had been discovered. A team from the US Defense Intelligence Agency had examined them a few days earlier and doubted that they were for biological warfare purposes. Despite this, the US and British governments were heralding this mobile equipment as proof of the accuracy of their assertions about Saddam's WMD. But Kelly was not impressed and appears to have been disturbed by the politicians' rush to judgement. He was contacted by *The Observer* and left its reporter in no doubt that the mobile laboratories he had seen were not for biological warfare agent production. Kelly was obviously aware of the sensitivity of what he had to say because he was not identified in the resulting article.[6]

Public evidence to the Foreign Affairs Committee

On 17 June the House of Commons Foreign Affairs Committee began holding public hearings. I took a great interest in its progress. The government was not cooperative. Despite this, the committee began a process of progressive revelation that would continue for the best part of a year through a sequence of successive inquiries. It took public evidence from the two Cabinet ministers who had resigned over the Iraq War.

Clare Short, who resigned from her post as Secretary of State for International Development after the war, was asked whether she believed the threat and the intelligence position were exaggerated. She replied that she thought the briefings she had received were reasonably balanced but that people were confused by the phrase 'weapons of mass destruction' and the implications of its use. She grappled with the confusing terminology and with what defined a capability as opposed to a programme. Even at that early stage, over a year before the Iraq Survey Group was to report, Short's recollection was that the intelligence picture she was given, almost certainly from MI6 or John Scarlett's Cabinet Office department, was more about laboratory work and the intention to develop a capability than the existence of stockpiles of weapons. What she may not have understood, perhaps because it was never explained, is that the step is quite small from the laboratory to a very significant offensive *biological* warfare capability that would potentially be a weapon of mass destruction. For some biological weapons to be strategically important it is not necessary to develop and hold large stockpiles over long periods of time.

Robin Cook had been Foreign Secretary throughout Tony Blair's first term. However, in the post-election reshuffle of June 2001, six months after the Bush administration took over in Washington, he was 'demoted' but still remained in the Cabinet as leader of the House of Commons. He resigned from the Cabinet in March 2003, before the invasion of Iraq, objecting to the imminent invasion. His explanation to the FAC of why he resigned was littered with misconceptions.

Liberal Democrat MP David Chidgey asked him a challenging and provocative question about the difficulty of controlling biological weapons. He said the FAC had previously been told that any quantity below 1,000 litres of anthrax would be almost impossible to discover in a place like Iraq. Was that the view of the intelligence services? Since even that amount of anthrax has the potential to do incredible damage to many people, was it impossible to remove the threat? If so, the only sensible policy would be to remove the organisation that would use that threat. Was this what the government believed and, if so, when did it decide that the only solution would be to pursue a policy of regime change rather than the suppression of weapons that were so difficult to find?

Chidgey was right. It is virtually impossible to be sure that a significant potential biological warfare threat has been removed. A sizeable stockpile of anthrax could be produced from a small initial stock within weeks or even days.[7]

Robin Cook's answer betrayed a degree of misunderstanding that I would not have expected from a minister with his reputation who, as

Foreign Secretary, was for several years primarily responsible for the issue of WMD disarmament. He thought these things were difficult to find, easy to conceal and had complicated the disarmament process until 1998. However, after 1998 he saw no compelling, urgent reason to believe that containment was not working in the sense of keeping Saddam in his cage. He seemed to think the problem Chidgey had described reflected the US attitude to arms control and that anthrax was not as much of a problem as suggested. He said Iraq's biological agents were not weaponised and could not be used for military purposes. Agents such as anthrax were extremely toxic and a menace to anybody near them, and it was fortunate that it is not particularly easy to weaponise biological agents. Cook said this was because weapons tended either to explode or incinerate, which would destroy the biological agent. He noted this difficulty of weaponisation was 'fortunate for humanity because it is actually quite easy to get hold of biological agents; it is fortunate it is not particularly easy to turn them into weapons'.

In fact anthrax is not too difficult to handle. In the Second World War at Porton Down, anthrax-laced cattle cakes were produced which would have been dropped on Germany if it had used nerve agents or biological weapons against Britain.[8] If anthrax is suspended in a liquid slurry it presents no great hazard until it is sprayed into the air and gets into the lungs. It can be handled reasonably safely unless the handler has a skin wound. Also there are vaccines that would allow people to work on anthrax with few other precautions.

Anthrax is quite a robust micro-organism (which is partly why it is such a concern) and even 1940s technology allowed the UK to produce bombs with light, fragile casings requiring only small burster charges. They were successfully tested on sheep but, in the process, the test ground on Gruinard Island, off the west coast of Scotland, was heavily contaminated and remained so until the late 1980s because the spores had not only survived being exploded in bombs but had lived on for a further forty years in the ground. At that time David Kelly led a decontamination programme. But spraying aerosols is a much more effective way of delivering biological warfare agent, which avoids high temperatures and mechanical shock and is also suitable for some more fragile agents. Cook obviously did not understand how great a risk biological warfare agents could be to 'humanity'.

Cook also said that he never saw any intelligence to suggest that Saddam had successfully weaponised anthrax. It is true that most of the information on Iraq's biological warfare capabilities pre-dated his time at the Foreign Office, but he had entered office only about two years after details of Iraq's biological warfare capabilities emerged in 1995 and he should have been well briefed on the subject before Operation Desert Fox in 1998. More recently, the September 2002 dossier had made reference to the Institute for Strategic Studies' 'net assessment' on Iraq's WMD,[9] which had reported that before the 1991 Gulf War Iraq had produced sixteen anthrax-filled warheads for its al-Hussein missiles, fifty R-400 aerial bombs and four drop tanks suitable for delivery from modified Mirage F-1 aircraft. Despite these and other mistakes, Cook was right to suggest that the threat from Iraq was being exaggerated.

Although the lack of understanding on the part of senior government ministers concerned me, the ministerial evidence that was to worry me more came from the man who had succeeded Cook as Foreign Secretary, Jack Straw. On 24 June, David Anderson, the chairman of the FAC, asked Straw, 'So far as the first document is concerned, September 24, which went through the proper processes, have any complaints been made by any senior intelligence officials about the use made of those documents?'

Mr Straw replied, 'None whatever, to my knowledge.'

His qualifier was important because there was no reason for him to know that I and a colleague had raised our reservations in writing with the senior officials on the Defence Intelligence Staff.

Campbell unleashed

The Foreign Affairs Committee interviewed Andrew Gilligan on 19 June and Alastair Campbell on 25 June. These televised events attracted much media attention. Unfortunately, they focused on a sideshow.

After resisting, the government eventually allowed Campbell to appear. He launched into a tirade against the BBC, repeating the charge that they were accusing No. 10 of lying about the 45-minutes intelligence and about the part Downing Street played in its inclusion in the dossier. It is a pity that the BBC was not nimble enough to defuse the argument, which was now being turned to the government's advantage.

There was much in Campbell's testimony to the FAC that has been overlooked. One of the more significant aspects concerns the importance of the dossier in the process that led to the war. Later, as the WMD case for war dissolved, and continuing right through the Chilcot inquiry in 2010, government witnesses, including Tony Blair, downplayed the dossier ('it was never a case for war') and the 45-minutes intelligence ('was not mentioned again by the Prime Minister after he introduced the dossier to Parliament'). However, at this point, Campbell told the FAC:

> The dossier in September 2002 was one of the most important pieces of work developed during the entire build-up to the conflict . . . The dossier in 2002 attracted, I think I am right in saying, more interest around the world. No. 10, the Foreign Office and the BBC websites virtually collapsed on the day. It had a massive print run. It was the product of months and months of detailed work with the intelligence agencies. It was a huge break with precedent. It was a very important document.

A few days after giving evidence to the FAC, Campbell arrived unexpectedly at the *Channel 4 News* studio to deliver another broadside. And whilst this drama was being played out, under the surface a tragedy of Shakespearian proportions was brewing. By now Gilligan had told his managers at the BBC that his source was David Kelly, and within a few days, as the FAC finalised its report, this became known to senior members of the MoD. Although I did not know it at the time, the concerns I had raised about the dossier in September 2002 were to be an important element in the aftermath of the storm that was soon to break.

The FAC report

In its report, the FAC said Jack Straw had told them 'that there had been no formal complaint from members of the security and intelligence services about the content of the dossier'. The Foreign Secretary himself had made a much more qualified statement. Had the FAC reflected his qualifications, I might not have felt compelled to take the matter up.

I was in a difficult position. My experience of the earlier Scott inquiry suggested that all relevant documents, including classified papers buried in DIS files, might be exhumed. If my memo expressing concerns over the dossier emerged, I might be asked to explain why I had not informed Parliament about it. I decided to seek advice.

My designated official contact for such matters was the deputy chief of defence intelligence. When I retired that had been Tony Cragg. Now it was a new man I had never met called Martin Howard. I wrote to him on 8 July.

[IN CONFIDENCE]

Dear DCDI

Having scanned the Foreign Affairs Committee report of its 'Inquiry into the Decision to Go to War with Iraq' I have some concerns. I am not clear whether I have any obligations with regard to these matters, nor the extent of any conflict which may exist between my responsibilities to the Department and the Government, and my responsibilities to Parliament. I write to seek your advice on this issue.

Your records will show that as ADI NBC ST, and probably the most senior and experienced intelligence community official working on 'WMD', I was so concerned about the manner in which intelligence assessments for which I had some responsibility were being presented in the dossier of 24 September 2002, that I was moved to write formally to your predecessor, Tony Cragg, recording and explaining my reservations.

The Foreign Affairs Committee appears to consider it important that the Foreign Secretary told them 'that there had been no formal complaint from members of the security and intelligence services about the content of the [September 2002] dossier'. I believe his evidence was, in fact, that he was not *aware* of any such complaint, and there is no reason to suppose he should have become aware of mine. Nonetheless, it is now a matter of record, and I feel very uneasy that my minute could be uncovered at some future date, and that I might be judged culpable for not having drawn attention to it.

I would be most grateful if you could consider this and advise me accordingly.

Yours sincerely
Brian Jones

I had sent the letter before David Kelly's name was made public. I was shocked when I heard he was involved. I was surprised again a few days later when it emerged that Kelly would give evidence to the Foreign Affairs Committee in an open session that would be televised.

Cameras on Kelly

David Kelly's appearance before the FAC was on Tuesday 15 July. The ferocity of the hottest spell of weather for decades had driven us to outdoor living in search of the intermittent, mostly imperceptible breeze. But compulsion dragged me from the relative comfort of our shaded patio to my chair in front of the television.

The hum of our own electric fan was joined by the sound of others picked up by the microphones in the House of Commons committee room. I had last spoken with Kelly in early January. Now his face seemed thinner and he looked understandably nervous. His voice, always soft, was somehow weaker than normal and tended to merge with the collective droning of the fans. The ones in Westminster were obviously losing their battle to keep the place cool. It was enough of a cauldron in the coldest of weather.

I was surprised to see Kelly sitting on his own before the committee. It is rare for a witness to sit at the table without the presence at each elbow of a colleague or adviser. But there was no one there for him, No one to turn to when the questions became tricky, to intervene on his behalf or offer whispered advice on how he might structure an answer, to remind him of something he might have forgotten. However, he could be an independent, sometimes slightly arrogant man, relatively inexperienced in the ways of Whitehall, and I thought he must have shunned offers of support.

Kelly said that, although he had met and talked to Andrew Gilligan, the information the reporter had attributed to his source 'did not sound like something I would say'. He was evasive when questioned about his contacts with other journalists. The committee asked him if he could provide a list and Kelly said the request should be made to the MoD. The committee seemed then to bully him, asking insistently when he could make the information available. Kelly's response – that it depended on the media scrum that was preventing him from gaining access to his own home – was something that was to influence me greatly in the weeks ahead. Finally, Kelly was questioned about whether he had met a journalist called Susan Watts; some statements she attributed to a source were quoted. Although this did not strike me as significant at the time, his very deliberate response that he had never 'met' her seemed a little odd.

I gained the impression that the committee believed what Kelly was saying, but it also seemed to think that the MoD was in some way constraining his ability to respond, leaving him in no man's land. It was a very odd inquisition and I felt sorry for my former colleague.

I am amazed that, even after watching this evidence, I did not recollect the exchanges that I had had with Kelly in September 2002 on the issue of the dossier. If I had still been working there would have been others to jog my memory. In the isolation of my retirement I had carelessly reaffirmed my hasty conclusion that the intelligence community dissent reported by Gilligan was reflecting defensive briefings from MI6.

The following morning, Martin Howard left a message on my telephone saying he had received my letter, which had been delayed in the internal mail. He was about to become a significant influence on my life but this is as close as I ever came to speaking with him. He would reply in due course and I should not be concerned, but could call him if I wished. I returned the call but he was not available and I had a brief discussion with his military assistant, who told me Howard had only wanted to reassure me that my letter had not been overlooked and that he would send me a reply shortly. On reflection, I suspect that Whitehall was keen that I should not contact either of the committees investigating Iraq at that time. I was not aware that on this same day Kelly appeared before the Intelligence and Security Committee, which held its meetings in closed session.

Kelly made a strong statement to the ISC about his positive view of the dossier.[10] He said:

> I think it is an accurate document, I think it is a fair reflection of the intelligence that was available and it's presented in a very sober and factual way. It's presented in a way that is not an intelligence document or a technical document, I think it is presented in a way that can be consumed by the public, it is well written.

That did not reflect the things he had said to Gilligan, Watts and Gavin Hewitt. It roughly reflected the views he had expressed to me in 2002 and January 2003, although he had never commented on the intelligence. I doubted that he was in a position to do so.

On 17 July there was a meeting in the office of Sir David Omand, the intelligence and security coordinator, at which he, Howard, John Scarlett and possibly others discussed the letter I had sent to Howard and a draft of a briefing note he was preparing for the Defence Secretary in advance of his appearance at the ISC. The detail of the discussion is not known, but at a minimum Omand and Scarlett were shown Howard's advice to Geoff Hoon.

Events near Oxford

On the morning of Friday 18 July it was reported that David Kelly was missing. Before I had time to properly absorb the significance of this, there was news that a body had been found in the Oxfordshire countryside near his home. I accepted almost immediately that the body was probably Kelly's, but I felt sure it would transpire that his death was due to an accident or some natural cause. I dismissed the thought that he might have committed suicide.

A lot of things had happened on the day Kelly disappeared. He had taken his last walk at roughly the same time as Andrew Gilligan was giving more evidence to a special session of the Foreign Affairs Committee, this time in camera. By now Kelly would have realised the significance of what the two members of the FAC had quoted at him. He had not seen Susan Watts's TV report based on his conversation with her because he had been in New York. Not only had he failed to disclose this conversation to the FAC but he had also avoided telling the MoD these details when asked about the same thing. It was obvious that the committee had now heard about similar conversations he'd had with two people. It would be clear corroboration that he had said more than he had been prepared to admit. As a man whose career as a scientist and an international weapons inspector was built on his absolute integrity, he would be shown to have lied before the nation and 'the high court of Parliament', as Andrew MacKinlay had so grandly, somewhat brutally, but nonetheless correctly warned him just two days previously. Kelly must have been shattered.

Capitol acclaim

At about the same time that David Kelly was dying on Harrowdown Hill, across the Atlantic the Prime Minister was addressing a joint session of Congress at the Capitol in Washington DC. He was greeted with a standing ovation. His speech was interrupted by applause about thirty times and his audience rose to its feet on about a dozen occasions. Blair seemed quite overwhelmed by it all, bursting with pride at this reception. He clearly enjoyed the adulation that was denied him in his own parliament and country. In fact he made reference to that contrast.

But the simultaneous events back home took the shine off a Blair triumph for the second time in a few weeks. Another public relations coup was ruined by the next episode in the developing drama. On the subsequent flight from America to Japan the news of Kelly's death was received, and it was not long before a reporter asked Blair if he had blood on his hands. It was announced that an inquiry into the circumstances surrounding Kelly's death would be established. Within hours it was further announced that Lord Hutton had agreed to lead the inquiry.

Ducking and weaving in Whitehall

My letter to Martin Howard concerning the FAC report would become a factor in relation to Defence Secretary Geoff Hoon's appearance before the ISC on 22 July. Howard signed a briefing minute on 18 July that included mention of the concerns I and a colleague had recorded about the draft dossier just before its publication.[11] Despite what my letter said, Howard chose to play down our concern by characterising it as an issue that was 'fully aired as part of the process of reaching consensus within the DIS and within the JIC'. It had been a minor local matter about wording. Howard recommended that Hoon should 'resist any calls from the ISC to disclose the identities of the individuals concerned, call them as witnesses or have access to their written comments to line management'. Although government witnesses would later be at pains to insist that our concerns were confined to the DIS, the Defence Secretary was provided with an analysis of them by the Cabinet Office Assessments Staff. This raises questions about the extent of that confinement and why the central intelligence machine was now involved. Howard's advice to Hoon was given a wide distribution within the MoD and copied to the intelligence chiefs, Sir David Omand and Sir John Scarlett, in the Cabinet Office. I was not aware that it existed until much later.

On 19 July, the inquest into Kelly's death was opened and adjourned, whereupon it was subsumed into Lord Hutton's broader task. The next day the BBC declared what it had learned from Andrew Gilligan on 27 June – that Kelly had been his source.

I began to see that the letter I had written to Howard was growing in significance. Despite the reassurances, I had received no reply by 21 July, so I telephoned his office and was told it was about to be sent. I did not know the ISC would be interviewing MoD representatives the next day.

When the ISC asked whether or not any DIS staff had expressed concerns about the drafting of the dossier, Hoon followed the advice given by Howard.[12] He said 'there had been a dispute' in the context of the 45-minutes claim about whether it was better to say that the intelligence was 'showing' or 'indicating'. He did not say that we had put our concerns in writing. Nor did his officials, including Howard, even when pressed on this matter after Hoon had left the hearing.

The chief of defence intelligence, Air Chief Marshal Joe French, appears to have given the impression that, before he decided to approve the draft dossier, the process for a normal JIC assessment had been followed. That is, that there had been this vigorous internal debate, including himself or Tony Cragg, on a draft that would be placed before the JIC for approval. No such debate had taken place. It had been curtailed by Cragg's unilateral decision.

Hoon said he thought it was a rather healthy indication that people had the self-confidence to say 'Hang on, we think this word is not quite as accurate as it should be' and that the system not only tolerated it but encouraged it.[13] The ISC agreed such debate was healthy and recognised that at the end of a discussion a decision needs to be made, and that the CDI makes the decision for the DIS.

Despite what I had said in my letter to Howard, our minutes were made to appear unexceptional and part of the normal process of debate that had been resolved in the usual way. The cover-up was working. But it had been planned to operate in secret. It later became clear that the Hutton inquiry was going to be more open. A few days before he was to give evidence on the first day of the Hutton hearings, Howard wrote to the ISC revealing that our concerns had, in fact, been put in writing. The committee decided to recall Hoon and other officials and they edged closer to the whole truth. The MoD decided now to show the ISC our minutes and this brought Report X to its attention. But the MoD still insisted that this was all part of the normal process and, although Hoon was criticised for failing to be more open, the ISC accepted it. The truth would eventually emerge but, as the Hutton inquiry approached, the government was falling deeper into a trap of its own making.

There was another aspect of the cover-up that began with the government's evidence to the ISC. It was maintained and developed throughout Hutton, through Butler and into the Chilcot inquiry. The impression was created that there was disagreement *within* the analytical ranks of the DIS and that most analysts were happy with the dossier. The only dissenters were the two that had put their concerns in writing. This was untrue. French and Cragg understood why they received the information about Report X in the way they did. It 'enabled' them to override the DIS analysts. Key players in the DIS, the wider MoD and the Cabinet Office who had received copies of Howard's briefing notes for Hoon had also received six pages of the consolidated DIS comments of 17 September 2002. Subsequent silence from all but us two had been the result of an instruction from Cragg, not an acknowledgement that they found the dossier acceptable.

Eventually, on 25 July, I received the response I had been waiting for from Howard. It was dated 23 July and said:

> Thank you for your letter of 8 July (which for some reason did not reach me until the middle of last week).
>
> I am grateful to you for drawing my attention to this. I assume you are referring to the minute you wrote on 19 September to DIST, copy to Tony Cragg, my predecessor. I was aware of this and regard it as an entirely proper expression of your views at the time. The Defence Secretary and the former CDI have also been briefed on your note as part of the preparations for the evidence they gave this week to the Intelligence & Security Committee. There is, therefore, no question of your being found culpable in any way for what was, as I say, a perfectly legitimate action. I do not think you need take any further action, but if you would like to discuss the issue, please feel free to get in touch.

I now realise that this was part of an attempt to keep me in the dark and to keep me quiet. At the time, I thought Howard was telling me he believed my worries were being dealt with in a straightforward way. But how could I rely on a committee meeting behind closed doors that was responsible to a Prime Minister who might be ducking and diving to avoid responsibility? But perhaps my mind was running away with ideas too Machiavellian to be credible, and there would be reassurance in the report of the Intelligence and Security Committee, when it emerged.

This had been a frantic period for those involved. Within the space of a few days, Kelly had given evidence to both committees, Gilligan had been recalled for a private session with the FAC, Kelly had been found dead, the Hutton inquiry had been announced, the BBC had acknowledged Kelly as Gilligan's source, briefs had been written for the Defence Secretary, the MoD had given its evidence to the ISC, the nature of the Hutton inquiry had been revealed and the ISC had recalled the MoD witnesses. Perhaps the pace of events and the consequential pressure on individuals explain some of the mistakes that were made.

CHAPTER EIGHT

August 2003: The Hutton inquiry begins

Hutton dawns

Lord Hutton opened his inquiry on 1 August to explain the way in which it would be conducted and to allow interested parties to raise any objections they might have to his plans. He decided that the inquiry would, so far as possible, be conducted in public but that it would not be televised or broadcast. However, he would use information technology to the greatest extent to make transcripts of evidence available to journalists in near-real time. The transcripts, together with items of documentary evidence, would be posted on the internet on a specially established website.

At about this time, I was contacted by a former colleague still at the Defence Intelligence Staff. He told me he was acting as the focus for the DIS on matters relating to Hutton, and said that Martin Howard would be giving evidence on behalf of the DIS. I was surprised because Howard had not been in post in the run-up to the war. I did not know Howard had been directly involved in interviewing David Kelly in the preceding weeks. My ex-colleague asked if I had held any meetings relating to the dossier before it was published. As I had been on leave in September I thought I could not have done so. He said that others recollected a meeting that included Kelly, but they thought it had been in August.

After the call I checked my diary and saw I had I had, in fact, returned to work earlier than I had recollected, on Wednesday 18 September, four working days before the dossier had been published. I called the DIS the next day and mentioned my mistake. My colleague said his own inquiries had revealed a greater certainty that there had been a meeting with Kelly, probably in August 2002. People recalled that two or three members of my staff had been present, together with two others, Kelly and another non-DIS MoD official. It was the mention of the name of the other individual that triggered my recollection. It was the only time I had met him. A process of recall began. My memories of those few days rushed back. I asked my contact to bear with me and over the next twenty-four hours I was able to piece together the sequence of events that is recorded in Chapter 5.

A shocking start

On Monday 11 August 2003, the first day of the Hutton inquiry hearings, Martin Howard was one of the witnesses. I switched on the television news at six o'clock and heard a disembodied voice say: 'As . . . probably the most senior and experienced intelligence community official working on WMD. . .' – the words popped up on the television screen as they were spoken – 'I was so concerned about the manner in which intelligence assessments for which I had some responsibility. . .'

Although I had written those words myself only a few weeks before, I held my breath, waiting to see what came next.

'. . .were being presented in the dossier of 24 September 2002. . .'

I was staggered.

'. . .that I was moved to write formally to your predecessor, Tony Cragg, recording and explaining my reservations.'

By now my heart was beating in a decidedly odd fashion. A flicker of panic acknowledged my past cardiac problems. I turned to my wife, who looked as shocked as I felt, and we stared at each other for a moment.

'That's my letter to Howard.'

'But you marked it "In Confidence", didn't you?'

'And now the whole nation knows.'

I could not understand why my letter rather than the original minute of September 2002 was appearing in evidence. I remain unsure why the government chose to do it. It was the headline event of the first day of an inquiry for which the media had cleared the decks. Could the document have been submitted before it was realised that Hutton would place so much in the public domain? Could the intention have been to keep me out of the equation by demonstrating that I was off the hook and would not be blamed for the intelligence blunder that would now be the Prime Minister's excuse for the absence of WMD in Iraq? From the outset, I was astounded by the deceptive nature of the evidence given by some government officials.

The intelligence evidence[1]

On that first Monday, Julian Miller, the chief of the Assessments Staff in the Cabinet Office, also appeared. Over the next week or so, evidence relating to the intelligence background on Iraq's weapons of mass destruction was also given by the chairman of the Joint Intelligence Committee, John Scarlett; his boss, David Omand, the intelligence and security coordinator; and Jonathan Powell, the Prime Minister's chief of staff. All except Howard had been in post during the preparation of the dossier and were still in those jobs. To say that they were economical with the truth would be euphemistic.

Howard followed the plan that had been developed for the Intelligence and Security Committee. There had been a 'very wide variety of views on different parts of the dossier and the language that was used in it'; 'two individuals expressed concerns about some specific language in the dossier to their line manager'; the concerns had been 'fully aired within the DIS; and those views were taken into account before the Joint Intelligence Committee finally met to review the final text and approve it'.

This struck me as clever spinning. Without actually saying so he created the impression of a healthy debate within the DIS leading to a satisfactory resolution. The whole matter appeared to have been taken before the full JIC. It would transpire that the JIC had never met to review the final text, or indeed any substantive text of the dossier before it was approved, out of committee.

Howard briefly touched on 'some intelligence which was finally reflected in the dossier which was compartmented and restricted to a very few individuals'. This was the intelligence in Report X that was used to 'spike' our concerns, effectively preventing us from raising an objection with more senior officials outside the DIS. But Howard did not explain this and the significance of this vague reference to Report X was not pursued by Lord Hutton or the counsel for the inquiry, James Dingemans, and it would be some time before it was mentioned again. Howard also provided incomplete information about the source of the 45-minutes intelligence – 'a single source, a well-established and reliable source we have reported before on other issues'. He did not mention the sub-source.

Miller followed the same line. Although he had held the pivotal role at the centre of the production of intelligence assessments for the most senior readership, I regarded Miller as an intelligence novice, like the leaders of the DIS. His home department was the MoD but he was not even sure about the existence of the Scientific and Technical Directorate of the DIS. He dismissed

DIS concerns that the dossier was reflecting excessive confidence in the 45-minutes intelligence report. Like Howard, he did not reveal the extent of uncertainty on the 45-minutes intelligence – 'Yes, it was a single source as we have heard, a reliable, established one.' He claimed confidence in it because 'our view was that . . . it fitted with other intelligence we had about Iraq's existing command and control arrangements'. This was a feeble suggestion. No one could doubt that, if Saddam had chemical weapons, he could use them in timely and effective fashion on the battlefield. He had done so against Iran on many occasions. A source telling you that could have acquired such unclassified knowledge in any one of a number of ways.

The actual intelligence we had of 'command and control' was based mainly on historic information. We had no up-to-date information on Iraq's recent military plans or concepts of use, as had been made clear in the JIC paper issued on 21 August 2002.[2] Less than three weeks later the JIC asserted that 'recent intelligence casts light on Iraq's holding of weapons of mass destruction and on its doctrine for using them'.[3] This reference was to the 45-minutes intelligence. Miller will have taken part both as chief of the Assessments Staff in overseeing the preparation of both JIC papers, and as a member of the JIC in considering and approving them. What he could not have known when he gave this evidence was that they would later become available to the public in the report of the Butler review.

Miller neglected to mention the more detailed arguments there had been about the 45-minutes material, and did not explain how it had been used as evidence that Iraq had undertaken extensive agent production.[4] The ability to use weapons in 'forty-five minutes' paints the picture of large numbers of chemical (or biological) weapons available ready for use with numerous Iraqi units deployed on the battlefield, or the availability of missile warheads. We had no collateral for this intelligence – details of the type of agent involved, its production, and the weapons into which it was filled.

Miller claimed he thought the problem with the 45-minutes intelligence had been resolved because the DIS had raised no more objections to such matters in response to the circulation of the 19 September draft of the dossier. He did not explain the lengths he had had to go to in order to achieve this. He did not mention Report X.

Ignorant of what had been going on in Whitehall and of Howard's involvement in it, and being in a state of mild shock at the audacity of what I was hearing at Hutton, I did not know what to do next. This was much more important than the error that I had felt compelled to raise with regard to the FAC report, and seemed to me to be misrepresentation. I could not let it pass without protest. However, although I was becoming increasingly suspicious that a cover-up was in progress, I could not be sure it was a deliberate deception. Howard was still new to intelligence.

But Howard, my official point of contact with Whitehall, was in a position to block or undermine any attempt to set the record straight if he was not behaving honourably. I began writing a second letter to him but I struggled. I could hardly ask him outright if he was deliberately misleading the inquiry. I consoled myself with the belief that there was plenty of time for me to decide what to do, and the urgency I felt began to recede.

It was revived on Monday 18 August. It was then that Hutton heard evidence from Jonathan Powell, the Prime Minister's chief of staff. In September 2002, a week before the dossier was published, he wrote a memo to Alastair Campbell that made two things clear. First he believed that Saddam had continued to produce and deploy chemical weapons, for which there was no clear evidence, and second, that there was no imminent serious threat, which was a sound judgement. He thought the argument in the dossier should be that if Saddam was not checked at this stage, he would become a serious threat. When it appeared, the foreword of the dossier reflected Powell's certainty about the existence of weapons, but neglected any accurate representation of the potential threat.

A second letter to DCDI

I felt I could not put my response off any longer and, by Wednesday 20 August, I had written a second letter to Martin Howard:

> IN CONFIDENCE
> Deputy Chief of Defence Intelligence
> Defence Intelligence Staff
> Ministry of Defence
> 20 August 2003
>
> Dear DCDI
> I have concerns about two aspects of the evidence that has emerged in the Hutton inquiry which I feel I should mention. I appreciate that you are in a difficult position, not having been in post at the time of the production

of the 24/09/02 dossier, and indeed never having met or spoken to me. However, I believe it is important that the information relating to that dossier should be as accurate as possible, and we may need to discuss how this might be achieved.

The first matter concerns my minute of 19 September 2002 to which I referred in a letter to you dated 8 July 2003. (I accept that, as you point out in your response of 23 July it was addressed to DIST and copied to your predecessor as DCDI.) One impression that it seems may exist is that this minute was part of the normal process of debate on intelligence assessments which are eventually to be considered for issue under the imprimatur of the JIC. It should be made absolutely clear that it was not. My minute, and the one it covered, were written in the belief that all discussion and debate about the dossier had already been drawn to a close. They referred to a draft on which, so far as we understood, comments of substance would no longer be taken. Our minutes were a statement at closure, recording that we were not prepared to compromise our professional judgement by allowing the impression to stand that we endorsed the dossier. This was an exceptional, rather than a normal, action in the process and that this was so is substantiated by the absence of any significant response to it. My recollection is that DIST sent me an email thanking me for my minute, and that DCDI never responded or discussed the issue with me in the several months following, up to my retirement.

Related to this first matter is the possible existence of relevant compartmented intelligence to which I did not have access. The information I received on this was, perhaps inevitably, very confused. However, I was unable to convince myself that information of direct relevance existed, or if it did exist, that it could have been adequately interpreted since no specialist appeared to be in the loop. Although I have not had access to my 19 September minute since I retired, I seem to recall qualifying my judgement with a phrase like 'on the basis of the intelligence which I have seen'. This should not be interpreted as an acknowledgement that I accepted it was likely that additional intelligence would satisfy my reservations. Indeed if such evidence existed, it should have led to a significant modification of the words in the main text to match those of the executive summary and foreword.

I do not understand why our exchange of correspondence on this was provided to the Hutton inquiry (and indeed, apparently, the ISC) and is now available to the public. The original minutes appear to me to be the most salient documents. I cannot recall that mine contained very much, if any, sensitive material that has not already emerged into the public domain, but even if it did, I am surprised that a suitable, useful redacted version cannot be made available.

The second matter concerns the discussion meeting on the dossier held on 19 September at which David Kelly was present. The purpose of that meeting was not to formulate comment on the dossier to be fed back to the Assessments Staff. It was a meeting of opportunity at which I wished to square a comment Kelly made to me that he was happy with the version of the dossier he saw on 18 September, with the level of dissatisfaction about it that some of my staff were expressing to me. By the time of the discussion meeting the final (19 September) version of the dossier had arrived and we had noted that changes we had believed to be significant, and had recommended, had not been incorporated. In a relatively short session (probably no more than 30 minutes) I came to understand the basis of the different views between Kelly and my staff and was satisfied that they did not conflict. In due course I finalised my 19 September minute and emailed it to the addressees.

The publication on the Hutton inquiry website last weekend of my letter to you of 8 July 2003 has given rise to some press speculation as to my identity. I was disturbed to see a report in the *Independent* newspaper of 18 August 2003 that a member of the FAC (Richard Ottaway MP) was urging me to contact the committee. I am not sure of the way ahead on these matters. I have no enthusiasm to give evidence in person to either the parliamentary committee or the Hutton inquiry. Apart from my preference for a quiet life now that I have retired, I could not afford the legal representation I believe I would need, especially in view of my lack of experience at the public interface and the intense media interest. However, I do believe that any possible misconception in relation to these matters should be avoided. I am most interested to hear your views.

Brian Jones

I received the request to give evidence to Lord Hutton's inquiry on the day I posted this letter, and perhaps that is why I received no response to or acknowledgement of it. The message from Hutton was passed through the Treasury Solicitor's Office via the MoD. The DIS would make documents relevant to my appearance at Hutton available to me if I needed to look at them.

The Treasury Solicitor is an entity that does not belong to the Treasury, but provides a legal service to the government as a whole. Its name, like so much in the British government, is a reminder of an historical association that is no longer relevant. My concern about the likely cost of legal representation evaporated as its services were extended to me free of charge.

I was told by one of the Treasury solicitors that the inquiry had scheduled me to give evidence on Tuesday 26 August – just six days away – but said the date was negotiable. They wanted to know how well I knew Kelly and about his involvement in the meeting on 19 September 2002. They also asked for the detail of any concerns that were expressed about the dossier by the participants in the meeting, or by the wider intelligence community. I asked if I was obliged to give evidence and was assured it was not compulsory. But no one who had been invited had so far declined. I told the Treasury solicitor that, due to a health problem, I needed to consult my doctor before submitting myself to what I felt would be a stressful occasion.

The next day I sent an outline draft of a witness statement to the solicitor. I assumed that my statement would be held in confidence but it eventually transpired the MoD had to see it for 'security clearance'.

My doctor examined me and said if I wanted to give evidence, I should. He advised me to keep an eye open for the symptoms of distress with which I was familiar and to walk away from the situation if they appeared. He wrote an explanatory note that I could show to anyone concerned if it became necessary.

It was only then that my wife and I decided whether I would give evidence. I was impressed with what I had seen of the Hutton inquiry. I had a contribution to make in ensuring the truth emerged, and if I did not appear there would be no grounds for complaint about the outcome. However, thinking back a few weeks to Kelly's experience, we dreaded the thought of a 'media' encampment in the small cul-de-sac on which we lived. I reasoned that my name would not remain secret for very long if I tried to conceal it. News reporters would work hard for the 'scoop' of revealing my identity. At first my wife was surprised when I suggested I should appear in public without concealment, but she understood my logic. I was retired so there would be no interference with any future work. The DIS had been significantly reorganised as I departed so there was little I would need to conceal. It was the right course of action.

More intelligence evidence

On Tuesday 26 August, John Scarlett gave evidence. He explained he was chairman of the Joint Intelligence Committee and head of the Intelligence and Security Secretariat in the Cabinet Office, reporting to Sir David Omand, the security and intelligence coordinator. But he insisted on drawing attention to the direct access he had to the Prime Minister.

Scarlett followed the line that had been well rehearsed by Martin Howard and Julian Miller before him. When asked about the 45-minutes intelligence Scarlett's reply lacked clarity: 'This was a report from a single source. It was an established and reliable line of reporting; and it was quoting a senior Iraqi military officer in a position to know this information.' It did not make clear that the Iraqi officer was a sub-source who had no track record of reliable reporting.

Asked if people were unhappy over the single-source nature of this intelligence, Scarlett said no one was unhappy, and failed to mention the problems with this intelligence that had been raised repeatedly in comments by the DIS on various drafts of the dossier. He argued that the 45-minutes intelligence report gained credibility because it fitted with previous intelligence on command and control.

James Dingemans drew Scarlett's attention to a significant message sent to those involved with the dossier from one of his own Assessments Staff drafters on 11 September.[5] It related to questions that had been received from the Prime Minister's Office on the first draft of the dossier. Could the names of individual Iraqis involved in the programme be used? Was there any intelligence that Iraq had actively sought to employ foreign experts, in particular in the nuclear field? They wanted more details on the items procured for their nuclear programme – how many did they buy, what was the significance to a nuclear weapons programme? Could we say how many chemical and biological weapons Iraq currently had by type? If we couldn't give weapon numbers, could we give any idea of the quantity of agent available?

There was a hint of an apology when the author of the message noted that the question about the type and numbers of chemical and biological weapons had been asked at least once before. In August 2002, there was a request from the Assessments Staff for everyone concerned to re-examine their databases for relevant intelligence. The repetition of the request was excused by the addition 'But No. 10 through the Chairman want the document to be as strong as possible within the bounds of avai[l]able intelligence.'

Scarlett could not recall the background to this email but did not deny that the questions came from No. 10. Presumably he understood their significance. The vagueness of the intelligence was recognised by No. 10, the chairman of the JIC and the Assessments Staff. The message from No. 10 was that the draft was not strong enough and it recognised exactly what information was required to bolster the case. Something more tangible was needed. This contradicted what intelligence officials had been arguing in their evidence so far – that the assessment was completely sound.

This critical questioning contained in the Assessments Staff message was typical of what intelligence analysts would expect. Answers to them would normally be a prerequisite of an assessment on which important policy decisions would be based. Such answers were not available on Iraq's chemical and biological weapons. The Prime Minister's 'defence' on the WMD issue was that the intelligence community and the JIC had presented him with a cast iron case. However, he had been repeatedly warned of the inadequacy of the intelligence, most recently at his meeting of 23 July,[6] and the picture had not changed.

When asked how the DIS concerns about the dossier were resolved, there was an economy in the explanations offered by Scarlett. He made no mention of Report X or Miller's need to invoke it.

Dingemans underlined the paucity of evidence in later drafts of the dossier by reference to Jonathan Powell's email of 17 September 2002 in which he noted that it did 'nothing to demonstrate a threat, let alone an imminent threat from Saddam'. Powell also noted that 'the threat argument will be a major problem in the press/parliamentary assault after the dossier comes out'. Elsewhere Powell had written, 'You need to make it clear that Saddam could not attack us at the moment. The thesis is he would be a threat to the UK in the future if we do not check him.' Scarlett said he was aware of Powell's view but took it to be a reference to what he thought should be included in any political statement that was made about the dossier. On this basis, Scarlett appears to have agreed with Powell's interpretation of the intelligence assessment, or he would surely have wished to correct a false impression emanating from someone so close to and potentially influential with the Prime Minister.

However, when Scarlett was given the Prime Minister's foreword to approve or at least comment on, presumably he felt he could support it, despite the fact it did not reflect Powell's advice. At least one member of the JIC – indeed a former chairman – Peter Ricketts, director general of the

Political Department of the Foreign and Commonwealth Office, thought the committee was responsible for what the Prime Minister said in his foreword to the dossier: 'The foreword was shown to and approved by the Joint Intelligence Committee, so the foreword was not some and separable part of the document that was written elsewhere, it was all cleared through the Joint Intelligence Committee.'[7]

The evidence from the politicians

On Wednesday 27 August, Geoff Hoon gave evidence. He contributed little on the intelligence background. However, reminded of a post-war lunchtime exchange with David Kelly, the Defence Secretary noted he had been seeing intelligence on Iraq for well over four years and the cumulative picture he had acquired is what convinced him about Iraq's WMD.

The following day the Prime Minister came to the inquiry. James Dingemans asked him about the genesis of the dossier and the reason for the focus on Iraq. Tony Blair argued that Iraq fitted a special category because it was in breach of United Nations resolutions and had a history of using weapons of mass destruction against its own people. He said that the publication of a dossier had been postponed early in 2002 because of the government's judgement 'that it would inflame the situation too much'. In reality, the document that would have emerged at that time would not have been nearly as inflammatory as the remarks that he had been making himself, most notably the assertion on 3 April 2002 of Iraq's possession of WMD. Blair believed that the situation had changed by 3 September because there was 'a tremendous amount of information and evidence coming across my desk as to the weapons of mass destruction and the programmes associated with it that Saddam had' and 'a renewed sense of urgency, again, in the way that this was being publicly debated'. With President Bush, he decided the issue really had to be confronted. The Prime Minister said he took the view 'that we really had to disclose what we knew or as much as we could of what we knew' in order to explain why the government believed Iraq was such a big problem. He said the aim of the dossier 'was to disclose the reason for our concern and the reason why we believed this issue had to be confronted'.

Blair has never given any detail about the 'tremendous amount of information' that was coming across his desk. He was not seeing *assessments* of that intelligence to support the certainty of his professed conviction about Iraq's WMD. He could not have been briefed about new and worrying information by the chairman of the JIC, John Scarlett, because the absence of substantial information continued to be a problem as the dossier was being drafted. Even when Sir Richard Dearlove brought him something new directly from MI6 on 12 September, he says he warned the Prime Minister that the new source was on trial. Blair's evidence did not reflect the uncertainty understood even at his inner circle meeting on 23 July, or offer any substantial evidence on how things had changed between then and the day the dossier was published, just nine weeks later. Furthermore, the public debate to which Blair referred had been stimulated by statements on the need for regime change in Iraq made by various members of the Bush administration and by himself and his own government.

Lord Hutton's question about No. 10's comments on a draft of the dossier in September 2002 might have come from an inspired New Labour backbencher: 'So you would agree, Prime Minister, that the wording that "No. 10 through the Chairman want the document to be as strong as possible within the bounds of available intelligence" is a fair way of putting your view and the view of your staff in No. 10?'

Blair did not hesitate to reinforce his position:

> Provided that is clearly understood as meaning that it is only if the intelligence agencies thought both that the actual intelligence should be included and that there was not improper weight being given to any aspect of that intelligence. In other words, given that the process was that they had to decide what it was we could properly say, then obviously we wanted to – we had to make this case because this was the case that we believed in and this was the evidence that we had, because all of this stuff was obviously stuff that had come across my desk.

This can hardly have been a slip of the tongue. The policy cart was placed before the intelligence horse. The belief came before the intelligence, and generated a clever plan to justify regime change in Iraq.

Dingemans asked if a comment made by Jonathan Powell about the relationship between the Prime Minister's foreword and the main body of the dossier was reflected in the final document. Powell had suggested, 'We need to do more to back up the assertions.'

The Prime Minister replied, 'I think so, yes; but I think the most important thing was I was very careful in my statement to make it clear what we were and were not saying.' But his assertion that 'Saddam is continuing to develop WMD' which can 'inflict real damage upon the region and the stability of the world' is neither substantiated nor explained anywhere in the dossier or in any of the JIC assessments he received.

Blair's recollection that the dossier was intended not to provide the immediate reason for going to war but instead to return to the issue of Iraq and WMD and deal with it through the United Nations conflicts with the understanding of the then British ambassador in Washington, Sir Christopher Meyer. In March 2002, six months before the dossier was eventually published, he wrote that Downing Street's objective was to make the case well enough to create a critical mass of parliamentary and public opinion that would support British participation with the US 'in any operation against Saddam'. There was no doubt that the context was military action and the intention of the dossier was to persuade more than simply inform. The political director of the Foreign Office, writing independently at about the same time, thought the purpose of the dossier was to get public and parliamentary support for military operations and it had to convince that the threat from Iraq was significant enough for British troops to die for.

When asked about the Commons debate on the dossier on the day of its publication, Blair chose quotes from his speech to show he was not suggesting an imminent threat, and the 'threat' he was talking about was a rather broader concept, more nebulous, perhaps, and something to do with acceptable standards of international behaviour. In reality his statement indicated his belief that Saddam might use his weapons within weeks of September 2002.[8] There was much in that speech that he chose not to quote.

The Prime Minister was asked about the concerns I raised about the dossier, and said he was not aware of them at the time. Dingemans continued by reciting to him a large extract from my letter of 8 July 2003 to Martin Howard. 'Had any of those complaints, as it were, worked their way up as far as the JIC or to you?' he asked.

The question seemed to unsettle the Prime Minister and he gave the following strange answer:

> No, they did not. I mean, I should say that this was a. . . the question of whether we produced intelligence, though, was a very, very difficult question. I mean, on the one hand it is not normal for you to do this. I

mean, intelligence, as I say in my witness statement, is intelligence and it has to be handled with care. On the other hand, the clamour for us to produce the reasons why. . . here was I saying, 'This is the situation with Saddam and weapons of mass destruction we have to deal with.' The clamour for us to produce the evidence for this was obviously very, very strong. So, in a sense, the 24 September dossier was an unusual. . . the whole business was unusual, but it was in response to an unusual set of circumstances. We were saying this issue had to be returned to by the international community and dealt with. Why were we saying this? Because of the intelligence. Not unnaturally, people said, 'Well, give us the intelligence insofar as you can.'

Going back

On the day the Prime Minister gave evidence, I returned to the DIS building in Whitehall for the first time since my retirement. I had been told I could visit the DIS to refresh my memory on the relevant classified papers and that they would be available in the office of the former colleague who had also expressed concern over the dossier.

It was a strained and strange experience. Entry into the secure area of the DIS was a complicated process for a visitor. My clearances had disappeared with my retirement so I could not be allowed to roam free. Fate decreed that I was collected from 'the atrium' by one of the two officials who had represented the DIS on the Cabinet Office drafting committee for the September dossier. I had not planned to see him but when I arrived others were busy on unexpected urgent tasks.

We sat in his office and chatted for a few minutes and I was able to clarify and confirm my recollections about various aspects he had been involved in before the phone rang to say those I had come to see were free. As we walked the 50 yards or so between offices he said something I found both reassuring and moving: 'I learned a lot from working with you, Brian. You are sorely missed, you know.'

I was caught off guard by this sudden, unexpected declaration. I found myself having to contain my emotion – the pressure upon me and the feeling of isolation was, perhaps, greater than I had realised.

Before speaking with my former colleague, I popped my head round the door of my old office. My successor was not in the room. I stood at the door looking around it for a few moments. It held good memories of many kind, generous, knowledgeable and wise people who had moved in and out of it to talk with me, but it had been about people rather than place and I did not miss it. I went next door.

A pack of classified papers was ready for me to read. After a few minutes' general discussion, I took the chance to talk over the decision I had reached: giving my evidence to Hutton openly, declaring who I was and what my job had been. I explained why I wanted to do so, but said I would not if my former colleague thought it would create problems for him or any other colleagues still serving. He thought for a moment and said there would be no problem.

I settled down to read the papers and refresh my memory. There were no real shocks, although I was surprised at the brevity of the note of concern I had written, and impressed by the detail and clarity of the one written by my colleague.

After a while we were interrupted by the director who had been my boss for the few months before I retired. We exchanged pleasantries, I thanked him for making the documents available and he said that for those few weeks in the previous September he had really not known what it was all about. I sympathised that he had been placed in such a difficult position. I sensed he was reluctant to leave but we had little to say to one another and he soon departed.

When I had finished the documents I handed them back before spending an hour or so mingling with friends and former colleagues at a lunchtime celebration for the impending retirement of two of them. It was a very reassuring interlude. They seemed pleased to see me and wished me well in my appearance at Hutton. I was surprised that most were not very familiar with the detailed background to the affair. I had already forgotten the impact of the incessant pressure on those who work in Whitehall, and how difficult it sometimes was for an individual to keep abreast of things peripheral to his or her immediate task. I wondered how they would react when they heard my evidence.

After the break, I crossed Whitehall and through Horse Guards, skirting the edge of St James's Park on my way to my final appointment of the day. As I did so, I thought back over the last few hours. Somewhere in the confusion of many discussions I had learned that the sensitive compartmented intelligence of Report X, denied to us in September 2002, had eventually been given a wider distribution. Of course I was not given any details about it, but I was left in no doubt about its value. 'Crap' was the description that stuck in my mind. I cut through Queen Anne's Gate towards St James's Park Tube station, thinking as I walked how much more confident I felt about the difficult days to come knowing that Report X had been every bit as weak as I had suspected it might be.

I located the Treasury Solicitor's Office in another of London's many anonymous government buildings. I recollected the experience I had at the time of the Scott inquiry when the QC representing my colleague, always scurrying between cases, was never up to date with the documents we had prepared at his unforgiving urgent request. My representative, Peter, went through my draft statement and made some recommendations for changes. I now regret agreeing to one of them. I was persuaded to omit mention of Tony Cragg's anger, as had been described to me by my boss, about the minute I had sent on 19 September 2002.

I mentioned the letter I had written to Martin Howard a few days earlier on 20 August and Peter said, with some authority, that I should not expect a reply. Although it did not occur to me at the time, that does suggest there was some discussion across witnesses within Whitehall. However, we agreed that the inquiry should be aware that I had written it and that we should send Lord Hutton a copy. He also said my witness statement would have to be vetted for security reasons and cleared by the MoD before it could be submitted to the inquiry. I was a little surprised by this but did not challenge it. In the event, Hutton did not reveal the full statement.[9]

Peter was surprised when I said a condition of my appearance would be that I wished to appear openly and be named at the inquiry. He seemed confused when I insisted that I should not be named *before* I appeared and wanted no other details revealed. I am not sure he fully understood or accepted my explanation but he said he would put my conditions to the inquiry. 'I am also representing another MoD witness,' he said, 'who is going to be called Mr A and will not actually appear. I assumed you would do the same.'

I told Peter before I left that I was worried about press attention before and after my appearance before the inquiry and he seemed very surprised that I anticipated there might be any great interest.

My submission to the Hutton inquiry was completed on Friday 29 August. I am not sure when it became available to the inquiry. That was ultimately under the control of the government. The inquiry team would have had little time to study it even if it had been sent to them immediately.

CHAPTER NINE

3 September 2003: My day in court

The day before

The night before I gave evidence, my wife and I stayed in a hotel just off Leicester Square that had been booked and would be paid for by the MoD. Expense had obviously been spared, but after thirty years in its employ I was not surprised by this.

We tried to take our minds off the pending 'trial' by watching a West End play. Michael Frayn's excellent comedy *Noises Off* seemed appropriate and did the job well. The premier of the British film *Calendar Girls* was taking place that evening at the Odeon in Leicester Square and we walked back to our hotel through the crowd from that event as it dispersed. The long hot spell had broken a few days earlier but our hotel room had not yet recovered and remained warm and sticky. Without air conditioning we needed to have the windows open. London, at least in the proximity of Leicester Square, is a city that never sleeps and that meant we did so only fitfully. I lay awake listening to the workmen clearing away the barriers and the temporary grandstand outside the cinema. As I thought about the ordeal to come and the evidence Hutton had accumulated so far, I found myself comparing the group of ageing ladies now represented on film revealing all except those bits that were, arguably, of most significance, with the senior officials and politicians who, a few hundred yards away, at various other venues in central London, had been doing much the same thing. However, whilst the ladies of the Women's Institute were perpetrating an innocent tease for charity, the other show in town was altogether more sinister.

The morning session

In the morning there was no interest in our arrival as we quickly gained entrance at the side gate to the Royal Courts of Justice. When we got to the courtroom I was relieved to see there was less than a full house. The

list of the day's witnesses included two unnamed 'MoD officials' – who
would be me and Mr A. Early on the evidence of a forensic toxicologist,
the assistant chief constable of Thames Valley Police and a named MoD
security official was taken, the small, unsuspecting audience relaxed almost
to the point of boredom.

We sat at first amongst a few 'official observers' none of whom I
recognised. In front of us, elevated to a strange degree high above the
rest of the room, was the bench at which Lord Hutton presided. It was of
light wood with modern, clean but uninteresting lines. Behind the bench
were rows of empty bookshelves. They gave the place a skeletal, temporary,
almost flimsy feel. Had it been a stage set, it would have been a poor one
that you would have expected to wobble precariously at the slamming of
a door.

Below the bench, another elevated tier was occupied by the stenographers
and the man operating the equipment that projected evidence onto two
screens, one each side of the bench, as it was being discussed by the
witnesses. At the right-hand end of this tier as we looked at it was the
witness box, which faced back across the width of the room. As I was about
to discover, there were two screens in the box for the witness to observe.
One contained, when appropriate, the written evidence that was being
discussed or questioned. The second followed the stenographers' record of
the proceedings as it was generated.

In the 'well' of the courtroom were several rows of tables stretching
across its width, each with what appeared to be a video monitor. This area
was occupied by industrious, mainly young, men and women. Although it
was never explained, these appeared to be the representatives of the various
parties concerned with the inquiry – their lawyers and officials from
the various departments of state. The heavy cabling that fed the screens
snaked untidily about the courtroom floor. Together with the irregular
positioning of VDUs, books, people and discarded coats, this created a
scene that bordered on the chaotic. I vaguely wondered about the Health
and Safety at Work Act. Amidst this modern, shambolic arrangement of
the animate and inanimate, directly in front of and below his Lordship's
plush throne stood, in complete contrast to all about him, the dapper
form of the neat and precise James Dingemans at a strange old-fashioned
lectern. Both performer and prop would have been at home in the
courtroom of a Victorian melodrama. This environment of contrast and
confusion was more familiar than intimidating to a retired civil servant

who had worked recently in Whitehall, where, in terms of both fabric and occupants, ancient and modern sat incongruously together.

Behind the bank of tables and screens, on a row of chairs that swept almost right across the back of the room, was the press – one or two faces familiar from the television amongst an anonymous pack of reporters. Recognising Nicholas Witchell, my wife recovered just in time from the stress and confusion of the moment to avoid greeting him like an old friend. Behind the press and slightly elevated in a small, shallow alcove were the few seats available to the public. We were aware that space had been made available in an adjacent room with closed circuit television screens for the overspill of media personnel and members of the public, but I doubted that it was occupied of necessity by anyone on this sparse and apparently uninteresting morning.

Although I tried to concentrate on the witnesses that went before me my thoughts continually turned to trying to fix in my mind the words and phrases I might be inclined to use and those things it would not be appropriate to say under these circumstances. I had decided not to be too pointed in my criticism, partly because it would be difficult enough for me to say so many things that would contradict not only the Prime Minister but many other clever, senior and experienced Whitehall operators. I also judged, perhaps to excuse my timidity, that a direct attack on the integrity of so many others would be counter-productive by giving the impression of a relatively junior person only too ready to puff up his own importance.

Suddenly, I found myself listening intently to a description of the samples that had been taken for analysis from the body of David Kelly and I became strangely and morbidly focused on the physical circumstances surrounding his wretched demise. Mention was made of urine samples, blood from a lung removed in autopsy, the contents of his stomach, a liver sample and a sample of fluid from inside the eye. My heart rate quickened, my temperature rose, my head began to spin and, for a moment, I thought I might vomit. It was perhaps the association of these details with the quiet man who had so often sat chatting in my office that caused me distress. I concentrated hard on ignoring what was being said, took several deep breaths and gradually came under control. I would not, after all, need my doctor's note.

When I eventually took the stand and announced my name and that I worked for Defence Intelligence on WMD there was a stirring and bristling around the courtroom. I dared not look up for fear of losing focus and confidence. My wife thought that many suddenly looked very serious, almost worried, as they tried to absorb the unexpected.

My evidence is well covered by the witness statement,[1] which reflected the detail I have provided in Chapters 5 and 6. The transcript of the hearing is available on the Hutton website.[2] I had two sessions: one each side of a break for lunch.

During the morning Dingemans gave me a chance to explain some important background. He began by asking about the definitions of the various weapons of mass destruction. Answering a variety of questions, I explained that the term itself was problematic and went on to explain why. I emphasised that chemical weapons had much less potential for causing mass casualties than most nuclear and many biological weapons. During the course of this exchange my mouth was suddenly dry in a way I had never experienced before and I realised how tense I was. I paused for a sip of water.

At this point, Lord Hutton intervened: 'Do I gather, Dr Jones, that there is perhaps some debate in intelligence circles then about the precise meaning of "weapons of mass destruction"? You are expressing your own view. Do I take it that there are others that might take a different view?'

'There may be,' I answered. 'I mean, I think "weapons of mass destruction" has become a convenient catch-all which, in my opinion, can at times confuse discussion of the subject.'

'Yes, I see,' said Hutton. 'Thank you, yes.'

Dingemans would have liked me to go further. 'You say there may be. Are you aware of anyone who does have a different view?'

I lacked the confidence to say that I suspected the Prime Minister had been doing this quite deliberately in talking up the threat and judged, anyway, that such a provocative assertion might divert attention from the underlying case. Instead, I said:

> That is difficult. I do not think I was ever in a situation where it was discussed in quite those terms. I think it was quite a frequent comment from myself and my staff about particular issues, that it is perhaps not right to use that general term to describe something that is more specific.

I did not add that the lack of response we received when we did raise such issues surprised me and led me to conclude that much of Whitehall prefers not to be tied to exact terminology, 'wriggle-room' being highly prized in the world of politics.

Dingemans asked me about the pressure I had said was on my analysts during the preparation of the dossier and he referred to the request from a member of the Assessments Staff dated 11 September, noting this section in particular:

> Can we say how many chemical and biological weapons Iraq currently has by type? If we can't give weapons numbers can we give any idea on the quantity of agent available? I appreciate everyone, us included, has been around at least some of these buoys before . . . But No. 10 through the Chairman want the document to be as strong as possible within the bounds of available intelligence. This is therefore a last call(!) for any items of intelligence that agencies think can and should be included.

He asked if that was the sort of pressure I meant. I said:

> No, no. They were quite normal and natural questions that would arise in the preparation of any particular paper. The pressure I was referring to, I think, was the frequency of drafts that were coming on, and the fact that my staff were being pressed to get their comments back to the Assessment Staff or, you know, to the interface with the Assessment Staff very quickly indeed.

On reflection I am disappointed with this answer. I was answering cold and off the cuff, but I now believe that when I returned to work after my holiday, on 18 or 19 September 2002, one of my staff showed me the memo as an illustration of the pressure involved. It did not register in the stress of the witness box that what I was being shown referred to a previous call for people to dredge their files and memories. Whilst such a request was not that unusual, it was unusual for it to be repeated. It was also unusual, to the point of being unique in my experience, for such a requirement to be linked directly to comments from outside the intelligence community, let alone No. 10. However, such detailed recall was beyond my capability on that difficult morning. Also, at that time I had not absorbed the full context and significance of the exchange that Dingemans had with Scarlett on this same document just a few days earlier.

Later, when Dingemans was asking about the concerns of my chemical warfare expert, an intervention by Lord Hutton gave me an opportunity to talk about the language of the dossier. He asked:

> Could you just elaborate a little on his concern? Can you give us examples of the nature of his representations not being accepted? Were they matters of language? Were they matters of assessing how serious a particular matter was? Were they on the basis that he simply thought some statements were wrong, in the sense that the information simply did not exist? I do not want you to go into security matters.

I replied, 'My Lord, they were about language, but language is the means by which we communicate an assessment so they were also about the assessment, yes.' I wondered if this was such a statement of the obvious that His Lordship might be offended by it. Or perhaps there was some perception underlying his question that I was missing. In the event my statement was to be seized on by several commentators as a good example of plain speaking in the midst of so much obfuscation.

'Quite. Yes,' said Lord Hutton in a way that I took as encouragement to expand on my statement and cover the slight embarrassment I was feeling. It was a chance to illustrate the detail that could lie behind the choice of a single word in an intelligence assessment compressed to the limit to make it 'readable'. Without realising its particular significance in terms of the sound-bites beloved by our media, I proceeded with a statement that was to achieve some prominence over the next several days.

> I mean – if I can just refer to a note I have here, because I wanted to be sure I was clear on this – they were really about a tendency in certain areas, from [my chemical warfare expert's] point of view, to, shall we say, over-egg certain assessments in relation particularly to the production of chemical warfare agents and weapons since 1998. Indeed, I guess that goes all the way back to the end of the Gulf conflict. And he was concerned that he could not point to any solid evidence of such production. He did not dismiss that it may have happened, and there was certain evidence that suggested that it could have happened, but he did not have good evidence that it had happened.

'Yes,' said Lord Hutton, but he wanted more:

> Could you just perhaps, and please say if you are not able to do this, but
> when you say that he was concerned about language and he was concerned
> that certain assessments were over-egged, can you give examples of that as
> regards the use of language? If you cannot, please do not speculate. I do
> not want you in any way just to speculate.

I did not need to speculate but I hesitated to be sure I framed my reply
accurately.

> I think – I think it is the difference between saying, for example – making
> a judgement that the production of CW agent had taken place as opposed
> to that judgement being that it had probably taken place or even possibly
> taken place. It was that degree of certainty in the judgements that were
> being made. I hope that helps.

Lord Hutton said, 'Yes. Thank you very much.' But I wasn't sure he meant
it.

Dingemans broached the same issue of language by reference to an
email exchange between Alastair Campbell and Scarlett. He was keen to
develop his theme but did so quite slowly, reaching the point eventually.
Reading from a particular email, Dingemans said:

> [Campbell] says '"Might" reads very weakly' and '"May" is weaker than
> in the summary'. Those are obviously points on language. You have made
> the point to His Lordship that intelligence personnel communicate by
> language. Is this the sort of comment that intelligence personnel might be
> passing to and from each other?

I was not sure if there was a degree of sarcasm in Dingemans's comment
and, if there was, whether it was directed at Hutton or at me. I dismissed
the thought from my mind and gave a direct answer:

> Yes. Those are the things which we spend hours debating. They are very
> important in this business – I mean, it depends on context and I cannot
> tell from what you have showed me there the context of those particular
> statements, so I could not comment on that. But the use of, you know, a
> 'might' or a 'may' does convey some uncertainty in the information you
> are trying to provide.

Dingemans continued:

> Can I take you, then, to . . . the reply? This is from Mr Scarlett to Mr
> Campbell. He says, 'Thank you for your minute.' He talks about reordering
> and other aspects. Then if we go down the page, at paragraph 6: 'Turning
> to your details points [*sic*], we have . . . strengthened language on current
> concerns and plans.' [Later] he says 'We cannot improve on the use of
> "might"' . . . but [elsewhere] 'The language you queried [which was "may"]
> has been tightened.' Is that the sort of response you would expect, as it
> were, between intelligence personnel discussing this type of issue, looking
> at the intelligence, and deciding what the language will bear?

I paused to be sure of my answer before saying that it was. Then Dingemans
asked: 'Mr Campbell told us of a distinction between presentation and
intelligence. How do you present your intelligence to others? How do you
communicate it?'

I was confused. 'I mean, we write reports, we give presentations. I'm
sorry, I am having difficulty with the question.'

'Sorry,' said Dingemans. 'Perhaps it was not as clear as it ought to be.
Did any of the personnel who were working under you know that people
within the communications side of No. 10 had been making suggestions
on the dossier?'

'I think there was an impression that they were involved in some way.'

'Were people happy or unhappy about this?'

I paused before answering. There was no doubt that my staff were
unhappy about what had been going on but it was hard to distinguish
between the general pressure and the suspected involvement of intelligence
outsiders, perhaps even some with a political motivation. I did not explain
this well. I tried to explain that there are all sorts of potential influences
on intelligence analysts. The job is about producing an assessment
dissociated from such influence. When there is inappropriate influence on
an assessment it is important for analysts to distance themselves from it.

Dingemans then quoted from the briefing note that Martin Howard
had prepared for Defence Secretary Hoon on 18 July before he appeared
in front of the ISC. At this stage I was not aware that this had been done
and did not place it in the context of the letter I had written to Howard
on 8 July. It was the part of the MoD brief that, for some reason I do not
understand, had been written by the Cabinet Office Assessments Staff and

purported to explain the concerns my colleague and I had raised, despite the fact they had not been sent to the Cabinet Office at the time (see page 128). But the important thing Dingemans wanted to raise was the intelligence received on 11 September (Report X). The brief had noted how Report X influenced the assessment in the dossier but that we had not seen it. Dingemans asked, 'And were you aware that further intelligence had been received that had not been seen?'

I replied:

> We are really talking now about the very end of the production, the dossier production process, for most of which I was away. But when I came back I looked at the information and had these concerns and, indeed, there was a suggestion – and I cannot remember how it came to be there, perhaps one of my staff mentioned it – that there was said to be additional intelligence that actually, had it been available to us, would have removed those concerns that we had.

'So you were aware that there was further intelligence?'

'I was.'

'Did you make any efforts yourself to find out whether there was this further intelligence, to see it for example?'

'I discussed the matter with my boss, my director,' I explained. 'Partly because it was suggested to me, I think, that he had seen it, he had seen that intelligence.'

'And had he seen it?'

'No, he had not. He told me that he had not seen the intelligence, although he was also aware of its existence and had been contacted by a senior official from MI6, and it had been suggested to him that the intelligence judgements that were being made in the dossier were in fact OK because of. . . and they were supported by this additional intelligence.'

'And did that satisfy you?'

'No, it did not. I mean, it would not anyway. I would always have to put a caveat on a conclusion which was based on something I had not seen. I mean, that is—' I stumbled and Dingemans found the word for me.

'Inevitable.'

'So I told him,' I continued, 'that was the case and that really we, you know, would have to express a reservation on the particular language in the dossier because of that.'

'Because you had not seen the intelligence?'

'Yes.'

'Did you ever see the intelligence?'

'No.'

'And do you now know whether or not it supported the stronger language?'

'No, I do not.'

Although the information about Report X had been mentioned once by Howard in passing on the first day of the inquiry, and had haunted the proceedings as subsequent evidence was given, it had not previously been brought so clearly into the open.

The 45-minutes intelligence was discussed next and Dingemans explored and exposed the concerns my staff had with it. I explained the problems we had with the source, the vagueness of the content, and the absence of good collateral intelligence to give us confidence in the report. Dingemans asked if David Kelly was aware of these concerns at the time. I explained that he was aware at that time, or shortly afterwards, from discussions with me and others in my branch, although I believed he had not seen the original reporting.

Hutton intervened with the suggestion that when it came to the reliability of sources the SIS was surely the authority. I was not sure I convinced him that analysts, especially technical experts, had a part to play in this process by considering whether the content of a report made sense.

Shortly after this, Hutton decided the court would rise for lunch. I now know that, after I had started giving evidence, the word had gone out that something unusual was up. There had also been some early coverage on the lunchtime news bulletins, and a host of journalists and others, who had thought it would be a quiet day at the inquiry, changed their minds. On our way back after the break we discovered a throng blocking the entrance to the courtroom. As we pushed our way through I became aware of generally pleasant smiling faces that watched our progress. Someone stuck a thumbs-up under my nose. I took it to be a sign of approval or encouragement. A voice said 'Well done', and there were muttered words of encouragement.

The afternoon session

The resumption of my evidence was delayed to allow Mr A to give his. This was necessary to accommodate the special arrangements that had been made to conceal Mr A's identity. He gave evidence from a building in Whitehall by means of closed circuit television. The interruption to my evidence was mildly annoying but, at the time, I thought it no real problem.

When I resumed, James Dingemans asked me how my chemical warfare expert reacted to the refusal of those drafting the dossier to accept his suggestions in the DIS returns. I said that he was unhappy that what he thought to be several very significant comments had been repeatedly ignored. I said this was unusual and tried to explain why. It was not easy. 'Well, I mean the whole dossier was unusual. It was not something we did. If I think about that in the same context as the normal product of the assessment process and the JIC assessment process, it would, in fact, be very unusual to arrive at a point where a paper was about to be published, not in the wider sense but published as a secure paper—'

'The JIC assessment finalised?' Dingemans interrupted.

'Yes – where significant differences remain. Part of that process in the normal production of a JIC assessment would involve a meeting within the DIS of analysts with our representatives on the Joint Intelligence Committee, at which arguments would be put to them, if there were outstanding issues, for them to take into the full committee to discuss. And that happened fairly often – that there would be one or two things and the chief of defence intelligence and his deputy would look at those and decide whether they would represent them or otherwise.'

'At the Joint Intelligence Committee meeting?'

'Yes, yes. And usually issues were either resolved before that or resolved as part of that process.'

Dingemans thought it necessary to expand my explanation. 'Because the chief of defence intelligence would say "Look, you are being silly about this; for reasons A, B, C I am not going to represent this argument in the Joint Intelligence Committee" or "You have persuaded me, I will see what I can do".'

'That is exactly it.' I was glad of his help.

'Did that happen in this case?'

'No. There was, I believe, a slight difference in process here, in that these latest dossiers were. . . the latest drafts of the dossier, I think, were being modified between major JIC meetings, as I understand. So I think some of these issues were – probably must have been, as far as I can see – dealt with out of committee, as it were, by members of the JIC.'

'Mr Scarlett told us that he set up a drafting committee, sub-committee, I hope I represent it fairly, from the Joint Intelligence Committee and his joint intelligence assessment staff which was responsible for drafting the dossier.'

'That is right, yes.' In fact it is not quite true because rather than include individuals from the JIC, apart from Julian Miller, the head of the Assessments Staff, who chaired it, it consisted of their representatives. It was similar to a Current Intelligence Group, which reviewed and modified draft JIC papers before they went to the committee.

'And that is what you refer to as being a slightly unusual process, is it?' asked Dingemans.

'No, no. The involvement of the Assessments Staff in the drafting of the papers was normal process.'

'What was abnormal?'

I thought Dingemans was making too much of this. I do not think either of us knew at this stage that non-intelligence personnel had been involved in the drafting group meetings, although he could have been pursuing that line of inquiry. I was trying to explain that there had been no normal meeting within the DIS at which each directorate could make their arguments to our own JIC members, the chief and deputy chief of defence intelligence, but I allowed myself to be sidetracked.

I continued:

> I think 'abnormal' is the wrong word. What was unusual or what did not follow the normal practice was that this was not a paper that was going through the process by which it was examined and argued over at a full meeting of the Joint Intelligence Committee at the stage that we are talking about. Unless there was an extraordinary one, of which I am totally unaware, I would think that the last meeting before publication, which was a Tuesday, would have been the previous Wednesday. And here we are into the Thursday and the Friday of that cycle.

By working through the dates we established that the later drafts of the dossier could not have been discussed by the JIC in a normal weekly session. I said I was not aware there had been an extraordinary meeting of the JIC to discuss the dossier and suspected there had not been one. Although Dingemans seemed very interested in this it was not what I was trying to explain was unusual about the process. However, it did get us eventually to the minutes of concern that my colleague and I had written near the end of the process.

I explained, 'I wrote a minute to my director making it clear that there were problems with this, and I copied that to my deputy director.' (I meant 'deputy chief of defence intelligence'.)

A document flashed up on the screen in front of me and Dingemans interrupted, 'Can I call up a minute and you can tell me if it is the right one? It is MoD/22/1.'

I recognised the minute I had written almost a year before, on 19 September 2002. 'Yes, that is the one.'

Dingemans 'introduced' it and read large parts of it aloud, asking me as he went along to confirm its accuracy or his interpretation of a particular point I had made in the minute or relating it to the evidence I had already given. When he had finished he asked, 'To a lawyer who reads people moaning about words [*sic*] all the time, it might seem that this is a usual sort of minute to write. Would that be a fair impression?'

I allowed myself to be led and replied, 'No, if we revert to our comparison with the normal JIC product, I think I had only had cause to express this sort of reservation after the shutters had come down, if you like, on one occasion, maybe two. I clearly remember one, but there may have been another. But, you know, in fifteen years of dealing with this process it was very unusual to have to do that.'

'Did you get a response?'

'My director – who, I should explain, was only recently in post, he had only been in post a few weeks, had come from outside the intelligence area – was, you know, having a difficult time then, shall we say, coming to terms with all this. And he did write me a note saying "Thank you for your minute", and I think that was the only response I had.'

'You got the impression he did not really mean it when he said "Thank you".'

The tension was broken by general laughter. When it stopped I said, 'He may well not have meant it, but I do not know – no, I cannot really comment on that. I mean, we had had a discussion about it, and he was aware of my reservations, you know, twenty-four hours earlier.'

Dingemans asked me if I could recall the discussion about the 45-minutes intelligence at the meeting I had held on 19 September 2002 that was attended by David Kelly, and he related it to a document he had about Kelly's conversation with Susan Watts, the *Newsnight* science correspondent. I had not been aware of that conversation, or the *Newsnight* programmes before then. The gist of a rather complicated exchange was that I said it did not exactly reflect what had been said at the meeting or the position of me and my staff, but it was a reasonable approximation. The main point of difference was that we had not suggested at the meeting or at any other time that the 45-minutes intelligence should be completely excluded from the dossier. Kelly had told Watts that some people had suggested it should.

Dingemans referred again to a section of the transcript of the Kelly–Watts conversation, which was now on the screen before me and which is reproduced below:

> DAVID KELLY: In your heart of hearts you must realise sometimes that's not actually the right thing to say but it's the only way you can put it over if you've got to get it over in two minutes or three minutes.
>
> SUSAN WATTS: Did you actually write that section which refers to the forty-five minutes or was it somebody else?
>
> KELLY: I didn't write that section, no. I mean, I reviewed the whole thing. I was involved with the whole process. In the end it was just a flurry of activity and it was very difficult to get comments in because people at the top of the ladder didn't want to hear some of the things.

'Was that a fair comment?' asked Dingemans, referring to Kelly's last statement.

I hesitated again. These were difficult questions to answer off the cuff and I did not want to level a trivial criticism of Kelly. However, he did seem to have exaggerated, by implication, the role he had played in preparing the dossier and the authority he had in the process. I said:

> I think David was involved in the whole process to the extent that he had visibility of the whole. . . the complete drafts of the dossiers, or at least by the time I returned from leave on the eighteenth I think he was seeing them. He did not contribute to the process of the analysis of the latest intelligence, so he was not involved to that extent. His description of the flurry of activity was certainly right and I think I have explained that. I mean, I think the end of that, 'because people at the top didn't want to

hear some of the things', whether that was the case or not, I do not know. It was certainly difficult to get the things done and it was more difficult than usual, and we were disappointed when we did not succeed. But the exact cause of that one can only guess at. One cannot. . . I was not in a position to know, and I do not know whether he knew any more than I did.

Suddenly Dingemans put me on the spot. 'If members of your staff had given this sort of information to journalists about the discussions that had taken place in your branch relating to concerns about the dossier, what would your reaction have been to that?'

If he had put the question directly about Kelly, I would have found myself unable to answer. But my heart sank anyway. The previous few days of the inquiry had been taken up with the moving evidence of Kelly's widow, Janice, and one of his daughters. I paused for what seemed like an age as I realised my answer would reveal what I thought of his behaviour. It would cast an ugly shadow across their fond memories. It would be speaking ill of the dead. I had hoped I would not be forced to admit the deep sense of betrayal I had felt personally, and on behalf of my team of analysts, when I first realised that Kelly was talking about matters he had learned, in confidence, in my office. Eventually, I found some clumsy words that were accurate enough but concealed the depth of my emotion: 'I would have thought they were acting well beyond the bounds of what they should have been doing. I would have been very disappointed and very annoyed.'

Dingemans moved swiftly on.

Can I take you to one final reference, CAB/29/15? This was Mr A's email. Just at the bottom of CAB/29/15 Mr A makes the comment: 'Another example supporting our view that you and I should have been more involved in this than the spin merchants of this administration.' Mr A has explained what he meant by that. Was there a perception, right or wrong, amongst DIS personnel that spin merchants were involved with the dossier?

Another difficult question caused me to give a disjointed answer. 'Well, "spin merchants" is rather emotive. I think there was an impression, right or wrong, and I do not know, I did not allow that to concern me as this process. . . I think there was an impression that there was an influence from outside the intelligence community.'

'And were people in the intelligence community happy with that?'

I almost answered without thinking carefully enough but I was wary enough to qualify my answer. I replied:

> No, I do not think. . . well, I cannot comment on the broader intelligence community. I think the people who had been involved on my staff and possibly others. . . I mean, one cannot make a general statement about this. But certainly those people that were working directly with me were concerned and unhappy; in the way I think I described earlier in my evidence, in the way that people can be unhappy. But I think there was a realisation that this was a different process; and I think, at the end of the day, what they were very keen to do is have any assessment reflect as accurately as possible the product of their work.

And abruptly, that was it. Lord Hutton thanked me for attending. We were led quietly out of the courtroom as the session proceeded and through the maze of corridors to the courtyard where, we were assured, a car would be waiting to whisk us to Waterloo station.

The escape

The courtyard where an MoD car should have been was at the bottom of a wide stone stairway. There was no sign of it. I glanced around anxiously, but could see no reporters or photographers. In the far distance, perhaps a hundred yards away, was the gate out onto the Strand. Together with our solicitors and the court usher, my wife and I walked slowly down the steps wondering at the absence of the car, grumbling quietly amongst ourselves and quite unaware that all the while we were being filmed and photographed. We would see ourselves on the television that evening and in the next morning's newspapers, courtesy of powerful telescopic lenses. Our discussion as we descended the steps looks much more earnest and considered than it actually was. After a significant pause our driver sauntered casually around the corner and led us to his vehicle.

Then, as we approached the gate, there was an inordinately long wait for it to be opened. When it did we nudged only slowly through the horde of cameramen who seemed to be alert and primed to catch us on our departure. Cameras were thrust against the windows and we tried to turn our faces away from them. Turning left, our car accelerated for a short distance along the Strand but at a set of red lights we drew to a halt. I heard a rumble of thunder. As it got louder we suddenly became surrounded by the unruly press pack. I realised I had been listening to the pounding of collective feet as they stampeded after us. Knowing the territory they had obviously anticipated the lights might change and took full advantage of their luck. There were cameras at every window again, and this time bodies draped themselves across the bonnet and a continual banging and thumping echoed around us as each photographer tried to persuade us to look into his camera. My wife looked terrified. I stared at the floor, upset at being the cause of her discomfort. We suddenly had some idea of how famous people, criminals or celebrities, must feel under such circumstances, as eager bodies jostled for position and we were immersed in an ocean of flashing lights. The solicitor, Peter, seemed as shocked as we were. My fear that we might be followed or spotted on our journey home was magnified.

When the lights turned green at last, the car quickly shed its load of bodies and moved off through a maze of streets which seemed to leave our pursuers far behind. We crossed the Thames on Waterloo Bridge and stepped from the car at the main station with some trepidation. But by the time we reached the concourse we were confident that we had not been followed. We were relieved to be on the train home.

Afterwards

We remained twitchy when we got home and spent the evening watching ourselves on the television. All the news bulletins we saw that evening covered my evidence and showed pictures of us leaving the court. Although I was initially highly sensitive to variations in emphasis, or minor misrepresentation, in retrospect I feel the coverage was fair.

There was some confusion about Mr A. The complication of him not actually appearing or being named created the impression that he was a serving intelligence officer. He was, in fact, a weapons inspector who, I now understand, had returned from his ongoing work with the Iraq Survey Group especially to give evidence. This would be why he did not want to be identified at that time. Some reporters understood who he was, others were less careful and described him as an intelligence analyst. A few went so far as to assume he was the intelligence analyst I had referred to as my chemical warfare expert. I felt this was particularly unfortunate because several of the comments made by Mr A, and the email he sent to David Kelly mentioning spin doctors, which attracted particular attention, were highly speculative. He had no experience of intelligence or the careful way in which we tend to present information. I had striven hard to eliminate speculation from my evidence, or to make it clear when questions invited a speculative reply. The media reports were generally not sufficiently discerning to identify the difference; I hoped that Lord Hutton was.

Several news reports made a great deal of the questions and answers about whether the JIC met to consider a near-final draft of the dossier. My suspicion that the dossier had been approved out of committee by the silence procedure excited considerable attention. This process is normally adopted only for minor modifications to final drafts that had been considered at a full JIC meeting. Perhaps the most significant thing is that the inquiry had not been made aware of this by government witnesses. Despite a show of openness, this was one of several areas where significant economies were being made with the truth. It was clarified in subsequent evidence to the inquiry that the JIC had not met to discuss the text of the dossier.

In one of the early evening television news bulletins, the Labour MP Eric Joyce was interviewed. I cannot recall ever having noticed him before. Whilst he did not draw conclusions from the day's evidence that were critical of the government, his comments seemed reasonably balanced and he warned against jumping to hasty conclusions. But by the end of the evening I was to recognise that Joyce was acting as the unofficial voice of the government. In the intervening few hours he had made a giant leap and was now 'on message'. I had become a junior official with limited visibility of important matters and was not really very important at all.

An item by Mark Urban on *Newsnight* included the suggestion of a turf war between MI6 and the DIS. On this occasion that had not happened, but his source clearly had a degree of insight. Over the years there had occasionally been disagreements between the two organisations, including on weapons of mass destruction, but mostly these were the result of inevitable and understandable tensions between individuals or groups trying to do difficult jobs when their judgements conflicted. After the cold war I had sensed that, in searching to reidentify its prime roles, MI6 had decided to increase its profile in the area of nuclear, biological and chemical weapons. I discussed it often with senior colleagues and line managers in the DIS. At one point MI6 sought help from us in identifying and recruiting experts to assist in their effort. However, my resources and the pool of relevant expertise in UK were both so small that I was unable to offer as much assistance as they needed. It may have appeared to them that I was protecting my patch and there was an element of that in my reaction. MI6 proceeded to recruit and develop contacts independently in the highly effective way that their status, freedom from normal civil service strictures and superior resources allow them to. Although the MoD and DIS senior management allowed me to enhance my staffing levels to a small extent it did not match the increasing WMD collection resource of MI6 or the trend of greatly increased investment in collection *and* analysis that our intelligence allies were making. As a consequence we were always hard pressed to keep pace with the growing volume of secret intelligence we were receiving and the explosion in the availability of open source information through the internet, and because of the political changes in Russia.

I take great pride in the fact that, although we had this problem, we never failed to identify, assess and brief on all the significant information that became available during my time at the DIS. During the process of sifting through the flood of new information, the judgement of what was important by my expert staff was of the highest quality. What we did not have time to do was pay enough attention to promoting our successes, or tending adequately to our interface with the collectors. There were times when MI6 felt some of the excellent intelligence they were obtaining, especially on the former Soviet Union, was not being significantly reflected in MoD policy. The increased effort they made in briefing MoD policy makers at first hand had little effect, and some in MI6 thought we in the DIS were not properly reflecting their efforts. Unfortunately, we did not often find the time to adequately explain the situation to them. First there was a high degree of resistance in MoD to recognising and accepting an uncomfortable new potential threat that would inevitably limit their freedom of military action, especially as there were no simple solutions to the problem. Second, there was a practical difficulty in translating an intelligence assessment quickly into a meaningful programme aimed at defence and protection. MI6 found it difficult to accept that other priorities drove the MoD.

At the time the dossier was being drafted relations had much improved. One of my key analysts was being shared with a short-staffed MI6 at my expense. My suspicions about the way the dossier was going were focused on the political influence. The failure by senior personnel, especially within the DIS, to adhere to the established rules seemed to be the main problem. Those involved were either too keen to bend to the requirements of No. 10 or too weak to resist them. There was no argument at the working level over access to Report X. The reasons for such decisions were usually well founded. It was our bosses' apparent weakness or inadequacy in weakly accepting the collectors' reassurance that we saw as the problem.

Neither my wife nor I slept well that night, wondering what the papers would say the next day and whether crowds of journalists might arrive on our doorstep. I looked tentatively between the curtains when I got up, and breathed a sigh of relief when I saw the street was empty.

Newspaper coverage was extensive and I was variously called a 'whistleblower' and an 'intelligence chief'. Since I had not publicly volunteered any information until asked to contribute by Lord Hutton, I did not consider myself to be the former, and I did not think the latter an accurate description of my previous middle-ranking status.

CHAPTER TEN

September 2003: ISC reports and Hutton hearings end

The ISC report

On 5 September, the Hutton inquiry took a ten-day break. During this interlude the report of the Intelligence and Security Committee was published.[1] The extent to which the two inquiries influenced one another is not clear. At this point the ISC report comprised all that was known about the secret ISC inquiry. When it started Whitehall had no reason to think it might lose its control of what was disclosed to it.

The ISC report started by defining the terminology it would apply but it did not always adhere to its own rules. For example, it was all-embracing in defining the term 'munition' to include 'warheads' as well as other systems such as bombs and projectiles, yet subsequently the report accepted the interpretation that 'munitions' in the 45-minutes intelligence excluded ballistic missile warheads and referred only to 'battlefield' weapons. This was one of several things that would influence government evidence in what was to follow at Hutton.

The report provided a misleading interpretation of the 'single source' issue. It accepted the argument that some famous 'single sources' had provided valuable information. The ISC did not understand that confidence in each source will have come from comparisons with other overlapping information of appropriate quality, confidentiality and independence. None of the evidence provided by the 45-minutes source could be corroborated or supported by collateral of this type.[2]

The ISC did not treat the Prime Minister's foreword as a separate political statement that was beyond its remit.[3] It noted that the first draft of the foreword had included the statement 'The case I make is not that Saddam could launch a nuclear attack on London or another part of the UK (he could not)' and said it was unfortunate that this point was removed and not highlighted elsewhere because it made clear that the government recognised that the nature of the threat that Saddam posed was not directly to the mainland UK. The committee opined that some might have been led to believe there was such a direct threat to the UK mainland and this might have influenced public perceptions and attitude to the invasion of Iraq.

With regard to the concern expressed by me and my colleague, the ISC referred to the sensitive intelligence of Report X that was available to only a few and commented, 'We have seen that intelligence and understand the basis on which the CDI and the JIC took the view they did.' At the time, I interpreted this as meaning that the ISC was convinced of the validity of the intelligence. Some months later, when I challenged a member of the committee about it, he claimed the statement was intended to be 'Delphic' in nature and that, whilst the ISC did not endorse the view, it was saying it understood how others might. I did not know that the ISC had been told that Report X had been withdrawn before it reported and, although this emerged later, it has never explained why it acceded to the government's request to keep this secret. In doing so, it had become part of the cover-up.

The ISC said it deplored as 'unhelpful and potentially misleading' the initial failure by the MoD to disclose that 'some staff' had put their concerns in writing to their line managers. It was further disturbed that, after the first evidence session, which did not cover all the concerns raised by the DIS staff, the Defence Secretary declined to give instructions for a letter to be written to the ISC clarifying them. Although some further information on the matter was later made available, the ISC did not recognise that anything unusual had occurred. The report's suggestion that the complaints procedures within the DIS should be tightened up suggests the ISC failed to grasp that without access to Report X we had no substantive grounds to do anything other than warn our line managers we were unconvinced and suspicious.

On 11 September the Defence Secretary, Geoff Hoon, made a statement to the House regarding the criticism of him by the ISC.[4] But, because the ISC had not investigated the matter properly, Hoon did not have to explain why he and his officials misrepresented the nature of our expression of concern. The contradictory evidence I had given to the Hutton inquiry just a week earlier was ignored by both Hoon and those who raised questions in the House. Although there was a good deal of more general criticism, Michael Mates, a senior member of the ISC, relieved the pressure on Hoon when he intervened saying:

> Is it not the case that when anyone comes to the House and says that a mistake has been made which he regrets, and that he will see that it does not happen again, the House is generous? The real answer to all this is that, ultimately, the committee was not misled. There will be plenty of opportunities to debate this matter, because the government are required to respond to our report, and there will then be a debate about it. I suggest that that is the time when we shall be able to go over this ground again.

Neither Mates nor any of his ISC colleagues appear to have revisited the part of their report that related to my expression of concern in the light of my evidence to Hutton. Mates's assumption about the government's response to the report proved to be optimistic. The committee had been misled, and the government was to take five months to reply and that would be lost in the deluge of incredulity that would swamp the Hutton report.

Another important observation in the ISC report drew attention to the Prime Minister's use of the phrase 'continued to produce chemical and biological weapons' in his foreword to the dossier. It noted the absence of detail on amounts of agents produced. They said this could have given the impression that Saddam was actively producing both chemical and biological weapons and significant amounts of agents. Indeed, in the period leading up to the dossier the Prime Minister had stated this was the case. But the ISC pointed out that the JIC did not know what agents had been produced and in what quantities despite having assessed that production had taken place. It said that this uncertainty should have been highlighted to give a balanced view of Saddam's chemical and biological capacity. In fact, there was sufficient warning about the inadequacy of the intelligence and the uncertainty in quantities in the formal JIC assessments, if not in the dossier, and the false impression created by the dossier was exactly the substance of my concern. The ISC was apparently unable to see the connection.

The ISC report also highlighted a JIC assessment in December 2002, less than three months after publication of the dossier, that said that Iraq's ability to use chemical and biological weapons might be constrained by its available stocks of agent and the difficulty of producing more whilst UN inspectors were present. Thus the JIC clearly acknowledged that it did not know the extent of Iraq's stocks of those weapons. This assessment raises the question of whether Report X had been re-evaluated and downgraded by this time. A few weeks earlier the JIC had believed its information underpinned the dossier. The later assessment suggests that the claims in September of the existence of clinching intelligence on the presence of stocks of weapons in Iraq had already been set aside. There had then been a pressing need to bring the DIS into line so that the Prime Minister could deliver the goods on Saddam just a few days later. What had caused the JIC to change its mind in the intervening period? Despite getting so close to the heart of the matter, the ISC could not bring itself to acknowledge the false impression the dossier had generated or the Prime Minister's role in achieving that.

Hutton resumes with the DIS chiefs

On 15 September 2003 the two senior officers who had been in charge of the DIS in 2002 were the first witnesses called. By now both had left the DIS.

The deputy chief of defence intelligence, Tony Cragg, had retired, having been in post as my boss's boss from 1999 until I left in January 2003. Unlike his predecessor, he was not a professional intelligence analyst. Given his lack of familiarity with intelligence and the huge workload he inherited, I could understand why he seemed a rather remote figure. From what I did see of him, I thought he found it difficult to come to terms with the different culture of intelligence compared to that of the policy world in which he had spent most of his career.

Cragg told James Dingemans that his principal task had been to manage the work of the Defence Intelligence Analysis Staff; he was also a member of the Joint Intelligence Committee. His description of the Directorate of Scientific and Technical Intelligence's work on weapons of mass destruction was brief. It was not wrong but did not acknowledge that my branch was by far the largest and most experienced group dealing with WMD, and ignored the fact that a neat line cannot be drawn between scientific and technical matters and most other aspects of the subject. Perhaps Cragg genuinely did not understand this. If not, it was a very convenient misconception for the cover-up of which he was about to become a part.

When asked about the dossier Cragg followed what was now established as the government line, playing down the significance of our expressions of concern. He reinforced the implication that the concerns were those of only two officers by not clarifying that the comments on drafts of the dossier sent to the Assessments Staff were coordinated DIS returns, not merely the views of individual groups or factions within the organisation.

When asked of the extent of his 'knowledge of comments or unhappiness' in relation to drafts of the dossier before he received my minute of 19 September, he replied that he had 'received no indication of further unhappiness, either on the part of Dr Jones and his colleague or anyone else in the DIAS'. He did not mention that on 17 September he had instructed the DIS coordinators that they should raise no further objections to the dossier.

Dingemans, occasionally assisted by Lord Hutton, tried to understand the sequence and detail of the various meetings that had taken place from 16 to 19 September 2002, and the nature of the concerns that Cragg's DIS staff were trying to resolve. The exchanges became ever more convoluted and confused because Cragg seemed determined not to mention Report X, which was central to his decision to override his analysts' concerns. I had drawn attention to this in my evidence, but no government witness had mentioned it so far. Cragg's seeming determination not to be the first resulted in his evidence becoming increasingly difficult to follow.[5]

But Dingemans continued to press. Why had DIS concerns over the draft dossier not been discussed at the JIC meeting on Wednesday 18 September 2002? Cragg said the DIS concerns had been raised at the final drafting meeting chaired by the chief of the Assessments Staff the day before. Cragg had called an internal DIS meeting a few hours after the drafting meeting. It had been attended by the two DIS officials who had been at the dossier drafting meeting, their director and my director. When asked to explain what those who had attended the drafting meeting had told him about the discussion of the inconsistencies that concerned the DIS, Cragg made little sense:

> They said firstly, on the actual detailed intelligence, recent intelligence underpinning the main text and partly the executive summary, that the Secret Intelligence Service, SIS, were satisfied that the source was established and reliable and they were. . . they supported the reporting, which had itself already been included in a JIC assessment on 9 September.

Dingemans thought Cragg was about to discuss the matter of Report X, and asked him to confirm that he was not talking about the 45-minutes intelligence. Cragg confounded him by saying he *was* talking about the

45-minutes intelligence. Cragg tried to explain but was digging himself a deeper hole:

> Yes. If I could just track back again. My staff also reported to me there had been a discussion, as I say, of the general context in which the new intelligence had appeared which convinced them that it was quite reasonable to take the line they did in the executive summary concerning the likelihood or the capability of the Iraqis to deploy weapons of mass destruction within forty-five minutes of a decision to do so.

Lord Hutton intervened, adding to the confusion and apparently not understanding the thrust of Dingemans's questioning:

> Mr Cragg, did part of this discussion relate to the point that I think Dr Jones had been concerned that the intelligence about the 45-minutes claim was single sourced, but then, as I follow the evidence, the SIS, at the meeting that you conducted or at the meeting in which you took part, said that they were satisfied about the reliability of that source? Was that what occurred? Have I understood it correctly?

Cragg persisted:

> SIS were present at the Cabinet Office meeting, my Lord. At that point. . . I was not there myself, but I understand from my staff that there was a discussion on the validity of the source, which would almost certainly have included whether it was single source. And the answer, I think, on the single source issue is that, as I believe Mr Scarlett said in his first appearance, my Lord, that single source clearly has to be looked at with some care; but this was a known source, established and reliable with a good reporting record. And the statements he was making, the intelligence he was providing was well in context of known Iraqi approaches. So in that sense – I think Mr Scarlett said it fairly clearly – there were no qualms about including this reporting.

'I see. Yes. Thank you,' said Lord Hutton, inscrutable as ever.

Dingemans jumped back in. 'What was your understanding about ownership of the dossier—'

But Lord Hutton had not finished yet. 'Just before you ask that, may I ask you: at the conclusion of the meeting which you attended, and you had knowledge that Dr Jones and his staff were concerned about the wording relating to the 45-minutes claim, what was your conclusion about the validity of their concerns?'

Cragg answered, 'I felt, my Lord, bearing in mind the views expressed by SIS and supported by the assessment staff, that their concerns had been dealt with satisfactorily. That was my judgement.'

'Yes. I see. Yes. Yes,' said His Lordship.

Dingemans then asked, 'And your view was then made known to the two directors who had attended?'

'We discussed this round my table, so they knew,' said Cragg.

'The director for science and technology was the line manager for Dr Jones, is that right?'

'He was, correct.'

Dingemans left his quest to draw from Cragg some mention of Report X and turned to other matters before returning to the issue of Report X a little later. The breakthrough came when Dingemans manoeuvred Cragg into introducing the minute in which I had raised my concern, at which point he quickly took the opportunity to quote from it: '[Dr Jones] says that: "1. A number of people have been involved in the generation of the Iraq dossier, which has involved a number of iterations. It is my understanding that some of the intelligence has not been made available to my branch."'

'That is correct,' agreed Cragg.

'He must have picked that up following the meeting you had had with his director.'

'Yes. I specifically asked his director to make it clear that some intelligence, not on the forty-five minutes but on the production issue, was not available to them because it was being held on a very small circle to which he was not party and, indeed, nor was I.' This was the first overt reference by a government witness to Report X and its significance in relation to the dossier. The JIC chairman, Sir John Scarlett, and other members of his committee, Sir David Omand and Julian Miller, had already given extensive evidence which could have been much simplified if they had referred to Report X.

Not only had Cragg now acknowledged the importance of Report X, but he revealed other important information about it. Report X had been about 'production', presumably of chemical and/or biological warfare agent or weapons, and he had not seen it himself or been personally briefed about it. He simply believed what had been relayed to him by my boss – an inexperienced newcomer. It shocked me that Cragg could have dismissed the serious concerns held by his own experts who were so much more knowledgeable and experienced than he and his directors. He apparently accepted the interpretation of the collector of the intelligence without challenge and saw no need to call his experts together for a discussion before issuing a firm instruction.

Having taken so long to get to this point Dingemans went over the ground again to emphasise certain aspects.

Cragg revealed:

> I was going to say, at the meeting chaired by the Cabinet Office on the seventeenth it was agreed that the SIS representative would make further representations to us about this material [Report X]. In the event, he spoke to my director of Science and Technology, who then himself spoke to Dr Jones to explain, firstly, that this was very tightly held intelligence and, secondly, SIS believed that it was good intelligence.

In fact, my director had allowed me to infer that Cragg had seen the intelligence. He did not explain that he had been the conduit for relaying the briefing and the reassurances about it from the SIS. I did not gain the impression he had been told that the information was from a source whose credibility was not yet established, or that he had asked critical questions. Having listened to my suspicions and heard of some of my previous experiences and listened to my explanation of the pitfalls, I suspect he became too embarrassed to admit what he had done. I remember asking him the specific question of whether Cragg had seen Report X. I wonder exactly what he said to Cragg.

Dingemans asked Cragg if the language of my minute of 19 September was strong. He replied, 'Yes. I was quite surprised to receive the minute, because we had gone. . . we had tried to explain what the situation was, certainly on the production issue and, as far as I can tell also perhaps, although I am not certain, on the forty-five minutes.' This directly contradicted all the previous attempts by government witnesses to pass off our minutes of concern as part of the normal process of discussion and is a clear indication that the Intelligence and Security Committee had been misled on this. The anger that my boss told me Cragg had expressed to him is also indicated in this reply.

Dingemans asked, 'And having received a document that surprised you, what did you do as a result of that?'

Cragg said he was satisfied with the text of the dossier on 19 September despite my minute. He was satisfied that the issues I raised had been resolved at the drafting meeting on 17 September.

Hutton asked Cragg if he had considered whether he should report my concerns to the chief of defence intelligence, Air Chief Marshal Joe French (by now Sir Joe), or to the JIC. Cragg explained that French was not in the office on the day I wrote my minute but that he saw it and 'took a view' the following day. He had not reported the matter to John Scarlett because he thought Scarlett would simply ask for the views of CDI and himself.

Dingemans asked about the minute written the next day by my colleague. Cragg explained he had been out of the office that day and had not returned until the day after the dossier had been published. As a consequence he had not seen my colleague's minute at all. His first sight of it was in preparation for giving evidence, at the inquiry several months after he had retired.

French gave evidence immediately after Cragg. I had seen rather more of him than I had of Cragg during their time at the DIS. He was always pleasant and took an interest, but I think he gained no great familiarity with intelligence on the subjects I dealt with.

French explained that he had been chief of defence intelligence from November 2000 to 17 April 2003, which included the period relevant to the dossier, and that he was responsible to the permanent secretary of the MoD and the chief of Defence Staff. He said he was also one of two deputy chairmen of the JIC.

Although he may not have intended to do so, in his early testimony French confirmed there was a significant variation from the normal DIS process for JIC assessments when it came to the dossier. There had been no formal DIS meeting to discuss the last draft of the dossier before JIC approval, as there would have been with a typical assessment. The relevant specialists were not given the opportunity to explain their views.

French insisted that my branch had no particular contribution to make other than on strictly technical issues and perpetuated the idea that known tactics and doctrine for the employment of chemical weapons played a significant part in establishing confidence in the intelligence concerned. In doing so he implied that there were disagreements on this issue between branches in the DIS. Dingemans challenged French on his suggestion that the concerns were restricted to my branch, citing the coordinated DIS comments on an earlier draft of the dossier. French tried, in a garbled and confused way, to deny the point:

> No, and I am not sure I would express it in those terms. . . we come back to the process where the staffs were invited to actually put their comments through. It was discussed in detail with the assessment staff, with representations not just from the scientific and technical personnel, which is what you are actually alluding to there, but a range of others who would have been experts in this field, and also those who contributed from the agencies within the Joint Intelligence Committee overall.

But Dingemans kept him on the hook. 'Is this document here from the science and technology group alone?' he asked, referring to a specific DIS coordinated response to the Assessments Staff.

French was forced to admit, 'No, it was an amalgam of the comments from across the Defence Intelligence Staff.'

'Which rather suggests, having amalgamated the comments, the Defence Intelligence Staff took the view that the 45-minutes claim was, as expressed in the dossier – they have given the date, 15 September – rather strong.'

'In the staff view at that level. Ultimately the document had to be cleared at the Joint Intelligence Committee level and I was content with the wording that appeared in the final draft. I come back to, again, this is a regular process. As Dr Jones's minute makes clear or infers [sic], he had had many of his points actually included in the document and we had actually got down to the last one or two points, which is where I had been informed on the twentieth [when he became aware of my concern] that these issues were still then in the minds of the staff.'

'Right,' said Dingemans, having established that French had overruled all of his staff, not just me, or even just my branch.

Lord Hutton wanted further clarification. 'Air Marshal, when you say it has to be clear at the Joint Intelligence Committee level, do you mean by that at the level of the JIC assessment staff—'

French's answer was confusing:

> Well, it goes through a twofold process, my Lord. One is for the assessment staff to present the draft, the final draft ultimately on the twentieth, to the Joint Intelligence Committee itself. And then ultimately for the committee members on the part of the Defence Intelligence Staff, myself, to say that I am content with the wording as it stood.

With regard to my minute, French said there was advice from Cragg saying he had satisfied himself on the main issues that were raised. French continued:

> I got this document the next day and, having obviously seen these issues or discussed these sorts of issues in the weeks leading up to this, I come back to the point again that this is heavily qualified in the intelligence that was available to Dr Jones and to people within his particular area of the DIS. And that what I had been through with the directors over the two or so weeks beforehand, the forty-five minutes, I think we have covered already; on some of the chemical and biological weapons issues, the intelligence there was on a very limited distribution; and as you quoted earlier, the ISC did consider this and, as they put in their own report last Thursday, they fully understood the conclusions that both the DIS and myself in this instance and the JIC came to on that limited-distribution intelligence.

Dingemans picked up on the reference to Report X. 'The limited-distribution intelligence did not refer to the 45-minutes claim?'

'No, it was chemical and biological issues.'

'So to the extent that Dr Jones was making comments about the 45-minute issue, that was or was not answered by the recent intelligence?'

French seemed lost. 'Not that chemical and biological. There was intelligence which I think was either 29 or 30 August which dealt specifically with the forty-five minutes.'

Dingemans continued to press him. 'We have heard of the reporting of that.'

'I have to keep reiterating, Dr Jones more specifically would be looking at the technical aspects of weapons, how they were put together, the effects of actually using them. It would be other parts of the organisation, who certainly had no quibble with the forty-five minutes, who would also contribute equally well to that discussion.'

Unfortunately he was not asked which part of the organisation had no quibble, and who was leading that argument, but I think Dingemans had already exposed the falseness of the statement.

'Having seen Dr Jones's memorandum, what did you do as a result of that?' asked Dingemans. French said he was content for the draft dossier to go to print.

French was asked if the JIC met in committee to approve the final version of the dossier. He said it had not but, in doing so, implied that the JIC had collectively considered earlier drafts. It is now clear that the JIC never discussed a substantial draft of the dossier in committee.

When pressed on the quality of the sourcing for the 45-minutes intelligence, French declined to put forward any logical argument. He referred, instead, to the ISC report – suggesting he believed an independent group of non-specialists were better placed to make judgements on intelligence than professionals.

Dingemans's inquisition circled for a while before returning to the 45-minutes claim. French repeated:

> I have accepted what they put in the report. Again, if you are looking at forty-five minutes I think it has to be understood that the intelligence that we were using in the Defence Intelligence Staff was not just an understanding of what the Iraqi forces may be capable of; we also had to put it in the context of our forces deployed to the region. We had had forces there continuously since 1991, and any potential conflict that might arise with them, we would have to make sure that we had an understanding that was passed on to our armed forces so that they could make the appropriate defensive measures themselves should they come under any sort of attack from these sorts of weapons.

I am not sure what French was trying to say here. Perhaps he meant that, in making our assessments in the DIS, we had to err on the side of caution because of our responsibility to our forces in the Gulf. This was certainly the case and I had carried that responsibility over the years, reporting twice or three times a year to the MoD's Nuclear, Biological and Chemical Defence Committee. My reports to that committee insisted that we should not drop our guard but I never went so far as to suggest there was 'no doubt' Iraq had chemical or biological weapons after 1991. The dossier was not an assessment for the MoD or the military, however,

and whilst I was concerned about sending a message that would give a
false sense of security to those military personnel who might read it, I still
wanted the assessment and the language in which it was expressed it to be
accurate and comprehensible.

After a lengthy exchange on the detail of Andrew Gilligan's report of his
conversation with David Kelly, French concluded with the observation:

> If there was any part that was not the intelligence, that was the foreword.
> The rest of the document was very much founded on intelligence and the
> issue of any concerns we have dealt with already, which were voiced by
> Dr Jones and someone else within his area. But ultimately I had made the
> decision on the part of the DIS that we were content with the final draft
> of the document.

This appears to disclaim what the Prime Minister had written but it was
not followed up. At this stage no other government witness had expressed
such doubts.

The evidence of 'C'

After lunch, Sir Richard Dearlove, 'C', gave evidence to the inquiry by
video link from 'another building'. He could see the inquiry but his face
was not shown. Since the existence of his organisation was no longer a
secret, perhaps this nonsense was intended to emphasise its continuing
mystique. He said he had been the chief of the Secret Intelligence Service,
'popularly known as MI6', since 1 August 1999. He had been in the
service since 1966. I recall a charming and entertaining talk he gave to
new members of the intelligence community when I joined in 1987, but
at Hutton in 2003 Dearlove was combative and pedantic.

When asked about the 45-minutes claim he responded, 'Can I just say,
you use the word "claim"; I think I would prefer to refer to it as a piece of
well-sourced intelligence.'

This seems now to have been a risky statement. No chemical or biological
weapons had been found in Iraq and he knew (although the inquiry did
not) there were already doubts about the sourcing of the 45-minutes
intelligence, and that the key intelligence report that supported it had been
withdrawn.

'Right,' said James Dingemans with the merest hint of sarcasm. 'When did you first become aware of this well-sourced piece of intelligence?'

There followed a familiar preamble about when and how the intelligence was reported and then Dearlove was asked to comment on the description of the 45-minutes source as an established, reliable and long-standing line of reporting. Dearlove was evasive. 'Well, I can, except I would not normally comment in public on the status of an SIS source; but a certain amount of this is already in the public domain.' He was persuaded to add, 'Yes, it did come from an established and reliable source equating a senior Iraqi military officer who was certainly in a position to know this information.'[6]

If it is correctly recorded this is an unusual source description. It may be that the word reported as 'equating' was actually 'quoting'. If it was, Dearlove chose not to correct the draft transcript nor to make it clear that the reliability of the secondary source had not been established.

Dingemans continued, 'That is at the end of August. On 3 September we have heard that the Prime Minister announced his intention to publish a dossier in relation to intelligence. What was the first you knew about the proposed publication?'

Further testimony revealed the central role played by Sir David Manning, the Prime Minister's foreign affairs adviser, at the interface with the intelligence community. I was not previously aware of Manning's closeness to the central intelligence machine.

Dingemans's style of questioning tended to mix up various issues in an apparently random way. He drew from Dearlove that, at the JIC meeting of 4 September, he had recommended that the JIC paper that was before the committee for approval be reworked to take account of new intelligence that included the 45-minutes report. Dearlove went on to say that at the next JIC meeting, on 11 September, there was a discussion of the dossier in which it was considered how to incorporate into it 'the previous JIC judgements on Iraqi WMD and the addition to that picture of any new intelligence that might be available'.

When asked if he was aware of any concerns about the 45-minutes intelligence, Dearlove said he was not. When asked if he was aware of any comment from the DIS relating to the 45-minutes intelligence, he said he was not. It is surprising that Dearlove was not told of his service's requirement to take exceptional action on 17 September in order to overcome DIS concerns. MI6 were asked to brief Report X to the chief and deputy chief of defence intelligence, who were outside the tight compartment in which it was being held.

When asked to comment on my minute of 19 September Dearlove used the 'it's only language' defence. Dingemans ignored this and introduced the 'single source' criticism, which 'C' defended in the same way as previous government witnesses had. Then, asked about the Foreign Affairs Committee's criticism that the 45-minutes claim was given such prominence in the Prime Minister's foreword and the executive summary of the dossier, he replied, 'Well, I think given the misinterpretation that was placed on the 45-minutes intelligence, with the benefit of hindsight you can say that is a valid criticism. But I am confident that the intelligence was accurate and that the use made of it was entirely consistent with the original report.'

As a member of the JIC and the originator of the intelligence, he had, of course, been uniquely well placed to correct the misinterpretation.

Lord Hutton needed an explanation. Dearlove told him:

> Well, I think the original report referred to chemical and biological munitions and that was taken to refer to battlefield weapons. I think what subsequently happened in the reporting was that it was taken that the forty-five minutes applied, let us say, to weapons of a longer range, let us say just battlefield material.

Dingemans intervened to ask if Dearlove agreed with the ISC that the 45-minutes claim was included so prominently because it 'was always likely to attract attention because it was an arresting detail that the public had not seen before' and that it was 'unhelpful to an understanding of the issue'. 'C' replied:

> Well, not entirely. But I think I would repeat what I said in answer to the last question. Given the misinterpretation of the original piece of intelligence, particularly as it was not qualified in terms of its relationship to battlefield munitions, this now looks a valid criticism; but I think the intelligence was accurate and that it was put to legitimate use in the drafting process.

Cross-examinations

The next stage in the inquiry allowed the representatives of 'interested parties' to cross-examine witnesses. The process was a lengthy one which went over much ground that had been covered before. Here I will pick out those exchanges which seemed most significant.

Geoff Hoon appeared for a second time on 22 September. Andrew Caldecott QC, counsel for the BBC, drew attention to the briefing paper for his appearance before the Intelligence and Security Committee which Martin Howard had written for him on 18 July. Hoon suggested that he had not considered the concern my colleague and I had expressed to be a serious objection that had remained unresolved, but his evidence was confused and confusing. On the 45-minutes intelligence, Hoon said he had always thought that it referred to battlefield munitions, but was promptly floored by the question of why he had stood back and allowed confusion, deception even, to persist on this matter when he could have clarified the situation. Sounding rather foolish, he said he did not consider that his responsibility.

Alastair Campbell was recalled later on the same day and Caldecott questioned him about the foreword to the dossier. Campbell had begun drafting it around 16 September 2002, basing it on a discussion with the Prime Minister and others. He said it was Tony Blair who had decided 'forty-five minutes' was a message worth including. Immediately, Campbell seemed to realise he had made a slip in pointing a finger at his boss but he was not allowed to gloss over it. Caldecott asked why, on or about 16 September, an account of the 45-minutes intelligence was being formulated in Downing Street before it had been finalised in the dossier itself.

Campbell replied:

> I was, I think, at the right time in the process, given that the foreword obviously was going to be an important part of the document overall, it would be the first thing that anybody getting the document would read, this was the right time to start drafting the foreword. I had a discussion with the Prime Minister, I think with David Manning, with Jonathan Powell, certainly with John Scarlett, and I based. . . I started a draft based upon what the Prime Minister wanted to say. And certainly that was one of the points that he felt was worth covering.

It may be that Blair's enthusiasm to emphasise the availability of WMD in 'forty-five minutes' was because he understood how it might chime with the Cold War 'four-minute warning' of nuclear attack that so many of the public would recognise and understand. In the event, it was a popular interpretation of the dossier – 'forty-five minutes from doom'. It appears that what the Prime Minister wanted to say played a greater part in shaping the dossier than the government was prepared to admit.

Sir John Scarlett was recalled for cross-examination the next day. His examination by Jonathan Sumption QC, counsel for the government, was designed to allow him to explain away some of the serious questions that had been raised. Scarlett painted a picture of a rising concern within the JIC through 2002 over the increasing capability of Iraq with respect to weapons of mass destruction. This was not evident to me, nor was it supported by information provided to Hutton or since.

The matter of Report X, which Scarlett and others had not mentioned in August, was carefully introduced by Sumption. Scarlett said he was aware of how it was used to overcome a problem at the last drafting meeting for the dossier. The exchange of questions suggested the intelligence was straightforward and reliable so that when it was briefed to the senior staff of the DIS they had no problem in endorsing the dossier. But no detail of the new intelligence emerged and nothing was said about its quality and reliability, although Scarlett knew that it had been withdrawn as unreliable.

Caldecott, for the BBC, asked whether it was made clear to the Prime Minister that the 45-minutes intelligence referred to battlefield munitions. Scarlett said, 'There was no discussion with the Prime Minister that I can recall about the 45-minutes point in connection with battlefield or strategic systems. Indeed I do not remember a discussion with the Prime Minister about the 45-minutes point at all.'

Scarlett went on to insist that the difference between strategic and tactical weapons in the context of many thousands being killed by them on the battlefield was semantic, thus contradicting Sir Richard Dearlove's suggestion that the misinterpretation of the intelligence was, as he saw it, significant. Scarlett thought it was not an important issue that a few newspapers, albeit with an overall readership of fifteen million, interpreted the dossier as referring to ballistic missiles. He added that it was not his immediate responsibility to correct headlines and if he had done so he certainly would not have had time to do his job.

Caldecott neglected to ask a vital question on this point. Having understood the scope for misinterpretation, did Scarlett check that Blair understood not only the detail of the nature of the weapons that were being discussed, but also the balance of probabilities associated with the intelligence assessments in the main body of the dossier? This much surely was his responsibility.

Towards the end of his cross-examination Caldecott turned to the matter of the minutes I and my colleague had written to our line managers on 19 and 20 September 2002 respectively, and my letter to Martin Howard in July 2003 reminding him of this with regard to evidence given to the Foreign Affairs Committee inquiry. Scarlett said he had seen both at a meeting in the office of the security and intelligence coordinator, David Omand. However, he refused to confirm counsel's suggestion about the seriousness of the original minutes, or that Howard's response to my letter was in any way misleading. Although the matter had been serious enough for a meeting to be called in the Cabinet Office by an official at the rank of permanent secretary (Omand), Scarlett insisted that the issue was a relatively minor matter dealt with entirely by the MoD.

James Dingemans revisited several of the issues covered earlier. Repeating a point he made in his testimony in August, Scarlett said he had not been aware in September 2002 of any DIS unhappiness about the dossier. Dingemans challenged this by reference to the earlier exchange between Sumption and Scarlett about Report X. He asked about the conversation Scarlett had with Julian Miller after the last drafting meeting about the need for a follow-up meeting at the DIS with regard to unhappiness about chemical warfare aspects.

Scarlett replied:

> That is not an expression of unhappiness. That was Mr Miller telling me that this point had been raised at the drafting group, and a number of points had been raised, but this one had in particular, and briefing was done; and I heard no more about it. So I did not know that there was any unresolved question and therefore unhappiness in DIS. I believed that that matter had been resolved to everyone's satisfaction.

'What did Mr Miller say when he said that the chemical warfare concerns had been raised with you or to you?' asked Dingemans.

'No more than that it had been raised, that the point about the compartmented intelligence [Report X] had been explained, that it had been agreed a briefing would be given to DIS senior management. That was it, I suppose. I do not remember precisely, but I would have logically thought: well, if this concern persists we will hear about it at a subsequent stage of the drafting process, or indeed at the JIC the next day, but we heard no more.'

Summary statements

Summary statements were made by representatives of the various groups and individuals involved on Thursday 25 September. To a large extent they reiterated the evidence that had been heard over the previous few weeks. Only a few comments require further discussion.

Jonathan Sumption made the first statement on behalf of the government. We must assume that it was agreed by the government and represented its views. He began by wrongly claiming that the process for the production of the dossier was the same as for any JIC paper. He described my evidence as 'a byway in the present inquiry' because I 'did not have access to the whole of the relevant material'. He claimed the 45-minutes intelligence was justified by the intelligence I had not seen (Report X) despite admitting it was also from a single unproven source, and he even hinted that there might be uncertainty about it, perhaps as a precaution in case the fact that Report X had been withdrawn ever emerged.

James Dingemans said:

> There was evidence from the then DCDI, Mr Cragg, and Air Marshal Sir Joe French, then chief of defence intelligence, and Sir Richard Dearlove, head of MI6, there had been a meeting within the Defence Intelligence Staff to discuss Dr Jones's unhappiness, and the chief of the Defence Intelligence Staff was content with the final claims made.

This was a rare mistake on his part. There is no evidence to suggest any such meeting took place nor had it been claimed that there was one. Unfortunately the error helped to underpin the government's wish to intimate that my colleague and I were the only analysts who were concerned about the dossier. But apart from that, I thought Dingemans was the hero of the Hutton inquiry. He coped magnificently in rapid fashion with huge volumes of information on a complicated matrix of subjects with which he was unfamiliar.

As he concluded, Dingemans made the following statement:

> Your Lordship is restricted to the terms of reference. As a matter of constitutional law and practice there are other institutions who have powers to examine matters beyond Your Lordship's terms of reference.

Stage 1 of the inquiry commenced in early August. Stage 2 concludes today. Somewhere along the way we lost a summer. I hope we exchange it for understanding.

His reference to the restricted terms of reference warned me that Lord Hutton's report might not be all that some expected.

The summer lost had been a glorious one in terms of the weather, but for me one of the darkest periods of my life had just passed. Unfortunately there was little relief on the horizon.

CHAPTER ELEVEN

October 2003–January 2004: the Hutton report

Waiting for Hutton

Lord Hutton thought his report would be ready at the beginning of November 2003 but it slipped into 2004. Despite urging everyone to wait for Hutton, on 17 December 2003 Tony Blair spoke out.[1] Shortly after the capture of Saddam Hussein and comments by Hans Blix on the failure yet to find WMD, Blair was asked if he was at all worried about the situation. He replied:

> Of course I would like the Iraq Survey Group to complete its work and to find whatever weapons Saddam had, because one thing is beyond doubt: he had them. And when Hans Blix says 'Well, there is no physical evidence', of course there was no physical evidence of the full extent of his biological programme for several years in the early 1990s, but it was only after the defection of his son-in-law to Jordan that we discovered the existence of that programme. So I don't think it is surprising that we will have to look for them, but I simply say to you: that he had them is beyond doubt, he used them, he used them against Iran, he used them against his own people. The evidence uncovered already is of a huge network of clandestine operations that are simply impossible to imagine without there actually being some purpose in these clandestine operations, and the purpose obviously was to conceal the weapons.

By now Blair will have been aware of the dearth of evidence obtained by the Iraq Survey Group. He probably also knew by this time of the decision of the Survey Group leader, David Kay, to quit his job because he thought there were no weapons.

A few days before Hutton issued his report, Sir Rodric Braithwaite, former British ambassador in Moscow and one-time chairman of the Joint

Intelligence Committee, observed in a thoughtful and brave contribution to BBC1's *Panorama* that my protests from the Defence Intelligence Staff would not have been undertaken lightly. He felt that John Scarlett had probably been drawn into the Prime Minister's 'magic circle' and influenced by that proximity to the highest in the land. He told me later that he thought he would have found such 'pressure' difficult to resist himself.

The *Panorama* programme also showed a clip from a previously unused interview with David Kelly from October 2002, some weeks after the dossier had been published. Kelly appeared to say he thought Iraq's weapons of mass destruction were an immediate threat. I was shocked to hear this. I could not imagine that he had gone on record to support the dossier after what he had told me and I doubted that he had spoken with the authority of the government. What he said appeared to contradict what he had told the three BBC journalists in the spring of 2003. However, further investigation revealed Kelly had given the interview wearing his UN biological weapons inspector hat and, therefore, had not necessarily been suggesting they were an immediate *military* threat to Britain so much as a general threat to the process of arms control and non-proliferation.

At last the report

Much was made of the efforts in hand to ensure the Hutton report was not leaked before it was released on 28 January 2004. Earlier in the month the Treasury solicitor heard there would be no criticism of me in the report and I was relieved. The Prime Minister was given a copy of the report twenty-four hours before its publication. Opposition representatives were allowed to read it 'under very secure conditions' a few hours before it was released. By then *The Sun* had announced that the report absolved the government in almost all respects and was critical of the BBC. I found that difficult to believe and, because the paper had strongly supported Blair over the Iraq War, I thought it must be an attempt to 'over-spin' what the report might say. I was wrong.

In the late morning, Lord Hutton held a press conference. He read the main conclusions of his report in his usual measured and unemotional fashion. Shortly afterwards Tony Blair presented the report to the Commons. There would be a full debate on it a few days later.

A review of the report

As James Dingemans had suggested he might, Lord Hutton stuck closely
to the terms of reference defined in the title of his 'Inquiry into the
Circumstances Surrounding the Death of Dr David Kelly CMG'. Issues
exposed in the evidence he had taken in August and September 2003 were
not mentioned if Hutton thought they did not impinge directly on Kelly's
death.

His main conclusion was that Kelly took his own life and no other
person was involved. He thought Kelly had done this because he had
suffered a severe loss of self-esteem resulting from his feeling that people
had lost trust in him and from his dismay at being exposed to the media.
I think this was a reasonable judgement.

Hutton could not rule out that

> the desire of the Prime Minister to have a dossier which . . . was as strong
> as possible in relation to the threat posed by Saddam Hussein's WMD may
> have subconsciously influenced Mr Scarlett and the other members of the
> JIC to make the wording of the dossier somewhat stronger than it would
> have been if it had been contained in a normal JIC assessment.

But despite this he thought the contents of the dossier were consistent with
the intelligence available to the JIC. Hutton did not distinguish between
elements of the dossier or say whether he considered the foreword to be an
integral part of it. He criticised Andrew Gilligan and the BBC but thought
the government had behaved honourably, although the MoD could have
shown more consideration of Kelly in the cursory way in which it advised
him of the disclosure of his name.

The report as a whole, which had taken Hutton much longer to write
than he first anticipated, has the despairing air of an author overwhelmed
by the volume and complexity of the evidence he had collected on matters
of which he had limited experience. Long tracts of verbatim evidence are
surrounded by sparse comments which fail to weigh relevant evidence he
had not reproduced.

One example concerns the conclusion: 'The "45 minute" claim was
based on a report which was received by the SIS from a source which
that Service regarded as reliable.' There was no further qualification or
explanation of that statement. Hutton had seen the original CX report

himself but perhaps he did not understand the reservation inherent in the source description. He did not explain why he dismissed so much of what he had heard about the uncertainty. The government had gone to great lengths to exclude or even conceal the important fact that the 45-minutes intelligence was not strong enough to stand on its own and relied on the additional intelligence of Report X to obtain DIS support for the dossier. But by the end of his hearings this much had become clear. Yet Hutton gives no indication of having recognised that this was significant in relation to the thrust of Gilligan's reporting on the dossier.

When he wrote his report, Hutton did not know that all the intelligence relevant to this issue had either been withdrawn as unreliable or was being re-examined. However, in addition to my testimony and the influence it had so obviously had on subsequent government evidence, the significance of Report X had been revealed in the Intelligence and Security Committee's report in ample time for Hutton to have taken account of it. Hutton convinced himself, against this evidence, that the government had absolute confidence in the 45-minutes intelligence at the time and this enabled him to say that

> whether or not at some time in the future the report on which the 45-minute claim was based is shown to be unreliable, the allegation reported by Mr Gilligan on 29 May 2003 that the government probably knew that the 45-minute claim was wrong before the government decided to put it in the dossier, was an allegation that was unfounded.

Hutton overlooked or ignored all that the DIS analysts had been saying about the 45-minutes claim before the dossier was published and the fact that their concerns had been formally documented and raised at the final drafting group meeting, chaired by Julian Miller, himself a member of the JIC. Hutton did not make it clear that their objections to the draft were 'resolved' only after this meeting when Tony Cragg made the unilateral decision that there should be no further expression of them. Hutton cast the whole issue in terms of my personal expression of concern, which was prompted by Cragg's directive. In ignoring the fact that I had arrived late on the scene after all the key decisions had been taken and was giving voice to the concerns of the real analytical experts, Hutton reinforced the impression the government was trying to create – that it was only one or two analysts that were concerned about the assessment carried by the dossier.

I believe it was not reasonable for Lord Hutton to conclude that Gilligan's allegation was without foundation. It would have been entirely reasonable if Gilligan had said, 'The government probably knew there was less than complete confidence in the 45-minutes claim when it decided to emphasise it in the dossier,' and this is close to what he actually broadcast.

Hutton believed that the JIC, which approved the wording of the dossier, had full access to the relevant intelligence information. But he had listened to evidence that made it clear that at least Cragg and probably even Sir Joe French did not see Report X. It had not been established whether it was withheld from other JIC members.

Despite my evidence, Hutton cast the concerns we had as being about 'wording' rather than 'assessment'. He recognised neither that there had been a shift from (inadequately) qualified assessment in the dossier to absolute certainty in the foreword nor that a clear expression of caution about the intelligence would have been appropriate. He considered 'the issue of [my] letter to DCDI on the Foreign Affairs Committee report' under 'Other Matters' but deferred to the ISC's inadequate conclusions on this.[2] Hutton had ample time to spot the discrepancy between what I said and what the ISC concluded. It is unclear whether he rejected my evidence on this.

Presenting the report to the House

Lord Hutton's statement was followed within minutes by a session on his report in the House of Commons.[3] The chamber was full and rowdy. It was not long before the Prime Minister mentioned the intelligence issue and referred dismissively to my part in it. He conceded his own declared requirement may, indeed, have had an influence on the dossier (albeit a subconscious one).

Donald Anderson, chair of the Foreign Affairs Committee, spoke in support of the Hutton report and Tony Blair without acknowledging that he had used his casting vote to produce a less critical report by his committee. A classic piece of parliamentary 'business' followed from Ann Taylor, the chair of the ISC:

> Does my Right Honourable Friend accept that the vast majority of members of Parliament are grateful for the thorough work that Lord Hutton has done and that the public will set more store by his judgments than the wriggling comments from the leader of the opposition? Does my Right

Honourable Friend accept that the findings of Lord Hutton parallel closely the findings of the report of the Intelligence and Security Committee, and will he confirm that the government will be able to produce their response to that report in advance of the debate next Wednesday, because it is clearly relevant? Will he also recommend to the House that all members who consider themselves informed on the matter should read the report by the Intelligence and Security Committee, which confirms what Lord Hutton said – that the dossier was not sexed up by anyone and that there was no political pressure whatever on the Joint Intelligence Committee?

Although her comparison of the reports exaggerated their similarity and her forecast of public reaction would prove hopelessly wrong, there was a procedural manoeuvre here that enabled Blair to effectively curtail debate on the ISC report. That report had been available for almost five months, since 11 September, and had identified many of the flaws in the government's defence of its behaviour without drawing the obvious conclusions. Members would struggle to absorb the voluminous Hutton report in the week before the main debate, let alone reread the ISC report and analyse the government response to it, yet to be released. Incidentally, Anderson and Taylor were elevated to the House of Lords when they retired from the House of Commons at the general election of May 2005.

I was very disappointed with Hutton and appalled with the line the government was taking. The pressure and inconvenience my wife and I had endured to give evidence appeared to have been for nothing. I was determined to try and set the record straight. I had admired the reporting of Paul Waugh on the inquiry and contacted him. *The Independent* was keen for me to provide an interview and write something about Hutton. I told them I wanted to thoroughly absorb Hutton's report before doing so and agreed to provide a piece for the following week. I did not realise until quite late why they came up with a target date of 4 February. It turned out to be the morning of the full debate on the Hutton report.

During the course of that intervening week, the government's triumph rapidly turned to disaster. Confused by the contrast between the report and the evidence they had followed for weeks the previous summer, perhaps also shocked by the convulsions that were affecting the BBC and the crass behaviour of Alastair Campbell, the public at large decided the Hutton inquiry had been a whitewash.

Response to the ISC report

By the time the government responded to Ann Taylor's ISC report it was almost five months old.[4] Because of its proximity to the storm over Hutton and perhaps also because it was dismissed as just another stroke of a whitewash-laden brush, the response to the ISC has largely been ignored. But there were points worthy of note.

The government did not accept the ISC's criticism that the dossier should have highlighted the uncertainty over Saddam's chemical and biological capacity. It did not accept that it should have made the document more intelligible for public consumption. It refuted the criticism that its assessments, after the return of inspectors in late 2002, failed to reflect the inhibiting nature of the inspectors' presence on Iraq's WMD capability. In its defence the government referred to a JIC assessment of March 2003 which indicated that chemical weapons remained, albeit disassembled.

The fallout from Kay's resignation

Meanwhile, there was something else that was not receiving the attention it warranted. The resignation of David Kay from the Iraq Survey Group on 23 January and the interviews he gave just a few days before Lord Hutton reported had little immediate impact in Britain. However, it compelled the Bush administration to take emergency action.

President Bush could no longer continue suggesting with confidence that the Iraq Survey Group would establish that WMD had existed in Iraq, so he decided to bury the issue until after the November presidential election. In a bold move he announced he had commissioned an independent inquiry into the intelligence failure over Iraq and that it would report in the spring of 2005, by which time Bush hoped, correctly as it turned out, that he would be safely re-elected.

Not only did this put pressure on Tony Blair to accede to the growing demand for an independent British inquiry, but it raised a problem with its timing. The next British general election could well coincide with the report of the American inquiry. What Blair hoped might, by then, be fading memories of the Iraq War would be rekindled at the wrong time. But the Prime Minister's hand was forced and, on 3 February, the day before the Hutton debate, he conceded an inquiry with terms of reference almost identical to Bush's. If timed correctly it might draw the sting from the US report. Trying to strike the right balance between allowing time for an adequate investigation and getting it out of the way well before the election, Lord Butler of Brockwell was asked to chair a review of intelligence on weapons of mass destruction that would report before the parliamentary recess in July 2004.

The first official indication of the Butler 'inquiry' came from the Prime Minister in his session with the Parliamentary Liaison Committee. This committee of committees comprises the chairs of the various select committees of Parliament, including the Foreign Affairs Committee. Appearing before it is a tough assignment for any Prime Minister, who needs to have the full spectrum of answers across all policy issues at his fingertips. Blair invariably dealt well with such situations, demonstrating an impressive recall of detail, an effective way with words and a barrister's mental dexterity. The Iraq WMD issue was one topic he was pressed on, especially as Kay's resignation and the ambiguities associated with it were beginning to resonate more loudly on the eastern side of the Atlantic.

By now the concerns we registered were looking increasingly justified but Blair continued to argue they were about the phrasing of references to the 45-minutes intelligence. But there was a significant shift in the government's line of defence:[5]

> I think that if we were to have let Saddam remain in office, in power, if he was in power today, with what we know incidentally, that irrespective of the issue to do with weapons being found, the evidence is absolutely clear from the Iraq Survey Group that he was developing programmes certainly for weapons of mass destruction and had every intention of making sure that those programmes were developed still further if he was given the chance to do so.

Pressed on this, Blair gave more ground: 'It is true, as I say, I have just accepted the fact, I have to accept, that David Kay has said that he has not found large stockpiles of weapons and he says that in his view he does not believe that that will happen.' Although the dossier did not refer to large stockpiles it carefully created the impression that they existed. Only once before, in the spring of 2002, had Blair made direct public reference to 'major' quantities of weapons, but here was a clear admission that this was his intended pre-war message. Now he had said unequivocally to Parliament that this is what he had believed.

Tony Wright, the chair of the Public Administration Select Committee, challenged him:

> If we just move to the intelligence judgment, when we met you here last July [2003], you said, and I quote you now, 'I stand entirely by the intelligence we put in the September dossier. I do not believe that our intelligence will be shown to be wrong at all. I think it will be shown to be right.' Do you stand by those assertions now?

Blair admitted:

> I have to take account of what David Kay has said in the last few days. He was the head of the Iraq Survey Group and I said all the way through, 'Let us wait for this survey group.' It is not a question, as it were, of changing our position; it is a question of recognising the fact that though there has been ample evidence of weapons of mass destruction programmes and capability, the actual weapons have not been found as yet in Iraq and the view of the head of the Iraq Survey Group is that he does not believe that the intelligence in relation to the stockpiles of weapons was correct. Now, that is exactly what we need to look into. I think it is sensible for me to say I have to take account of that. I said, 'Let us wait for the survey group.' The survey group has come up with certain findings. All I ask, again as I said earlier, is that people do not clip one part of what he is saying and not take the rest of what he is saying, because the rest of what he is saying is ample justification for the decision to go to war.

If the dossier had referred to the existence of programmes rather than actual weapons, the concerns of the DIS analysts would have evaporated. On the other hand, I doubt that the Prime Minister could have won the support of Parliament and the country for war on the basis of programmes rather than stockpiles of weapons.

Blair mentioned that the Foreign Secretary would be announcing the details of the next inquiry later in the day. Although he had not wanted one, an inquiry would at least enable him to defer questions on WMD until it reported. It excluded any requirement for further comment on David Kay and the Iraq Survey Group. However, through Blair's complicated interpretation of the message to be taken from Kay's resignation, it can be seen that he had already accepted the Iraq Survey Group's main conclusion. But a clear statement to that end would be delayed for many months.

Debate on the Hutton report

My first public comment on the Hutton report appeared in *The Independent* on the morning of the Commons debate on the report.[6] The main point of my article was that the responsibility for the 'intelligence failure' on Iraq WMD lay squarely with the members of the JIC because the advice of the expert intelligence analysts had been ignored. I stated clearly that I thought our concerns had been finessed out of existence by reference to the intelligence in Report X, which we were not allowed to see.

The article generated much comment on radio and television news before the debate but before the day was out, it had been overtaken by other developments. More newsworthy diversions were thrown up on the floor of the House of Commons that day.

The Prime Minister opened the debate in a generally hostile atmosphere. From the outset he was repeatedly interrupted with questions and points from all sides of the House. Most of them were ignored, avoided or diverted. Tony Blair remained buoyant. Eventually he came to 'the concerns by the people in the Defence Intelligence Staff', which he characterised yet again as being about the 45-minutes intelligence. After several interventions and interruptions, Blair referred to my newspaper article. Following further interruptions from the public gallery he managed to make this statement:

> I was dealing with the issue of today's story about Dr Jones, and I was saying that there are really two issues. One is whether there was some missing intelligence that was not seen [Report X], and the other is obviously about the evidence of Dr Jones himself. I was saying, and I repeat, that Dr Jones is an expert in this field and is highly respected. But on the forty-five minutes there is no missing intelligence. Dr Jones saw all the intelligence there was to see on it. So, incidentally, did Lord Hutton. The intelligence referred to in the article which he did not see was, I am told, about the production of chemical and biological warfare agents. He did not see it, because the Secret Intelligence Service put it out on a very restricted basis owing to source sensitivity. His superiors, however, were briefed on the intelligence. It does not bear on the 45-minute point at all, and the ISC itself saw this CW intelligence and was satisfied with it.

Misrepresentation of the nature and extent of my concern was central to the government's defence. The separation of the 45-minutes intelligence from the sensitive intelligence of Report X was disingenuous. It was less to do with the time than the availability of weapons. Report X was important because it 'confirmed' what the 45-minutes intelligence implied. To have been able to make his argument the Prime Minister would have been thoroughly briefed on both. What is now known is that when he made this statement, Report X had been withdrawn as unreliable six months earlier. It is barely conceivable that he was sent into the chamber without being told about it. The ISC had been told about it shortly after it was withdrawn. This meant that several members of all the leading parties were in the chamber and aware of this background. There can have rarely been a more obvious example of important information being withheld from Parliament or of the apparent connivance in this of an oversight body of parliamentarians.

According to Blair, my superiors had been 'briefed' on Report X. But if they had not had the opportunity to consider and digest an actual document it would have been difficult for them to form an independent judgement. Since my director, who briefed Tony Cragg, did not see a written report, it raises the question of whether anyone in the DIS saw one.

Although the full debate can be read in Hansard, I record a few exchanges here to highlight that at least some members had no trouble in understanding the points I made in my article and Blair's persistence in trying to misrepresent what I had said and written.

Alex Salmond said:

> In his article this morning, Dr Jones says that he formalised complaints about the September dossier because he did not wish to see himself and other experts scapegoated for the failure to find weapons of mass destruction. Will the Prime Minister make it clear that he would not want to subcontract any such responsibility, but would accept it, as Prime Minister?

Blair replied:

> I have made it clear throughout that not merely do I take full responsibility for the decision to go to war, but that our security services – I shall come to this later – do a magnificent job for this country. I hope that nobody in the House doubts their worth to the security of our people, or that they are immensely dedicated public servants.

This seems to imply not only that the 'security services' were really to blame but also that I was, in some unreasonable way, criticising them.

Lynne Jones, Labour MP for Birmingham Selly Oak, emphasised another important point:

> Brian Jones suggests that the particular intelligence information [Report X] was made available only to a limited number of people. He suggests that it was confined to the chief of defence intelligence, and not even shown to his deputy. He also suggests that those to whom that intelligence was made available were not sufficiently knowledgeable to be able to assess its importance. Can my Right Honourable Friend comment on those suggestions?

The Prime Minister spun back, ensnaring the ISC in the web of deception and cover-up:

> I can comment on them, and it is helpful that my Honourable Friend intervenes in that way. First, the particular intelligence that she is talking about is not intelligence on the forty-five minutes; it was intelligence on the different issue to do with chemical and biological weapons. The ISC considered this in its report. It was not seen by everyone within DIS. The procedures of SIS are that where there is a very sensitive source it will go on a restricted access to people, but they were briefed on the details. However, people on the Joint Intelligence Committee were able to know exactly what the provenance of that intelligence was and exactly what its significance was. But the point that I was making was that it does not relate to the forty-five minutes. What has happened – it is perfectly understandable, because this gets extremely complicated over time – is that people have conflated a different piece of intelligence with assuming that there was some secret bit of 45-minute intelligence that was not seen. Lord Hutton saw all that there was to see on the forty-five minutes.

It is interesting that the Prime Minister knew in great detail about the circumstances and access of the ISC to the sensitive Report X, but not that they were also told it had been withdrawn as unreliable.

Another Labour member, Jim Knight, who represented South Dorset, offered Blair some shelter:

> Does my Right Honourable Friend agree that those who are quoting Dr Jones should also look closely at the evidence given by Dr Kay to the Armed Services Committee on 28 January? He said, for example: 'All I can

say is if you read the total body of intelligence in the last twelve to fifteen years that flowed on Iraq, I quite frankly think it would be hard to come to a conclusion other than Iraq was a gathering, serious threat to the world with regard to WMD.'

The Prime Minister agreed, of course.

My Honourable Friend is absolutely right. I shall come in a moment to what Dr Kay said. I should like to say exactly what the point is that Dr Jones was making in the course of his evidence. The whole issue was gone into in minute detail by Lord Hutton. It is true that Dr Jones was expressing concern about the strength of the language used to describe the 45-minutes claim. But it is important also to contextualise that. In his evidence, to be found at page 120 of the Hutton report, he makes it clear in an answer to Lord Hutton that 'the important point is that we at no stage argued that this intelligence should not be included in the dossier . . . We thought it was important intelligence.' In other words, he was not even saying that it should not be in the dossier. He then said that he thought that the references in the foreword 'were too strong' and that what he believed was that instead of saying that the intelligence 'shows' this it should be that the intelligence 'indicates' this. I agree that there is a difference between the two. But let us be quite clear. It is hardly of earth-shattering significance in terms of how the whole dossier would be perceived. In any event, I do not pass judgement on whether it was right to say 'indicates' or right to say 'shows'. That judgement was made by the Joint Intelligence Committee. It never reached this difference within the DIS. In the Joint Intelligence Committee as a committee it did not reach the chairman of the committee, let alone Downing Street.

I had explained in *The Independent* that the real problem was one that, if not 'earth-shattering', was very important. It was part of a process that led to Britain's direct involvement in a disastrous war and much pain and anguish to many British families. It was about the exaggeration involved in Blair's insistence that he had 'no doubt' Iraq had WMD. He has never explained exactly what persuaded him he could make such a statement.

The Prime Minister moved with breathtaking ease from dismissing our apparently unreasonable fears that there were in fact no WMD to accepting the point we had been trying to make without the vaguest acknowledgement that it was anything to do with our concerns.

> Let me now turn to whether the intelligence on which we relied, in part, to go to war was correct. Originally, as the House knows, I wanted to wait until the Iraq Survey Group had reported fully before any investigation occurred. Last Tuesday, however, David Kay, the outgoing head of the ISG, gave evidence to the Senate Armed Services Committee in Washington which, frankly, cannot be ignored. More important still, it is now clear that the ISG itself, under its new chairman, will not make its full report any time soon.

This is an interesting insight on the part of the Prime Minister. How he knew the Iraq Survey Group would not report soon is something I will discuss in the following chapter.

In another interruption of Blair's opening speech, the Conservative MP for Croydon South, Richard Ottaway, an FAC member, asked:

> The Prime Minister says that all the intelligence about the forty-five minutes was made available. As he will be well aware, it has subsequently emerged that this related to battlefield weapons or small-calibre weaponry. In the eyes of many, if that information had been available, those weapons might not have been described as weapons of mass destruction threatening the region and the stability of the world. When did the Prime Minister know that information? In particular, did he know it when the House divided on 18 March?[7]

Blair replied:

> No. I have already indicated exactly when this came to my attention. It was not before the debate on 18 March last year. The Honourable Gentleman says that a battlefield weapon would not be a weapon of mass destruction, but if there were chemical, biological or nuclear battlefield weapons, they most certainly would be weapons of mass destruction. The idea that their use would not threaten the region's stability I find somewhat eccentric.

It had been suggested that he had not taken sufficient care to establish the dangers that those he sent to war would face – for example the nature of the enemy's weapons and the hazards they posed. The Liaison Committee had pressed Blair on this point the previous day but he had assured them that he was confident he had asked all the relevant questions relating to the intelligence on Iraq's weapons of mass destruction.

When Michael Howard replied for the opposition, he commented in some detail on my article:

> It then became increasingly clear – I commented on it – that people were misled about the 45-minute claim. If the Honourable Gentleman has not read Dr Jones's article in *The Independent* today, I suggest that he do so. There are some things that can and should be done in relation to these issues, however, that do not need the report of that inquiry. Some things could be done now. Writing in *The Independent* today, Dr Brian Jones has made a specific request to the Prime Minister to publish now the intelligence which he was not shown at the time [Report X], but which he says lay behind the government's key claims that Iraq was actively producing chemical weapons and could launch an attack within forty-five minutes of an order to do so. The Prime Minister has referred to that intelligence today in his speech. It clearly exists. Dr Jones says that it should now be released. Given that Saddam Hussein has been overthrown, even if that intelligence came from a source that was sensitive when Saddam still ruled Iraq, Dr Jones clearly believes that it is no longer sensitive now, although he went on to say that, if there is a reason of sensitivity, the Prime Minister should state it clearly. It seems to me that the request made by Dr Jones is entirely reasonable. I hope the Prime Minister will respond to it. If he chooses not to, I hope that the Secretary of State for Defence will deal with it in his winding-up speech.

There has never been any response to that request. It has simply been ignored. This is hardly surprising since the government was concealing the fact that Report X had already been withdrawn.

Later, Ann Taylor reiterated that the ISC was not blaming ministers but was saying that the issue was badly handled by intelligence professionals.

More fallout from Hutton

In mid-February, I met with a *Panorama* team which was keen for me to participate in a programme that examined the intelligence background to the Iraq war. Disappointed with Hutton, I felt that something like the true story should be made available to a bigger audience than the *Independent* readership, and a *Panorama* programme offered that potential. I was worried, though, that their editing of a filmed interview might, inadvertently or not, misrepresent my position or even give the impression that I was straying into the area of official secrets. They offered some reassurances and I said I would think it over.

A few days later I agreed to an interview. My decision had much to do with the generally positive reaction to my article and interview in *The Independent*. I had the open support of a former chief of defence intelligence, Sir John Walker, who went on record about my authority and expertise on WMD intelligence. I also had encouraging private messages from a number of former colleagues at the DIS who got in touch to express their appreciation for my defence of them and of intelligence generally.

CHAPTER TWELVE

December 2003–April 2004: The Iraq Survey Group and the Butler review

Inside the Iraq Survey Group

In December 2003 and the early months of 2004 there was much happening behind the scenes at the Iraq Survey Group.[1] Its independence had never been formally defined or practically established. Some of those who worked for it felt strongly that it should be completely independent and the chief investigator, David Kay, generally insisted on this, but there were important occasions when it was not free from political interference, particularly during the period surrounding Kay's resignation and before the man appointed to replace him, Charles Duelfer, had properly found his feet.

There was a strong presence of CIA officers within the Survey Group, participating as an integral part of the organisation but sometimes appearing to operate as a separate entity. At the group's headquarters, in the Perfume Palace within Camp Slayer, there was a specialist CIA contingent separated from the rest by a green door behind which 'the rest' could only guess what was going on. The CIA quarters were tightly secured against all but a handful of other Americans.

Kay had taken charge of inspections in June 2003. In October he delivered a progress report to Congress.[2] It was sparse. No weapons had been found but there were suspicions that needed further exploration. After that the Survey Group began to unravel.

George Tenet, the CIA's then director of central intelligence, records that on 19 November he heard rumours that Kay intended to resign. Tenet called him and told him he would not allow him to 'embarrass the President in that way' but suggested he return to Washington for a break.[3] Kay left Iraq on 7 December and some of his staff suspected it might be for good, although he did not tell them so.[4] It may be that when he left he was not sure himself. Perhaps he needed time away from Iraq to think through the situation.

Tenet has claimed that Kay had become disgruntled over organisational issues, pressure to release Survey Group intelligence staff to assist in a crisis in the counter-insurgency requirement, and a general lack of progress.[5] However, there is little doubt that Kay thought the task was drawing to a close. Before he left Iraq, he had called in an experienced former colleague from Australia to help write the final report. It could be that Kay came under pressure from Tenet and others in Washington not to go public but that he ultimately felt he had to speak out. He clearly concluded in December 2003 that there were no significant weapons in Iraq, but the statements he made were vague enough to allow the politicians to prevaricate.

David Kay had been pressing his colleague, Rod Barton, to come to Iraq for some months. Initially it had been to apply his long experience as an inspector but in the end it was about writing the report. Barton had refused to become involved until some important administrative problems had been resolved. Unfortunately, by the time Barton arrived in Baghdad in December 2003, Kay had already left for Washington. During December, in Kay's absence, Barton provided strategic guidance to the organisation and gave technical advice to the investigating teams. In a sense, for a few weeks he was filling in for Kay by default. Major General Keith Dayton, the Iraq Survey Group's director, approved this temporary situation.

Barton understood that a report was required by the US Congress by the end of March 2004, agreed with Dayton that this was something he should tackle and started pulling it together. As his work progressed he could see that this was likely to be a substantial report given how much had already been achieved. Most of the investigation had been done and, as Kay was soon to say publicly in Washington, a reasonably comprehensive picture had emerged, albeit one that did not accord with the original expectations of the departing Survey Group's chief investigator or the political need of the American, British and Australian governments.

By mid-January Barton had a draft some 200 pages long. Dayton was aware of this and expressed no concern. On 19 January Barton had an unexpected visit from Martin Howard, the UK's deputy chief of defence intelligence. Howard was ostensibly visiting members of the Defence Intelligence Staff who had deployed to Iraq as part of the Survey Group. He came to Barton's office and asked about the report he had heard was being prepared. Barton did not show Howard a draft but gave him a fairly comprehensive outline of it. Barton thought Howard seemed 'pretty well clued up' on the Survey Group's progress and could probably have worked out what the report was likely to say. Howard told Barton he did not like the idea of a report at this stage and would prefer to wait until the Survey Group found something substantive, by which Barton assumed he meant weapons.

A day or so later, with Howard back in Whitehall, there was a three-way video conference between London, Washington and the leaders of the Survey Group team in Iraq at which the planned report was discussed. Howard had spoken about the matter with Sir John Scarlett, who confirmed that they would rather not have a report at this stage. Barton said he understood the US Congress had a requirement for one and the CIA deputy director, John McLaughlin, confirmed a report was needed by late March. Barton continued on his substantive report for a few more days.

Kay eventually resigned from the Iraq Survey Group in Washington on 23 January 2004, but sometime during the first half of the month Charles Duelfer had been approached to replace him. Duelfer was the deputy director of UNSCOM in 1998 who, as explained in Chapter 3, had reportedly been implicated in a failed attempt to oust Saddam. On 15 January Duelfer met with McLaughlin at CIA headquarters and accepted the job.[6]

On 28 January Kay told the US Senate Armed Services Committee: 'We were almost all wrong, and I certainly include myself here.'[7] That was something of a generalisation but Kay was in an embarrassing situation and, doubtless, under considerable pressure not to be as frank as he would clearly have liked to be. I can understand the temptation to blur the implied criticism of the administration.

The next day in a television interview, Kay said that he did not wish to waste any more of his time in Iraq – that he might just as well spend it searching for Atlantis as continue the Survey Group mission. He explained that his belief in Iraqi WMD had been 'based mostly on the reports of people coming out of Iraq, that is, defectors'. With his lack of intelligence experience and technical expertise, perhaps he had been given highly selective and biased briefings to prepare him for his job. For whatever reason, Kay laid the blame squarely at the feet of the intelligence community.

Kay provided no indication of the reaction of George Tenet and President Bush to his resignation but implied that he had the courage to disappoint them. There can be little doubt that his abrupt decision to go, and his announcement that there had been a serious intelligence failure, was what forced the President to establish the independent inquiry he had been resisting for so long.

Kay seems to have conducted the investigation in Iraq with an open mind despite his declaration before the event. He was prepared to accept he had been wrong. Although Bush's announcement of the inquiry implied that he was accepting that the Iraq Survey Group would find little or nothing tangible, Tenet was not prepared to accept that.

The DCI plays hardball

George Tenet's response was to challenge David Kay's view in a speech at Georgetown University a few days later. It was important to let people know that Kay's resignation should not be seen as the end of the Iraq Survey Group. He denied that the Survey Group project was '85 per cent finished', something Kay had said before he left Iraq.

Tenet's speech was deeply flawed in many respects. He tried to argue that whilst the intelligence assessments fell short of certainty, they were worrying enough to justify military action. On the one hand, he played down the firmness of the assessment by quoting the National Intelligence Estimate (NIE) of October 2002, which did not express certainty on the existence of WMD in Iraq, and on the other he tried to justify his personal representation of a more robust interpretation of the evidence in the presidential daily briefs and in his own representations to President Bush.

The intriguing explanation, later clarified in his book, was that in the autumn of 2002 several reports, too sensitive to inform the NIE, came to him from foreign intelligence partners. The sources were characterised as 'established and reliable'. The timing, part of the source description and some of the detail described by Tenet are similar to British intelligence reports I saw at the time.

According to Tenet, one source said the nuclear weapons programme was active, well funded and of intense interest to Saddam, who was told it was progressing and that a weapon could be available 18–24 months after the acquisition of the appropriate fissile material. Chemical weapons were being produced and stockpiled, including mobile launchers, weapons of last resort 'which would be fired at enemy forces and Israel'. The source said Iraqi scientists were 'dabbling' with biological weapons with limited success but the quantities involved were not sufficient to constitute a real weapons programme.

A different sensitive source with access to senior Iraqi officials said in a stream of reporting that he believed that prohibited production of chemical and biological weapons was taking place, and that biological agents were easy to produce and to hide. Furthermore , Saddam's inner circle believed, as a result of the UN inspections, Iraq knew the inspectors' weak points and how to take advantage of them. The source said there was an elaborate plan to deceive inspectors and ensure prohibited items would never be found.

Tenet said this information made a significant difference to his thinking, solidifying and reinforcing the judgments of the NIE. He conveyed this firmer 'view of the danger posed by Saddam Hussein' to the nation's leaders because he could not ignore or dismiss such reports. His examples were not convincing. The intelligence he quoted lacked the detail that might underpin their credibility. They could have been little more than informed speculation based on common sense, a limited amount of general reading and a desire to impress the collector. Either Tenet's own analytical capability and general appreciation of intelligence were inadequate to understand this, or he cynically judged that most of his audience lacked the experience and knowledge to challenge his interpretation.

A surveyor's view

Although we did not have the evidence to be convinced that Saddam held significant stockpiles of chemical or biological weapons, a problem remained. Why, if he did not have them, did he not provide a more complete declaration to gain relief from sanctions, albeit with the intention of reconstituting Iraq's programmes when things quietened down? Did Saddam understand that was an option?

A former Iraq Survey Group inspector, Hamish Killip, told me he thought Saddam would have understood it was one possibility but it was a tricky matter for the regime.[8] Many in Iraq, including some high-ranking members of the General Staff and scientific establishment, continued to believe that Iraq possessed such weapons. For Saddam to allow such an impression to remain would deter neighbouring countries and discourage internal dissent. Both Kurds and Shia rebels feared chemical weapons from experience. And the defiance of the West added to the Leader President's perception of his prestige in other Arab states.

The ruling clique were not affected by sanctions and continued to prosper. Beyond the insiders, the few senior Iraqis who knew the truth were without political power. The handful of insiders that had power and knew were probably only the President himself, his sons, two or three other members of the family, the Vice Presidents, the President's secretary, Abid, and perhaps a few in the armed forces high command. Eventually, they found that they had painted themselves into a corner. There may have been periodic attempts by some, advised by senior officials in the know, to reveal the truth. Unfortunately it had all gone on so long that the leadership would not bite the bullet. As time passed, the President withdrew from day-to-day interest in government, becoming preoccupied with more personal projects. The fear surrounding him meant others were too paralysed to take any significant initiatives. The regime was slowly imploding, but that was not recognised by Western intelligence or other analysts at the time.

Killip had a high opinion of David Kay, whose sometimes arrogant and bombastic nature was married to an inquisitive approach and an open-minded attitude which seemed to be well suited to the job required of him. Importantly, Kay was prepared to challenge his own preconceptions.

Whitehall interferes

Until David Kay upset the applecart, the defensive line in London had been that no one should prejudge what the Iraq Survey Group would find. His resignation and comments might have been expected to halt the pretence that stockpiles of chemical or biological weapons might be found and, as I have discussed, the Prime Minister appeared to begin to hedge his bets in evidence to the Parliamentary Liaison Committee a few days later. As it turned out, it would be many more months before a line was drawn under the question of whether there were any WMD in Iraq. Hamish Killip and Rod Barton, each from his own perspective, explained to me how this came about.

Before he left Washington, Charles Duelfer was sent the 'lengthy draft text' of the interim report Barton had been assembling. He has said since that he decided then that the Iraq Survey Group would not announce any of its conclusions before it had completed them all, not only on the range of Iraq's activities but also on its 'decisions and policies'. On his way to Baghdad, Duelfer stopped off in London on Monday 9 February.[9] He saw Tony Blair and told him of his plans, and that he intended to provide a short status report to Congress in March.

Duelfer arrived in Iraq on 12 February, the same day as George Tenet. Tenet introduced Duelfer as his new representative and chief investigator. The introduction took place at a gathering of about a hundred Survey Group staff in the main hall/operations room of the Perfume Palace. Tenet alone wore a flak jacket when he addressed the gathering in the thoroughly secured facility, prompting Killip to wonder who he thought might be out to assassinate him. Tenet called up 'Charlie', as he referred to Duelfer, putting his arm around him, and saying something like 'This guy's weird as shit, but he knows a hell of a lot about Iraq'. Duelfer looked embarrassed.

Tenet asked the headquarters staff, 'Are we 85 per cent done?' referring to Kay's estimate of Survey Group progress. There was a muted response suggesting not. Apparently, that was not enough for Tenet. He needed them to be adamant because that is what he had told the world a few days earlier at Georgetown University, so he repeated his question, 'Are we 85 per cent done?' and the audience repeated 'No' a little louder. He then told the Survey Group staff that WMD were out there and urged them to 'get out there and find [them]'.

Barton believes that this underlined the serious difference in view between most of the senior Survey Group personnel and the CIA/Washington axis that had been emerging in the preceding weeks. The Washington view was clearly one that suited London. However, Barton, who was having regular meetings with all the Survey Group inspection team leaders about their progress, insists the general view of the experts was that they *had* almost finished. In some areas, particularly the chemical area, and to some degree in the biological area, there was still some work to do but overall, there was general agreement that Kay was right. Barton insists that the essence of the final report that was eventually published in October 2004 had actually been written during his early time at Camp Slayer in January and February. In other words, the key findings in the report he had almost completed before Duelfer arrived would be those of the final report.

Hamish Killip gave me a similar assessment. He thought that, although Kay was by then the subject of 'severe criticism' from Tenet and Dayton, his views were a good summary of what most of the experts who had been involved for many months in the investigations really believed. He recalls Kay's conclusion as being that, except for long-range delivery systems, there were no actual weapons to be found. There was some evidence of activities related to WMD and still a few incomplete investigations, for example consideration of why the regime had not been keener to demonstrate non-possession of WMD.

On the day following Tenet's bravura performance, Dayton's boss, the director of the Defense Intelligence Agency, Vice Admiral Lowell Jacoby, also visited the Iraq Survey Group. Killip recalled Dayton's announcement the day after, 14 February, that the group's next report would not contain any of the assessments or annexes they had been feeding to Barton. Instead a 25-page interim report would explain what the group had done since September 2003. Killip said he thought it likely that Dayton had changed his mind on instruction from his Washington visitors.

Barton's recollection is that Duelfer imposed a compromise between what London and Washington wanted. A report was needed in Washington, but London's concerns were met because, although Duelfer decided to issue one, he made it short and inconclusive. Duelfer told Barton to set aside the substantive draft he had produced and write a short version.

Barton explained that when he challenged Duelfer, the latter claimed he was not responding to any political pressure but argued that he had been there for too short a period to come to firm conclusions about anything. Barton argued hard with Duelfer, pointing out that by the time he was required to report to Congress, he would have had six or seven weeks to come up to speed. And after all, he was not coming to the matter cold. Duelfer had been the deputy executive chairman of UNSCOM and had looked at all the issues as a researcher and an academic. Barton assumed Duelfer had been briefed in Washington before he came out to Iraq and he had experienced people to brief him now. Barton told him it would be wrong to hide the information they already had.

It is interesting to note that before Duelfer had arrived in Iraq, the senior Survey Group staff in Baghdad were still expecting to produce a substantive report within weeks. But Blair had announced on 4 February 2004, during the Commons debate on the Hutton report, that the ISG would not report 'anytime soon'. The day before, at the meeting with the Liaison Committee, he had seemed to imply that the work of the Survey Group had come to an end with Kay's resignation. He appears to have learned overnight that the group's report would be held back. In his Georgetown University speech on 5 February, Tenet had said that the work of the ISG was far from complete. The decision about the report, which was presumably taken in Washington, would not be announced to members of the Survey Group for another ten days.

Barton said there were many important things that could have been clarified at that time: for example matters that had been raised in Colin Powell's presentation to the UN Security Council in February 2003. The mobile laboratories were something that the Iraq Survey Group had already investigated very thoroughly. It was thought that two of them had been found in the spring of 2003 and they were prematurely heralded as the proof that Iraq had possessed WMD. David Kelly had examined one of them in June and concluded it was not for biological warfare agent production. Barton had seen the evidence of all the experts who went through the trailers over the months. Their conclusion was that 'they were nothing to do with biology'. They were hydrogen generators, as had been claimed by the Iraqis. But a senior CIA official working for the Survey Group told Barton this was an issue that could not be discussed. It did not matter what they were or what they were for, he did not want to know. Politically, it was too difficult to write about, Barton was told. When he took the matter to Duelfer, Barton recalled the reply, 'I'm not interested in that. We're not putting that in the report.'

Killip took a personal interest in the mobile units and the two trailers that had been brought to the headquarters in Camp Slayer. He confirmed that the Survey Group experts had concluded that the trailers were designed and constructed as hydrogen generators for the Artillery Command of the Republican Guard. Their use for biological warfare agent production was judged to be wholly impractical. This conclusion had been explained in detail in a video conference to experts in London and Washington, none of whom had challenged any part of the case against them being for mobile biological warfare agent production. Indeed, that much, without any detail, had been confirmed to me by a former colleague in London in mid-December 2003, long before I spoke to Killip or Barton. Killip, separately from Barton, raised his concern about this with Duelfer on several occasions without success. The interim report of March 2004 made no mention at all of the trailers.

Powell had also told the UN Security Council of 'convincing' intelligence on an ammunition storage point for transhipment of chemical warfare munitions and on aluminium tubes for a nuclear centrifuge programme. These issues had been thoroughly investigated by the end of 2003 and the conclusions were negative. The 'official' line at the end of February 2004 was that the Iraq Survey Group could not reach any conclusions on these matters, but that was untrue. Conclusions had already been drafted and agreed covering most of the areas of concern.

By this stage Killip thought that the Survey Group had lost objectivity and balance. Anything, however slight, that might confirm the existence of weapons or related programmes was being investigated in detail, consuming resources. Anything that might indicate the opposite tended to be ignored. Anything that supported pre-war assessment was good news. Any contradiction of pre-war assessments was judged suspicious and exhaustively re-examined. Washington demanded a higher standard of proof for unfavourable assessments after Tenet and Jacoby visited the Survey Group in Baghdad than had previously been the case.

When the draft of the second interim report was eventually circulated to the capitals, Washington, London and Canberra, for comment, it had become little more than a press statement giving the false impression that it was too early to make any assessments. Killip thought important information was being withheld from the coalition governments. Barton recalled that when the comments on the short draft report were received, Canberra's were constructive, largely editorial and caused him no difficulty. Many of the CIA's suggested amendments were useful, but Barton thought there were a couple of blatant attempts to change the Survey Group's findings. However, London suggested that certain material be added. Duelfer showed Barton a message from Sir John Scarlett listing a number of what Scarlett called 'nuggets' that should be included. Although Barton felt he must continue to respect the classification and not reveal to me the contents of that message, he had no hesitation in stating his belief that the additions suggested were designed to leave the impression that, contrary to the Survey Group's judgement, WMD might still be found. Killip's recollection is that he was shown a similar list of 'nuggets' from London, sent on 8 March. He thought they had been selected either because they confirmed specific pre-war assessments or suggested that Iraq was pursuing an active WMD programme. It looked like an attempt to sway the Survey Group's report in a particular direction.

Scarlett was in a very unusual position on this matter. He clearly had an interest that the findings of the Iraq Survey Group should match the assessments for which he bore responsibility as closely as possible. He also knew that the intelligence on which those assessments were based was in tatters.

On 7 September 2004, about a month before the substantive Survey Group report was eventually issued, the House of Lords was to hold a debate on the Butler report. The debate had been delayed by the summer recess of Parliament. It is appropriate to consider one element of it here, although it does not fit chronologically with the account I am offering.

Lord King, a former Defence Secretary who was the first ever chairman of the Intelligence and Security Committee, questioned Baroness Symons, the government's spokesperson in the Upper House. He asked about allegations that Scarlett had sought to influence the Survey Group report, mentioning the matter of 'nuggets'.[10] King thought this 'a serious matter because it suggests further involvement in what would appear to be the presentation of intelligence, which many might have thought was not appropriate action to undertake in that way'.

Symons explained that Scarlett wrote to Duelfer in March following a request from Duelfer to set out items from the earlier classified Survey Group report which the UK believed could usefully be included in the interim report. She added that it was Duelfer himself who 'made it absolutely clear that the decision to publish a shorter interim report was entirely his and not the result of pressure from the British government or any other government'. The issue of a curtailed report had not been raised by King or anyone else in the debate. In ignoring the important question of why Scarlett was involved in a matter beyond the scope of intelligence, Symons had revealed the sensitivity of the government to the fact that the more comprehensive report that could have been produced by March 2004 had been shelved.

To his credit, Duelfer resisted attempts to change the nature of the draft short report in a way more suited to the British and American governments and their suggestions were rejected. This in itself suggests they were unreasonable.

Resignations

Hamish Killip recalled that by March he had concluded that the only substantial work left for the Iraq Survey Group to do was on 'procurement' and on the intentions of the regime with respect to WMD. However, by this time there was a constant turnover of Survey Group staff, diminishing resources and a reducing level of expertise in the organisation. Killip thought the leadership had lost the enthusiasm to complete the task. Charles Duelfer was talking of a final report in June or July, but the commander of the group, General Dayton, was mentioning ever later dates, some as far removed as January or February 2005, which would be after the presidential election.

Now Killip began to question whether it was reasonable to risk the safety of staff in what he believed had become an attempt to justify pre-war intelligence judgements rather than an impartial effort to establish what the status of Iraq's weapons of mass destruction had been. He was worried that British lives were being put at risk unnecessarily. He had lost confidence in the integrity of the Survey Group and felt that if he stayed it would be seen as an endorsement of the organisation. He left in mid-March. He told me that he had written to the director of the Proliferation and Arms Control Staff of the MoD, through which the British contingent of the Survey Group was employed, explaining in detail his reasons for resigning. He had copied this letter to the Defence Intelligence Staff as it was the main London interface with the Survey Group, and to the relevant department at the Foreign Office. This letter formed the basis of evidence he gave to the Butler review in early April 2004. He did not think it appropriate to describe to me the content of the letter or his evidence but it seems reasonable to conclude that the information he provided matched what he had told me about his experience and views of the Survey Group up to his resignation.

Rod Barton believed the interim report of March 2004 would be a poor document that did not explain what the Survey Group knew. He decided to resign as soon as the final draft of the report was completed. He felt the report was symptomatic of a wider malaise in the group – 'there was no real objectivity in the investigation and it seemed that a lot of the direction, particularly in the chemical and biological areas, was coming from Washington'. He left Baghdad on 23 March and returned to Australia, shortly after John Gee,[11] another senior Australian, had decided on a similar course. But before he left Barton told Duelfer that he felt so badly about the report he had written that he did not wish his contribution to it to be acknowledged. Duelfer disregarded this request and sent a letter to Canberra praising Barton's contribution with no mention of any negative factors. On 29 March Barton formally resigned. In the final paragraph of his letter of resignation he reflected that it was a sad thing to see the efforts of so many years on such an important issue undermined by the distortion introduced by those unwilling to acknowledge their mistakes.

The conclusions of Killip and Barton were to be reflected later by Arthur Keller, a retired CIA officer. He recalled his own experience with the Survey Group in 2003 and 2004 in a newspaper article in 2007:

> In candid moments most of the Group's members had quietly acknowledged by late 2003 that Iraq had no banned weapons for us to find. But we kept searching for another year, until shortly after the November 2004 elections. Like a zombie, the group was kept alive long after it should have expired, seemingly because the only way to minimise the political damage of the truth was to let the White House announce, 'Our teams are still looking for Hussein's arsenal.' [12]

On 30 March 2004, Charles Duelfer presented the Iraq Survey Group's interim report to the US Congress. He said they had not found evidence of stocks of weapons, as some had expected, but were looking at other aspects of that. They continued to receive reports all the time that there were hidden weapons, so it was something they had to pursue. Although a full record is not available, Duelfer is reported as saying that he was given a torrid time.

So it transpired that David Kay's determination to leave the Survey Group, because he was sure the work was done and there had been no WMD, had the effect of concealing the certainty of that conclusion from the public at large for almost a year. The need to appoint a new man in his place provided an excuse to spike the production of the substantive report he had set in train and delayed the final pronouncement on the absence of WMD in Iraq. The British government could continue to use this as a shield until after the Butler review had reported. It is a considerable indictment of those involved that they were prepared to delay the emergence of the truth about Iraq's WMD for personal or partisan political reasons.

Later in 2004, Duelfer asked both Barton and Killip to return to work with the Survey Group. Killip was given some reassurance about the future approach and recognised that it was important to try and ensure that the final report, albeit later than it needed to be, would be honest. At first Barton remained reluctant because he was worried that the work might still lack objectivity. But he retained a degree of respect for Duelfer from his past experience of working with him in UNSCOM and listened to his assurance that things had changed. Barton says Duelfer told him, 'If you don't believe me, if you don't believe I am objective now, talk to some of the others in the ISG. Don't believe me; listen to what they say.'

By now Killip and others were able to tell Barton that things really had changed and with some reluctance Barton agreed to Duelfer's request. The men who had spent over a decade of their lives wrestling with this problem could not resist the opportunity to be in at its end. Barton first went to London to review the final report that was being put together there. He was impressed by the standards he saw. The draft stated clearly at last that there had been no significant stockpiles of WMD in Iraq since about 1991.

However, a question mark remains over Duelfer's influence when he arrived on the scene to replace Kay in 2004. What were his motives in disregarding Barton's earlier request not to be associated with the March status report, and why was he so keen to persuade Barton and Killip back to Baghdad so late in the day? Duelfer had a reputation as being politically astute and his strategy may have been to blunt the personal criticism of him implicit in the earlier resignations of such highly respected experts and in Barton's letter of resignation, and to diffuse the lack of credibility of the earlier report.

Evidence for Butler

Both the Conservatives and the Liberal Democrats formally withdrew support for the Butler review shortly after it was announced. Despite this, Michael Mates, a Conservative member of the Intelligence and Security Committee, decided to ignore his party's decision. Given his long service and current membership of the committee, I was surprised to learn that he had to be made a Privy Counsellor in order to participate in the review. Presumably the now 'Right Honourable' gentleman had greater access to secrets than previously. That gave me cause to doubt that the ISC had had as much access to secret intelligence in its own inquiry the previous summer as was now intended for Butler.

The review team was made up of five members in all. It was led by Lord Butler of Brockwell, a former Cabinet secretary and head of the civil service. As well as Mates it included Ann Taylor, chair of the ISC and former Labour Party chief whip; the Rt Hon. Sir John Chilcot GCB and the Rt Hon. Field Marshal Lord Inge KG GCB DL.

Shortly after the Butler review was announced the MoD told me that I would be expected to give evidence. I had no great desire to do this because by now I lacked confidence in the inquiry process in general. As the deadline of the period for potential witnesses to contact the review approached, a former DIS colleague called to ask if I was going to give evidence. He urged me to do so. Somewhat reluctantly, I sent an email to the inquiry. The secretary to the review telephoned me soon after to say that Butler had intended to invite me to give evidence within the next few weeks. I offered to provide a written statement covering those matters I could deal with at an unclassified level and this was accepted. The date for my appearance was set for 21 April and arrangements were put in hand for me to get into the Cabinet Office by more discreet means than the main entrance on Whitehall.

Over the next two weeks I worked up a submission.[13] I provided a copy of the witness statement I had written for Lord Hutton's inquiry. I defined my understanding of the term 'weapons of mass destruction'. I also discussed the nature of my perception of intelligence in general and as it related to WMD in particular. I explained my view that the UK had seriously neglected the analytical element of the intelligence process. I expressed concern that the DIS was semi-detached from the rest of the intelligence community and argued that its leadership had latterly lacked intelligence experience. I suggested that the JIC membership probably represented a good balance to set intelligence requirements and review performance, but that the high proportion of the membership who were intelligence users was not appropriate to a committee having responsibility for issuing intelligence assessments. I expressed the view that serious consideration should be given to enhancing the scientific and technical presence on the Assessments

Staff and at the higher levels of the intelligence community. I also drew attention to the damaging effect of the culture of internal competition for resources that had developed recently in Whitehall, which generated competition within the intelligence community when the management objective should have been to ensure that there was a sensible balance in their activities, which needed, in the main, to be complementary. The effort expended on propaganda to ensure that customers reported favourably on the performance of the individual agencies was wasteful of resources and counter-productive to all-source intelligence assessment. I suggested the possibility of establishing a single coherent intelligence organisation that embraced both collection and assessment, independent of any particular department of state and its policy requirements, arguing that the advantage would be the elimination of departmental bias and a potential improvement in efficiency. I said that consideration should be given as to how to promote the independence of the intelligence community leadership, and how a post or posts with greater experience of intelligence analysis might be introduced at the higher echelons of the present or a revamped central organisation.

Specifically on WMD intelligence, I gave my view that, partly based on an exaggerated expectation of intelligence to define the challenge, the capability of UK forces to protect themselves against the use of biological and chemical weapons was over-estimated. For this reason I felt that the greatest restraint should be exercised on the commitment of our forces to possible chemical and biological warfare environments.

I made it clear that at the time of the production and issue of the Prime Minister's dossier on Iraq's WMD in September 2002, and up to my retirement in January 2003, there was no convincing evidence that Iraq had significantly progressed its nuclear weapons programme following its dismantlement in the 1990s. Also, although suspicions remained, the evidence supporting the existence of an offensive chemical and biological capability was of a much lower order than it had been in 1990 before the first Gulf War.

I noted that intelligence estimates are rarely absolute statements and made no claim that modifications to the dossier to fit the DIS assessment would have provided a totally accurate picture, but I did claim it would have been significantly closer to the reality.

Bush fails Blair on the road-map

Whilst I was engaged in this retrospective analysis for Butler, the world was moving on in important ways. Tony Blair had highlighted the Israel–Palestine problem as an important factor in the aftermath of 9/11. He appeared to have made progress with President Bush on it in the intervening period, and the inference for many was that this was encouraged by Britain's support of the US administration on Iraq. When arrangements were made for the Prime Minister to visit Washington on 15 and 16 April 2004, immediately following a visit to the US by Israeli Prime Minister Ariel Sharon, there were expectations that an announcement of progress and a significant step forward might be made. Such a development would have lifted some of the weight from Blair's weary shoulders.

Unfortunately Sharon took a firm step back from the 'road-map' that Blair had persuaded Bush to publicly endorse, offering withdrawal from Gaza only in exchange for a hardening of policy on the West Bank; Bush, facing re-election in just over six months, had little choice but to accept. This left no tangible positives to be announced at the end of the summit press conference and left the British Prime Minister embarrassed in the rose garden of the White House. When Blair failed to acknowledge even the merest hint of a setback, and tried to place an entirely optimistic spin on the wrecked road-map, there was an outcry in UK. It suggested to me that his broader vision of using the inevitability of the US invasion of Iraq to move towards a broader settlement in the Middle East was less of a priority than I had hoped.

We were to learn many months later that progress on Israel/Palestine had ceased to be a condition of Britain's participation in the invasion of Iraq sometime between April and July 2002.[14] By then the requirement was that the situation in that part of the Middle East should remain 'quiescent' during the lead-up to the war.

Giving evidence to Butler

I gave evidence to the Butler review for the best part of a couple of hours on Wednesday 21 April 2004. It was a very different experience compared to Hutton. I travelled to London by train on the day I testified, walked across Westminster Bridge and used a discreet entrance to the Cabinet Office. A short walk within the secure zone of Downing Street brought me past No. 10. As I looked across at that familiar black door it occurred to me that, although I had spent fifteen years working within a hundred yards or so of the Prime Minister's residence, and spent many hours in the adjoining Cabinet Office, it was more than twenty-five years since I had stared directly at this famous building. The last time was in the late 1970s, before the Provisional IRA succeeded in changing our way of life, when anyone could stroll along Downing Street and do as we and so many thousands of others had done – stand our children in front of the door next to the policeman and snap them for the family album.

The Cabinet Office, parts of which I knew reasonably well, is a complicated warren of a building. Architecturally it ranges from the Middle Ages through to the unattractive, utilitarian construction that prevailed in the 1960s, which is, fortunately, concealed behind a more elegant, older facade. I was interviewed in a large well-lit room in a more modern wing of the building on a floor with which I was not familiar from my working days.

As I entered, the large figure of Lord Butler loomed at the door and greeted me warmly. He shook my hand, thanked me for coming and ushered me to a single seat at one of the short sides of a rectangular table. I was introduced to the other members of the review team who flanked him, two on each side. The atmosphere was anything but intimate. Butler himself led the process. Although imposing, he radiated a charm that did much to dispel the austere, functional surroundings. He thanked me for my written submission, which he said was helpful. He noted that they had heard from others much of what I had written about the general nature of intelligence and its organisation in UK and that they would be considering that aspect. He assured me they would take my views into account but said they would not question me on such matters in the interview because they wished to focus on Iraq and the dossier.

The questioning came mostly from Butler himself. I will not go into any detail about it, partly because it would repeat what I have already written about in earlier chapters, partly because I did stray into areas that referred specifically to the views and actions of individuals which must remain private or to intelligence which I am bound to keep secret, and partly because the committee and I agreed to share certain confidences about some of the detail involved.

Compared to Hutton there was a much greater emphasis on the mood and atmosphere that prevailed at the time the dossier was published. Lord Butler's probing was polite but firm. Michael Mates, to my right, the burly prop to the chairman's giant lock-forward, seemed quiet and rather sullen and although his few questions were asked in typical bluff style, I knew of old that this former army officer was a much more reasonable man than he sometimes sounded. Lord Inge, closer to me but still quite distant, seemed hunched, distracted and uncomfortable and asked only one or two questions, but I suspected he was concentrating deeply on what was happening. He looked strangely smaller than I knew him to be. Sir John Chilcot, sitting opposite Inge and to my left, was very quietly spoken and pleasant, and asked a number of questions in an open and sympathetic manner.

When it was Ann Taylor's turn the mood changed. A neat, well-groomed and buttoned-up woman of middle age, she posed her questions politely but in a distinctly combative way. Her attitude would have fitted either of two interpretations – devil's advocate for the review team, or politically astute defender of the government. Although I understand she was the only member of the review team with a scientific background and may have been invited to be a main interrogator along with Butler for that reason, I thought her approach seemed unnecessarily defensive of the government position and aimed as much at influencing her colleagues as questioning me. I felt there was something slightly sinister about her performance.

The only aspect of the interview that it is important to record here is that I was sometimes not able to answer questions, as I had had no direct visibility of most of the dossier process or because I was not familiar with the detail of the intelligence, having been retired for over a year by now. This prompted me to recommend that the committee should interview my former section heads. They were the real experts on the intelligence and on the scientific and technical interpretation of it. Since the Butler interviews were taking place in secret there was no reason to exclude them. I had anticipated that I might want to do this and had made an effort to talk to the three individuals concerned in the previous few days. As a courtesy, I had spoken to their boss about it and he was happy for me to do this. I had managed to speak to two of the three; one had been enthusiastic to do so, the other somewhat ambivalent. I am pleased to note that my advice was taken and they were called to give evidence. I was told some time later that Butler had privately reflected that his review might have been better served if he had requested more witnesses from the middle ranks of the civil service.

When Butler firmly ended the session I felt much had been left unsaid, but there was nothing I could do about it. As I prepared to leave the room the review team broke for lunch and one or two shook my hand and thanked me for giving evidence. Taylor approached me and asked rather abruptly what right I had to be writing about these things in the newspapers. I was offended by the tone of her challenge but tried not to show it. However, I am not easily bullied and said that I assumed the terms that applied to me were much the same as those that applied to former members of the government such as Robin Cook, who had recently published *The Point of Departure*. I told her that where things were not covered by the Prime Minister's exemptions for the Hutton inquiry, I followed the accepted practice of clearing what I wrote with the Ministry of Defence. She did not seem very pleased with my answer.

CHAPTER THIRTEEN

May–July 2004: *Panorama* and the Butler report

Interviewed for Panorama

In the first half of 2004, between the Hutton and Butler reports, I was approached by the BBC's *Panorama* for an interview which would form part of a new programme on the Iraq War. I wanted to understand what the programme was trying to achieve and I spent many hours exploring this with a team of producers. I stressed I had to be careful of my obligation not to reveal official secrets, and I wanted to avoid providing gratuitous background that might help proliferators or terrorists. They were sympathetic to both of these requirements. Eventually, I was persuaded by the suggestion that my views would reach a larger audience through television and eventually agreed.

A day was set aside for the interview itself, which in the event took two. I was impressed with the knowledge and dedication of the *Panorama* team. They worked with open but challenging minds. They examined what I told them with meticulous care and their insistence on coming back with detailed questions seeking comprehensive explanations before they would allow any particular point to be made was often frustrating and sometimes downright annoying. The presenter, John Ware, and I took some time to establish our territory on the first day. We had to get used to one another's style and language. Occasionally he would try to lead me into places I was not prepared to go and, for a while, we were both frustrated by the way things were progressing. The message I wanted to get across was simple: intelligence analysts were not responsible for the intelligence failure that led us to war. They wanted to probe as deeply as possible but they came to understand my limits and accepted the situation. Over a few days between sessions I had time to consider how I might better tackle some of the issues and the second day's recording went much better. Several hours of discussion between Ware and me were filmed. I did not know what they would use, who else would be involved or how the programme would turn out. I worried that my contribution lacked coherence, perhaps because I had to weigh every answer to ensure I would not cross into forbidden territory.

In the end I was delighted with the programme, shown just three days before Butler presented the report of its review.[1] It was visually powerful in parts, reminding me of the violent physical and human consequences of the matters I had been discussing and become a little detached from. A major revelation, confirmed a few days later by Butler, was that Report X had been withdrawn by MI6.

I was surprised and particularly pleased at the appearance in the programme of John Morrison, a career DIS analyst who had risen to the post of deputy chief of defence intelligence. I had worked with him over several years and he had been in my direct management chain in the late 1990s. He made a brave contribution to the programme that clarified several important issues, such as what constitutes a 'threat'. We had not always seen eye to eye on some management matters, but Morrison confirmed my reputation as the leading intelligence authority in Whitehall on WMD intelligence. I was equally surprised and delighted when a former chief of defence intelligence, Sir John Walker, followed up with a few words of support for my position on the radio the following morning. Over the next few days I was pleased to hear from several former colleagues applauding my part in the programme.

The report of the Butler review

The Review of Intelligence on Weapons of Mass Destruction, led by Lord Butler, reported on 14 July 2004.[2] The requirement for Butler to report before the summer recess in mid-July had placed important constraints on his committee, as reflected in the report's reservation 'we do not pretend that ours can be the last word on every aspect of the issues we cover'.

I understand the Butler review had to be assertive in extracting more evidence than 'the system' wished it to see, but still the government was able to dictate what could and could not be exposed to the public under its limiting terms of reference. Michael Mates later told the Commons that papers which the Butler report could not reveal had 'flown between very senior government representatives and ministers, which will make certain people's eyes water when they see them'.[3]

Methodology

The Butler report briefly explained how the committee had set about its task. It started with formal Joint Intelligence Committee assessments and asked 'the agencies' (MI6, GCHQ and MI5) for a full list of the underlying intelligence. This was not the most effective approach because the agencies were not concerned with 'all-source' intelligence. The most comprehensive intelligence archive on WMD was held by my old branch and in the files of the Cabinet Office Assessments Staff, which should have been trawled as well.

There is no indication that the review looked at *early* drafts of JIC papers and the exchanges of information between the Assessments Staff and the various contributors. If it had done so, a more complete picture of the intelligence background would have emerged. Hutton had provided a glimpse of the DIS's comments on early drafts of the dossier, which revealed something of the debates, misconceptions and disagreements over assessments.

JIC products are short summaries of a large body of information, analysis and effort, the tip of an iceberg. They are targeted at a busy senior readership from various departments and backgrounds and are consensus products that do not reflect all the nuances of opinion across the intelligence community. They are not always tailored to answer the highest-priority questions for each individual customer. Other studies informed but were not always reflected in the JIC products on which the review team appears to have based its deliberations.

Thus the Butler review was not nearly as rigorous or comprehensive as it might first appear. Although the committee of intelligence outsiders was assisted by advisers from the intelligence world, they did not include specialist all-source analysts or experts in the relevant subjects. Furthermore, I learned some years later from a very reliable source that the committee had agreed from the outset that it was important to try and preserve public confidence in the intelligence services.[4] Whilst at one level this is understandable considering the security environment that had developed, it is an obvious contradiction when the performance of the intelligence community is the subject of review.

Main points

The review included countries other than Iraq, presumably to show intelligence in a better light than a study of Iraq alone. This will have contributed further to the problems of an over-burdened committee with a short deadline.

It is not known how the other countries – Libya, Iran and North Korea – were selected. They did not include all of the other 'countries of concern' on which significant intelligence collection and assessments had taken place. Performance on some of the excluded countries would not have appeared in such a good light as the ones that were chosen.

The review acknowledged that chemical and biological weapons, which were the main WMD of concern in the case of Iraq, are much more difficult intelligence targets than nuclear weapons. The intelligence on the other countries studied was mainly about nuclear weapons. The other countries selected all *had* programmes to acquire nuclear weapons – Iraq did not. Something that exists is easier to establish than the opposite. Therefore, the conclusion reached by the review, that the performance of the intelligence community on WMD was generally 'impressive', was not based on a valid analysis. But despite having reached a conclusion, the review did not do the obvious thing and address the critical question of why Iraq was different.

The most significant difference from my perspective was the existence of an overriding government policy imperative that did not apply in the other cases. Intelligence assessments on WMD, more than on most subjects, will rarely be definitive. They will raise suspicions and provide guidance, but they will not often provide unequivocal evidence. It is vital that this is understood in the context of any decisions about pre-emptive military action in the future. Unfortunately, the review did not quite draw that conclusion.

The review took up the point I had made in my evidence about the JIC assessment of 9 September and its influence over the dossier. It agreed that the assessment was written to inform military and other contingency planning, and examined a range of possible scenarios in which Iraq might use chemical and biological weapons. And whilst it was right for the JIC to make precautionary judgements about the scenarios for such a purpose, it was not right to take those judgements up into the dossier without considering or explaining that background or giving warnings.

The ISC reached a similar conclusion, the review noted, and it said that experienced readers would have seen these warnings in the original JIC assessments and taken them into account. But the public, through reading the dossier, would not have known about them. It said the Prime Minister's description, in his statement to the House of Commons on the day of publication of the dossier, of the picture painted by the intelligence services in the dossier as 'extensive, detailed and authoritative' may have reinforced any impression the public gained from his foreword that the intelligence was even stronger than it appeared. The review concluded, 'We believe that it was a serious weakness that the JIC's warnings on the limitations of the intelligence underlying some of its judgements were not made sufficiently clear in the dossier.'

Not only had the Prime Minister read the warnings and, presumably, discounted them but he also chose not to consider them as part of the 'information' he wanted to make available to the public. I was delighted that these points had been emphasised in Butler. However, the review concluded that the outer limits of the intelligence were *not* exceeded in the dossier. It did not say if it considered the foreword to have stayed within those bounds. It is not clear whether the review took the foreword to be an overtly political statement, in which case it may have been beyond the scope of the review, or whether the intelligence community could be held accountable for it in any way. This is a major flaw in the report.

The review reported that almost all the 2002 reporting from MI6 on Iraq's WMD had either been withdrawn or was under suspicion. What intelligence outsiders will not have appreciated is that uncertainty on this scale was without precedent. The report made it clear that the vital Report X was withdrawn in July 2003 because the sourcing chain had been discredited. Butler said that Report X had provided 'significant assurance to those drafting the dossier that active, current production of chemical and biological agents was taking place', but it did not go far enough. It did not emphasise that Report X was used by the chief of the Assessments Staff, with the knowledge of the JIC chairman, to convince the chief of defence intelligence and his deputy that they could safely disregard the advice of their experts who had not seen the report.

In my evidence I had told the review of my suspicions from the outset that a single report could contain information that allowed anyone to reach such a firm conclusion so quickly. In February 2004, before I knew it had been withdrawn, I asserted that Report X had been used as a device to finesse the disagreement of the experts in order to facilitate a more robust dossier than was otherwise possible. My call for the contents of Report X to be revealed was echoed on the floor of the House of Commons but was ignored by the government.

In the subsequent Commons debate, Tony Blair was to say he did not know Report X had been withdrawn until shortly before the Butler report was published. Officials and ministers who knew about the withdrawal of Report X in February 2004 had a responsibility to ensure the Prime Minister was alerted when it was discussed in the House.

The review found no reason why I or my experts should not have been shown Report X and asked to assess it, so acknowledging indirectly that my suspicion of sharp practice may have been well founded. When the experts were eventually shown Report X before it was withdrawn but, presumably, after the war, it took them only a few hours to dismiss it as doubtful on the basis of its content. But the Butler committee, which presumably had also seen Report X, made no direct comment about its quality. If the committee, which said it was struck by the thinness of the intelligence, thought Report X insubstantial it should have said so much more clearly.

Whether the content of Report X was good enough to justify the decisions taken by those senior people who saw it is a question that remains unanswered. This was a potential indicator of the performance of the country's most senior intelligence officials. They had judged the intelligence to be reliable, assessing its contents to be credible enough to support a case for war. The review made no comment on whether that judgement was reasonable. The effectiveness of the leadership of the intelligence community could hardly be divorced from the review's requirement to make recommendations for the future gathering, evaluation and use of intelligence on WMD. Leadership is a fundamental element in equipping the community to do the task required of it.

Both Butler and the ISC should have made their views on the credibility of Report X absolutely clear. If, as seems likely, the report was not credible, it was important to reveal that the senior people involved lacked not only the knowledge and ability to undertake critical assessments themselves, but also a knowledge of the limits of their capabilities and when they needed to seek expert advice. If the JIC was not incompetent, then there must be doubts about the integrity of the officials concerned. This was a judgement that the public had every right to expect the Butler review (and the ISC) to make, even if similar consideration with regard to the politicians involved was beyond their terms of reference.

Butler on forty-five minutes

Butler examined the 45-minutes claim as one of a number of 'Specific Issues' but did little to resolve the uncertainty that surrounds it. During the drafting of the dossier the DIS contended that the CX intelligence report which contained the claim was 'vague and ambiguous', and the review supported that contention without saying it in as many words. Butler expressed the suspicion that the intelligence was included in the dossier because of its 'eye-catching character' but concluded it should not have been used 'without stating what it was believed to refer to'. It is not clear that the review addressed witnesses directly on what that belief was, but it deferred to the ISC.

The ISC report had said that the Assessments Staff judged the 45-minutes claim to relate to 'chemical and biological battlefield munitions'. This was not a judgement that could be made with any certainty because of the vague and ambiguous nature of the intelligence report, and it did not coincide with the view of the analysts and Assessments Staff as reflected in the 9 September JIC assessment. Butler seemed to acknowledge this by suggesting that a form of words which I included in my evidence to the review would have more accurately represented the intelligence report. The description I used was: 'A source has claimed some weapons may be deployable within forty-five minutes of an order to use them, but the exact nature of the weapons, the agents involved and the context of their use is not clear.'

Finally, Butler noted that the review had been informed that the validity of the 45-minutes intelligence had come into question and the reliability of its reporting chain was in doubt. Thus, not only was the content of the report vague and ambiguous, but its sourcing was also doubtful.

If we consider the detail about sources in the Butler report, Sir Richard Dearlove's suggestion that the intelligence assessment of it was a misinterpretation of the information provided by his service, and other information now in the public domain, we may allow ourselves a speculative interpretation that more detail was known than was revealed to analysts.[5] Further clarification of this was, and still is, obviously in the public interest. Sir David Omand, the security and intelligence coordinator at the time, has suggested that in August–September 2002 'the search was intensified quickly for any relevant intelligence, and that was sweeping up material that was not of first quality' and that 'the 45-minute warning should never have appeared [in the dossier]'.[6]

Whatever the complete background to the 45-minutes intelligence, it remains difficult to believe that the Prime Minister was not kept fully in the picture. He was aware in late July 2002 of the absence of sufficiently convincing intelligence on Iraq's WMD.[7] He did not disagree with colleagues and officials who assessed it was inevitable that America would go to war. He had to convince both Parliament and the public that Britain should join in and ensure the maximum security of the troops he would commit to action. Alastair Campbell said it was Blair himself who was keen to give the 45-minutes intelligence prominence in the dossier. Sir Richard Dearlove judged it appropriate to advise the Prime Minister of the arrival of the intelligence issued as Report X in a face-to-face meeting on 12 September 2002 and it is unlikely that the 45-minutes intelligence was not discussed in that context. Yet Blair had told Parliament that he was not aware of the nature of the weapons concerned in the 45-minutes intelligence until after the war. Perhaps at this point he was trapped. It was an embarrassing and damning admission because it suggests he was careless of the detail of the case for war he was putting before the nation and failing in his duty of care for the armed forces. Clearly he should have asked the relevant questions. Even if the pressures of the moment had prevented him from doing so, it was reasonable to expect that the information would be brought to his attention. The terms of reference of the Butler review may have disbarred it from questioning Blair's behaviour, but it should have asked intelligence officials why he had not been told.

It would have been difficult for the Prime Minister to admit this knowledge to Parliament in the midst of the Hutton inquiry, as the Commons would have likely thought it important information that should have been disclosed in the dossier debate on 24 September 2002, or in the various parliamentary debates and discussions leading up to the war. However, if the real justification for the war was different to the one made by the government, owing less to Iraq's existing WMD capability and more to other factors, some of them not directly concerning Iraq, the Prime Minister could not admit that a mere detail of intelligence on current capability was insignificant in his greater strategic analysis.

A flawed intelligence process

Intelligence clearly contributed to the publication of a dossier that misled Parliament and the public at a critical time on the path to war in Iraq. The Butler report concluded that there were numerous problems that contributed to this. But it did not identify the major flaw – that MI6 occupied a role that dominated the intelligence community to an extent that unbalanced it and skewed its final product.

Weakness in source validation procedures used by MI6 was volunteered by that organisation as an important problem. The Butler report was complicated and vague on this but nonetheless sufficient for the government to persuade many people that it was a major reason for the overall intelligence failure. However, the source description as well as the content of the CX report on the 45-minutes intelligence told analysts it had to be treated with caution. Sir Richard Dearlove says that he warned the Prime Minister that the sensitive source of Report X was untried. The content of Report X also appears to have lacked credibility. Because of the disproportionate influence of MI6, the actual and potential contribution of expert analysts to the issue of the credibility of sources *and* their information did not weigh as heavily as it should have in the process leading up to the war. Nor is it adequately reflected in the Butler conclusions. Whilst recognised as a problem by the review, it was not explicitly identified as symptomatic of the real problem that exists in Britain's intelligence machine. A related aspect of the MI6 problem is that, in my experience, it, more than any other collector, was inclined to brief unassessed intelligence to senior politicians and officials. Indeed, it may be that the other agencies were, and perhaps still are, stimulated to follow suit for fear of being eclipsed by MI6.

I believe the source validation issue was used by the government, with the collusion of those senior officials who shared the blame, as part of the attempt to cover up what really happened.

Butler considered an accusation made by the former United Nations weapons inspector, Scott Ritter (see Chapter 2). Ritter, an American, had claimed that in the late 1990s MI6 were involved in a propaganda exercise relating to Iraq's WMD capabilities called 'Operation Mass Appeal'.[8] Butler confirmed that MI6 was active in 1998 in an effort to ensure information held by UNSCOM on an Iraqi programme for the nerve agent VX was placed in the public domain. I was not aware of this until it emerged, after I retired. In the event MI6 action was not necessary because the relevant UNSCOM report was leaked to the press in Washington. However, this information does provide a rare glimpse of one of the activities of MI6 that go beyond the collection of intelligence and into the realms of direct government policy support. The conduct of activity of this sort can have an impact on the collection and assessment of intelligence that is not adequately accounted for in the British system. If other collectors and analysts remain unaware of particular operations (as they usually do) the open source information can trigger an irrelevant collection effort or lead to false indications being factored into analysis.

The personal specific issue

The way in which the DIS is run contributes to the imbalance in the intelligence community and my own part in the Iraq WMD affair illustrates this. I was surprised to see it referred to as the 'specific issue' of 'Dr Jones's Dissent' in Chapter 6 of the Butler report. I was pleased with the conclusion of the committee that, 'given the vagueness of the underlying intelligence', I was right to 'raise concerns about the manner of the expression of the "45 minute" report in the dossier and about the certainty of its language on Iraqi production and possession of chemical agents'.

However, casting this matter as personal to me tends to obscure the fact that I was representing the broader view of DIS analysts. The failure of Butler to underline that my dissent represented the reservations of the DIS experts as a whole, which had repeatedly been put to the Assessments Staff, is an important oversight. It is disappointing that Butler declined to address the fact that the chief of defence intelligence, Joe French, and his deputy, Tony Cragg, failed to respond to the 'dissent' of me and my colleague. Butler suggested Lord Hutton had addressed the issue, but he had not. Hutton hinted that it was covered by the ISC. It was not. This matter is highly pertinent to the specific requirement for Butler to make recommendation on 'the future gathering, *evaluation and use* of intelligence on WMD' [my italics] as requested by the Prime Minister. Although the recommendation that future deputy chiefs of defence intelligence should be experienced intelligence analysts presumably reflects a judgement of sorts, a clearer statement would have been more constructive and less easily dismissed. If this had been done it would have been less easy for the MoD and the government to prevaricate and effectively shelve the recommendation in its later response to the review.

I learned for the first time from Butler that Report X had not only referred to the production of biological and chemical weapons, but had involved the building by Iraq 'of further facilities'. Once such information had been received, the next step in the normal intelligence assessment process would have been to search for confirmatory evidence. Any indication of the location of the new facilities would be followed up with careful analysis of imagery for earlier evidence of the construction of buildings or structures with signatures that related to the particular agents said to be in production. I do not know if the intelligence contained any detail that would have been useful in this regard. If it did not, as it came from an unproven source, it would not have attracted any significant credibility. If it did, then directed collection and expert analysis could have supported or cast doubt on the information. I have seen no evidence that such follow-up analysis was undertaken either before the dossier was published, or before the war that eventually followed.

Butler boldly suggested that 'the JIC had no reason to know that it [expert analysis] had not happened'. But that is wrong. At least five members of the JIC (the chairman, the chief of the Assessments Staff, the chief and deputy chief of defence intelligence, and 'C') – almost half the membership – appear to have been aware of this fact. This would exclude the suggestion that the use of unqualified intelligence was a consequence of accidental and innocent oversight.

Because it was constrained to cover a timeframe up to March 2003, Butler could not comment on the government's attempts to conceal the deception in the three previous inquiries and elsewhere. However, the cover-up reflects important light back on to the original issue and is highly relevant to the process of investigation. The next stage of the cover-up was about to begin as the Butler report was debated in Parliament. However, before dealing with that, I compare the Butler findings with my own evidence and recommendations.

Comparisons

Without mentioning that it had been neglected, the Butler review emphasised the need for better-balanced analysis in the British intelligence process, noting that the DIS was semi-detached from the community and recommending measures that might draw it closer. It also endorsed my view that the DIS leadership should include a career analyst. It recommended increasing the scientific and technical competence of both the Assessments Staff and the JIC itself and made suggestions about the selection of future JIC chairmen.

However, Butler saw no need to change the composition of the JIC to increase the presence of experienced intelligence analysts. It did not acknowledge that any problem was generated by factions within the intelligence community competing with one another, or recommend a wider review of intelligence to consider whether the formation of a single intelligence organisation independent of departmental influence was desirable.

Initial reaction in the House

Within minutes of Lord Butler's press conference the Prime Minister was on his feet in the House of Commons.[9] He agreed with all that Butler said and argued that the report demonstrated that those involved had acted in good faith, whilst acknowledging that 'the evidence of Saddam's weapons of mass destruction was indeed less certain and less well founded than was stated at the time'. Blair said that Sir Richard Dearlove accepted the conclusions and recommendations of Butler's report on behalf of MI6 but shouldered the blame himself. Exactly what he was taking responsibility for was not clear because somehow he was right to have been wrong – who could argue that the removal of Saddam was a bad thing? Using the broader terms of reference he had set for Butler, Blair continued to employ his device of conflating the issues of Iraq's WMD and the WMD ambitions of international terrorists. This would later sit uncomfortably with his attempts to separate them in relation to the bomb attacks on the London Underground in July 2005. His words wandered, apparently aimlessly at first, between Iraq on the one hand and global terrorism and 9/11 on the other, until, in a way that a detached majority would not notice, the two had somehow become inseparable.

The Prime Minister carefully selected quotations from both Butler's report and the JIC papers reproduced in them. On the one hand he spiked the guns of Michael Howard, an opposition leader already weighed down by his own rash statements in support of the war. And on the other, he isolated the phrases and sentences that he claimed had chilled his blood.

Howard's response was weak and he was subjected to particularly merciless interruption. One incident reflected particularly badly on the process of inquiry. In asking the House to respect Howard's right to be heard and threatening to suspend the session, the Speaker identified two members for special rebuke. One of them was the member for Dewsbury, Ann Taylor, the chair of the ISC and member of the Butler Review Committee. She was warned against further 'interference'[10] and was, I am told, waving a copy of the Butler report triumphantly above her head.

The Liberal Democrat leader, Charles Kennedy, failed to make any telling points and the Prime Minister escaped relatively unscathed, using the volume of his own side to support the assertion that before the war, not only Kennedy but 'everybody believed the same thing about WMD'. Given the strong position in which the Liberal Democratic Party now found itself, as the only party that argued against the war, I was repeatedly disappointed at Kennedy's failure to press home his advantage.

The newspapers were less kind to Blair and some were clearly frustrated by Butler's refusal to blame anyone for the 'litany of failure' he had identified. I was said to have been 'vindicated' and was very pleased with the almost universal recognition of how the DIS, apart from its 'amateur' leaders, had stood out against a mistake that seemed obvious to the analysts. Unfortunately, that satisfaction was soon to fade as, in the face of incessant spin from the government, the media appeared to accept that the only suitable shorthand for what had happened was an 'intelligence failure' which embraced the entire intelligence community.

The Commons debate on Butler

On 20 July, for the fourth time in less than six months, the Prime Minister made a lengthy defence of his decision to go to war with Iraq.[11] He repeated, as he had done a few days before, the government's acceptance of the conclusions and recommendations of the Butler report and listed the measures already taken or in process.

MI6 would conduct a wide-ranging review of intelligence relationships in Whitehall. This suggested not only that MI6 and its inadequate validation process were the major cause of the problem, but also that Blair saw it as the nation's dominant intelligence authority. In reality, the relationships between the various parts of the mechanism are the responsibility of the chairman of the JIC and his boss, the intelligence and security coordinator, not MI6, and this was quietly recognised when the actual process began.

I was pleased when Blair said:

> None of the disagreements that Dr Jones had with specific items in the dossier actually came to the JIC or the government. That is not to say that they were not important, but the fact is that they did not come before the government. As a result of the changes that we intend to make, such a thing will not happen again in future.

This was a revision of his earlier dismissive references to my 'disagreements', as he called them. They were no longer 'hardly earth-shattering'.

The Prime Minister repeated the highly selective quotations from the Butler report that had worked so well the previous week. He asserted that on the basis of the relevant JIC assessments, it could be concluded that Saddam Hussein was a 'WMD threat', and that he had intent, programmes and actual weapons. But the term 'WMD threat' has no clear meaning. He invited people to infer that there was a threat that Saddam would use WMD in a way that affected our national security. But the JIC itself came to no such conclusion. If it had done, it would have been a primary function to draw attention to it. It clearly did not regard Saddam to be such a threat.

Blair conflated and simplified a rather complex statement by the United Nations Security Council made in Resolution 1441, on the notion of Iraq being a threat to UK. The resolution recognised 'the threat Iraq's non-compliance with Council resolutions and proliferation of weapons of mass destruction and long-range missiles poses to international peace and security'. Blair's spin on this was:

> The UN resolution accepted as a fact that Saddam was a WMD threat. Once that was secured, the question was whether we would enforce the UN resolutions or not. Our intelligence community – like the UN and, as far as I am aware, most intelligence services in the world – certainly believed that Saddam had WMD weapons, capability and intent.

Whilst it may be true that many intelligence services thought it quite likely that Saddam had some chemical or biological weapons, it was not true to suggest most thought them a threat or that he had any intention to use them in the short or medium term.

Michael Howard's attempt to tie Blair down on his misleading description of the depth and quality of the intelligence was met with the threat of more selective quotations from the JIC papers in the Butler report. However, his quotations from the 9 September JIC assessment were blatantly contrary to Butler's criticism of its misuse.

Later in the debate, Robin Cook made a telling contribution: 'The root problem is that intelligence was used in order to sell policy, so it was required to be much more firm and definite than intelligence can ever be. Intelligence was not used as the basis on which to make policy.' Cook thought that the Prime Minister failed to pay much attention to the detail of the intelligence because it was not really the basis on which policy was being formulated.

The view from the Lords

It was not until after the summer recess, on 7 September 2004, that the House of Lords considered the Butler report.[12] Leading for the government, Baroness Symons ploughed a similar, if less theatrical, furrow to the one the Prime Minister had laid down in the other place.

Lord Butler made a contribution in which he said that the review committee did not doubt the good faith of the Prime Minister and the government in concluding that Saddam Hussein had concealed stocks of chemical and biological weapons and suggested this view was shared by most other countries and by Hans Blix. But he said the government's dossier did not make clear that the intelligence underlying those conclusions was very thin, even though the JIC assessments had clearly stated that. He invited people to reach their own conclusions about how grave a fault that was in the context of the lead-up to the war. His committee regarded it as a serious weakness that came home to roost as the conclusion about deployable stocks of chemical and biological weapons have turned out to be wrong.

Butler said that, although his committee was critical of the dossier, it thought many people were responsible and that John Scarlett should not carry the can alone and be made to sacrifice his appointment as chief of MI6. The committee thought it would be in the national interest for Scarlett to be the next head of the SIS if he was the best person for the post. However, he had certain personal responsibilities as chairman of the

JIC. The entire JIC was responsible for a very serious and costly error of judgement. If accountability is a critical factor in public life and it is not appropriate that a whole committee pays some penalty, then surely it is the chairman who should do so, especially as his involvement went far beyond that of just chairing the JIC. Perhaps Butler was suggesting that officials should not be penalised when politicians, who bear equal responsibility, are beyond the scope of his terms of reference. If that is the case then the purpose of the whole review must be called into question.

Lord King asked further questions about Scarlett's position in the light of evidence that emerged during the summer. It was suggested that he had interfered in the business of the Iraq Survey Group in an inappropriate manner. I discussed this matter in Chapter 12 in relation to the Survey Group's activities.

Report of the Iraq Survey Group

The Iraq Survey Group's *Comprehensive Report*, dated 30 September 2004, was issued on 6 October after Charles Duelfer attended a Congressional hearing in Washington.[13] It concluded that no large stockpiles of WMD were in Iraq and there was no evidence of significant production of any chemical or biological weapons after the first Gulf War in 1991. However, the Survey Group also concluded that Saddam's strategic intention was to preserve the capability to reconstitute his WMD programmes and stockpiles when sanctions were lifted.

Considering the chemicals that were available, the infrastructure that existed and the views of Iraqi scientists, the Survey Group concluded that in March 2003 Iraq probably had a capability to produce large quantities of some chemical warfare agents within three months. Our intelligence estimate in 2002 had a range of timescales from weeks to months. The Survey Group also believed that Iraq retained the capability to weaponise chemical warfare agent when the need arose. But it found no credible evidence that any 'field elements' (presumably meaning military units deployed outside Baghdad) knew about plans for chemical warfare use during the invasion, suggesting that the 45-minutes intelligence report was false.

The Iraqi Intelligence Service (IIS) had maintained a number of undeclared covert laboratories to research and test various chemicals and poisons, primarily for intelligence operations, right through to the invasion in 2003. The network of laboratories could have provided an ideal, compartmented platform from which to continue chemical warfare agent research and development or small-scale production efforts, but there were no indications it had happened or was planned.

The Survey Group found that the IIS played a key role in the Iraqi biological warfare programme from its inception in the early 1970s until the final days of Saddam's regime. Iraq's actions between 1991 and 1996 demonstrated that the state intended to preserve its biological warfare capability and return to a steady, methodical progress towards a mature biological warfare programme when and if the opportunity arose. The Survey Group believed Iraq could have re-established an elementary biological warfare programme within a few months of a decision to do so, but there was nothing to indicate this was planned. It noted that a biological warfare capability was 'technically the easiest WMD to attain' and that 'Iraq retained technical biological warfare know-how through the scientists involved in the former program'. Legitimate civilian biological facilities and equipment were found that could have been used for the production of biological warfare agent. These conclusions accord with our assessments of Iraq's capability in 2002.

The IIS operated a series of laboratories in the Baghdad area that worked with biological materials. Iraq should have declared these facilities and their equipment to the UN, but they did not. Neither UNSCOM nor UNMOVIC had been aware of their existence or inspected them. Some of the laboratories possessed equipment capable of supporting research into biological warfare agents for military purposes, but the Survey Group did not know whether this occurred. Although there is no evidence to link this activity with the development of biological warfare agents for military use, it suggests that our assessment on this in the 'possible scenarios' paper of 9 September 2002 was well founded. We warned that even if stocks were limited, small quantities of agent (such as those that might be produced in the IIS laboratories) could be used in focused strikes against key military targets.

The Survey Group confirmed that the pronouncements by senior British, American and Australian spokesmen about trailers captured in 2003 were premature. They were not mobile biological warfare agent production units but had been built exclusively for the generation of hydrogen. They could not have been part of any biological warfare programme.

Important revelations and admissions

Publication of the Iraq Survey Group report was obviously a great
embarrassment to the coalition governments. The Blair government dealt
with it, and other matters, on 12 October 2004 using a statement in the
House on the death of Ken Bigley, a British hostage who had recently been
beheaded in Iraq, as a distraction from other important announcements.[14]
After the headline statement, the Foreign Secretary, Jack Straw, turned to
the Survey Group report. He argued that, on the basis of what the group
found, the invasion of Iraq had been justified. In passing he said the MI6
reporting on the 45-minutes intelligence and on the mobile biological
warfare production trailers had been withdrawn.[15]

On 13 October 2004, Tony Blair was asked during Prime Minister's
Questions about the discrepancy between the intelligence and the Survey
Group report. During the course of a response to Charles Kennedy he
confirmed that the leaked memorandum he had received from his foreign
policy adviser, Sir David Manning, dated 14 March 2002 was genuine.[16]
When challenged about the legality of the war, the Prime Minister explained
that the justification for war had been based not on the intelligence or on
Iraq's possession of WMD but on Saddam's failure to comply with UN
Security Council resolutions. But he did not acknowledge what Manning's
and related papers and memoranda clearly revealed – that the intelligence
argument about Iraq's possession of weapons was an essential element
in the government's successful attempt to condition public opinion to
support an invasion.

Response to Butler

In March 2005, the Foreign Secretary presented the government's full
response to the Butler report to Parliament.[17] The previous July Tony
Blair had said implementation would be the responsibility of MI6 but
subsequently it had been transferred to the security and intelligence
coordinator, Sir David Omand. Although in mechanical terms this was
the coordinator's function it equated to moving the job of gamekeeper
from the poacher to the poacher's friend.

Omand established the Butler Implementation Group (BIG) as 'an
oversight group of senior officials'. The membership of BIG and their

affiliations has never been revealed. At its behest, individual departments and agencies looked at conclusions specific to them and 'a senior foreign office official' led a study on the broader matters. As with BIG, the membership of the study team was not declared. It has not been revealed whether the conclusions of the study team, in whole or in part, were included in the report it sent to ministers, nor is it known which of the ministers from the three departments of state with intelligence community assets saw the report and whether all who did see it accepted all its conclusions.

Before the government's response to Butler was published, the news management process had already provided misleading briefings, which repeated that 'intelligence was to blame' but added that 'it will never be allowed to happen again'. In January 2005 an unidentified senior official revealed the main themes of the draft response:[18] BIG had concluded that in future all intelligence must be scrupulously tested to ensure its credibility, that intelligence analysts must be sceptical of all reports provided to them by collectors, and that of course they must be properly trained. The implication was that these had been shortcomings that contributed to the intelligence failure. But the JIC and its senior members had overruled the analysts and insisted the new intelligence did not require the normal scrupulous testing and sceptical analysis.

The official statement of response by Jack Straw simply added to the cover-up that had been started in the summer of 2003. He said MI6 had already taken steps to improve things. But the improvements he listed had not caused the intelligence failure on Iraq. None of the MI6 reports I saw justified the exaggerations of the Prime Minister's foreword to the September 2002 dossier or the firmness of its executive summary.

The agreement that was said to have been reached between the DIS and MI6 on the distribution of sensitive reports sounded remarkably like the one that had existed under most circumstances throughout my fifteen years in the community. The distribution of especially sensitive reports had always been a matter of discussion between organisations when necessary.

Despite the Prime Minister having fully accepted all the Butler report's conclusions in July 2004 only some of those relating to the DIS were now to be implemented. Butler recognised the need for more intelligence experience at the top levels of the DIS and considered that the deputy chief 'should, unless there are good reasons to the contrary at the time when a particular appointment is made, be an intelligence specialist'. The MoD could not agree to this. Although it recognised the advantage of doing so, the post required a skills base wider than intelligence alone and the people already in intelligence were not often up to it. However, the hopelessly wrong decisions made by my three line managers and the head of the Assessments Staff in September 2002 suggest a lack of intelligence experience might in fact be the more dangerous result. This response highlighted the incoherence of the intelligence community because it showed how departmental preferences can override intelligence requirements and implied that the centre was not inclined to interfere. Similarly, the additional funding from the centre recommended by Butler to provide the DIS with a degree of independence from the pressures and priorities of MoD department was ignored. One recent chief of defence intelligence complained to me that several years later MoD priorities remained generally unsympathetic to the special needs of the DIS.

Butler recommended that the size of the Assessments Staff should be reviewed and enhanced to keep pace with 'the full scope and volume of the requirement', but this was hardly met by the proposal to increase its present staff of thirty by about ten. Apart from the intention to introduce a single desk officer 'with scientific experience' into the Assessments Staff, the government ignored the Butler recommendation to improve scientific representation in the central machinery. It argued that its chief scientific adviser could do it in his or her spare time. What is needed is a dedicated effort to increase the degree of cultural cross-fertilisation between scientists, intelligence analysts and policy staffs. This will only be achieved when more people who originally trained as specialists operate in non-specialist posts throughout the community and, indeed, throughout the civil service.

Accountability moments

President Bush was re-elected in November 2004, just a few weeks after the Iraq Survey Group had reported, and described this as his 'accountability moment' on Iraq. During the 2005 general election campaign in Britain Tony Blair, refusing to engage in further detailed argument about his rationale for joining the Bush invasion, simply asked the electorate to accept that he had had to make a tough decision over Iraq.

Blair has never acknowledged that the intelligence assessments from the JIC on Iraq's weapons of mass destruction were equivocal. Nor has he ever said that, when he considered the coherent bigger picture, he decided the stakes were so high for Britain that a degree of licence was necessary in composing the vision he presented to Parliament and the public in order to persuade them to support the US. But it seems likely that this is the risk he took in what he believed were the nation's best interests. If this was his rationale, at some convenient point after the war, when the risk had failed, Blair had ample opportunity to explain the dilemma which faced him. The main purposes had been achieved. Saddam had been removed, and Britain had demonstrated its solidarity with the United States.

Blair was now in a position to achieve an even more favourable outcome for his country. A frank admission and explanation of the mistake he had made would have been well received in Europe, understood by the American people at large, and limited some of the damage that has followed in Iraq and in Britain. When it became clear, in December 2003 or January 2004, that no weapons of mass destruction or significant related programmes existed in Iraq, the Prime Minister should have explained the motives that had driven him and resigned. It has been suggested that my own contribution to the post-Hutton debate helped to make Blair think seriously about doing so,[19] but I had never challenged Blair's integrity.[20] Perhaps he recognised that his own responsibility was greater than I knew. However, I have no doubt now that Blair's failure to resign damaged Britain's reputation and security, the institutions on which sound governance is based, and even the democracy which we prize above all else.

Blair's resignation could have provided a watershed after which the post-war presence of British troops in Iraq might have been more easily dissociated from the flawed case that had been advanced in support of the invasion, reducing animosity towards them. It might also have helped to defuse the anger and alienation so clearly felt in Britain's Muslim community. That feeling doubtless contributed to the July 2005 terrorist attacks in London, for the suicide bombers left video evidence citing British participation in the invasion and Blair's subsequent re-election as reasons for their action.

The re-election of New Labour in 2005, with a much-reduced majority, did not allow Blair to claim the absolution from blame that Bush had done. Blair fought the election having announced that he would stand down in the period of the next government. There was an assumption,

which eventually came to pass in 2007, that he would be succeeded by
Gordon Brown, who as Chancellor of the Exchequer had presided over
a sustained improvement in the economy which would be an influential
factor on the vote. Although Brown had said little about Iraq before this,
the tightness of the contest and his likely succession to the leadership placed
him under pressure to comment. He volunteered that he had supported
the decision to invade Iraq and still thought it had been the right thing
to do. The continuation in power of those responsible for the Iraq War
meant the discontent rumbled on for the rest of the decade, leading to an
unprecedented fifth inquiry, which began in 2009.

CHAPTER FOURTEEN

2005–2010: Intelligence oversight and the Chilcot inquiry

The ISC and the implementation of Butler

The task of overseeing the government's implementation of the Butler report became the responsibility of the Intelligence and Security Committee. The inability of the ISC itself to satisfactorily investigate the Iraq intelligence failure, and its unexplained decision to withhold from Parliament information about the withdrawal of important intelligence, cast some doubt on its authority and competence to deal with this matter. The existence of such doubts in official quarters was later suggested by Gordon Brown's declaration shortly after he became Prime Minister in 2007, that he would be looking at means to improve the arrangements for overseeing intelligence, clearly implying he thought the current system inadequate.

The first glimpse of the ISC's oversight of the implementation of Butler appeared in its annual report in July 2006. Its tone suggested that the affair might be drawing to an end. However, I thought the ISC had allowed itself to be hoodwinked by the government and its intelligence agencies so that two of the key recommendations, the ones that went close to the real root of the intelligence failure on Iraq, were being neglected in favour of the implementation of other initiatives that resulted from the convenient extrapolation of some of the Butler conclusions. These gestures, although of potential value to the intelligence process, were largely irrelevant to the Iraq intelligence failure.

In particular, the failure followed as much from weaknesses in, and the lack of influence of, the national intelligence *analysis* capability, as from the intelligence *collection* effort, for which MI6 was made the scapegoat – presumably because its current and prospective leader were seen as having been instrumental in promoting unreliable intelligence reports.

Butler had explained that Britain's analytical capability, particularly on WMD, is vested mainly in the Defence Intelligence Staff. In particular, the government, still led by Tony Blair in 2005, dismissed as impractical the suggestion that one of the two most senior DIS officials, who sit on the Joint Intelligence Committee, should under all but the most exceptional circumstances be an intelligence analysis professional. Butler thought this was necessary to ensure that at least one individual was familiar enough with intelligence to understand the advice of expert analysts and was experienced enough to recognise its importance and confident enough to represent it in the JIC. With two intelligence novices leading the DIS in 2002/3, this had not been the case in the run-up to the Iraq War.

The second recommendation concerned the introduction of financial arrangements to provide the DIS with some independence from its MoD paymaster. Such provision would free it to pay greater service to the central intelligence requirement, so that it could pursue important elements of its task unconstrained by the strictures dictated by the culture and competing priorities of a department heavily engaged in military conflict, which consumed both financial and human resources. However, although additional central funding had been made available to the intelligence collection agencies and there had been some enhancement of the small Assessments Staff in the Cabinet Office, there appeared to have been no provision for the matching reinforcement of the DIS. With heavy cuts to defence expenditure forecast, the future of intelligence analysis was apparently ignored. It was not even mentioned in the ISC report.

For these reasons, I wrote to the new chairman of the ISC, Paul Murphy, in July 2006, explaining my concerns in some detail and suggesting, with a greater degree of diplomacy than I display here, that his committee should be careful not to be misled by the government. Because I had already contributed to media coverage of the Iraq WMD issue, I reassured Murphy that I would treat my letter as private between me and his committee, save for an information copy as a courtesy to Lord Butler.

Suspicious that I was being ignored, I prompted the ISC through its secretary in September, and received a cool but polite reply asking me to keep the matter in confidence but leaving me with the distinct impression that my letter was indeed being ignored. It advised that I would hear no more from the committee but should look out for its next annual report to see if it said anything relevant. I responded that since there would be no further discussion between us I saw no reason to keep the fact or detail of my original letter confidential. This drew a rapid response from the secretary and an eventual personal letter from the chairman assuring me they were taking the matter seriously and asking me to keep it in confidence. Although I remained unconvinced and I made no further promises about confidentiality, I decided to wait for the next annual report, which Murphy had told me to expect around July 2007. When it had not appeared by November, I asked the secretary when I might expect to see it. It was sent to the Prime Minister on 4 December and published the following month.

Eventually I received a copy of the report with a covering letter on behalf of the ISC dated 29 January 2008. Although it expressed gratitude to me for bringing these matters to its attention, and it explained in general terms what it had done, neither the full report nor this letter provided me with any indication that the ISC had given the points I had raised any consideration at all. The discussion it reported it had conducted with the current chief of defence intelligence produced a simple reiteration of the government's response to Butler with regard to the post of deputy chief, and the financial issue continued to be ignored completely.

That is why I have decided to disclose my vain attempt to interact constructively with the ISC, and the discourtesy which I think it has shown me towards my contribution. The Brown government's continued neglect of the Butler recommendations on bolstering intelligence analysis and improving the independence of the DIS from the MoD seemed especially serious in the light of the recently proposed cuts to defence expenditure. Gordon Brown's 2007 promise had not been followed through before his government was voted out of office in the 2010 general election.

During the period after the Iraq War, Ann Taylor, now Baroness Taylor of Bolton, chair of the ISC throughout the Iraq crisis, was appointed as a defence minister; Murphy was reappointed to a Cabinet post and replaced as chair of the ISC by the former Foreign Secretary Margaret Beckett, who carried a certain amount of baggage on the Iraq issue; and she in turn, when subsequently appointed to a ministerial post, was replaced by the former Foreign Office minister Kim Howells. This suggested that any intention on Brown's part to institute truly independent intelligence oversight was not a high priority.

Some aspects of intelligence, particularly those at the centre, as well as its oversight, could be affected by the 2010 strategic defence review. It appears that the ISC has been in abeyance since the dissolution of parliament for the May general election until at least August 2010.

The Chilcot inquiry

A high level of public discomfort about the origins of the Iraq War persisted after the re-election of the Blair government in 2005, past Tony Blair's resignation in 2007 and throughout the period of Gordon Brown's premiership. Occasional calls for a further public inquiry could not be quelled, but were deferred by government promises of a full inquiry once British troops had been withdrawn from Iraq. UK combat operations in Iraq ended on 30 April 2009 and withdrawal was completed before the mandate for their presence in the country expired on 31 July that year.

On 15 June 2009, Brown announced there would be an inquiry to identify the lessons to be learned from the Iraq conflict. Like the Butler review, it would be conducted by a committee of Privy Counsellors, and Sir John Chilcot, a former senior civil servant who had been a member of the Butler committee, was asked to take the chair. His committee comprised the historian Sir Lawrence Freedman, professor of war studies at King's College London since 1982; Sir Martin Gilbert, an author and expert on political and military history and international affairs who had lectured extensively on those subjects; Sir Roderic Lyne, a member of the diplomatic service from 1970 to 2004 and British ambassador in Moscow from 2000 to 2004, who had previously held a number of senior positions in the Foreign Office and No. 10; and Baroness Prashar, chair of the Judicial Appointments Commission, president of the Royal Commonwealth Society and a crossbencher in the House of Lords.

Brown originally indicated that Chilcot's Iraq inquiry would be held in camera. But there was a considerable outcry at this and by the time it was officially launched on 30 July 2009 Chilcot appeared to have negotiated a considerable degree of openness. The terms of reference were very broad, covering the period from the summer of 2001 to the end of July 2009, and encompassing all aspects of the Iraq war and its aftermath.[1] Chilcot said that his inquiry would be held in public to the greatest extent possible and intended to include in its report all but the most sensitive information essential to Britain's national security.

However, as the initial public hearings approached there were suspicions that Whitehall intended to exercise considerable control over what the inquiry would be allowed to publish, and what it could refer to during its public sessions. The inquiry agreed to participate in a protocol with respect to sensitive information.[2] This promised the committee access to all government documents, including the most sensitive, provided committee members and their support staff were appropriately vetted and undertook to respect the rules for handling and disclosure of such material. The inquiry was required to obtain written clearance from the originating government department for the release into the public domain of any classified material, and the government, through the Cabinet secretary, would have the final word in the event of a dispute over what could be revealed.

It came as a surprise when, on 11 January 2010, after several weeks of public hearings during which reference to some of the sensitive documents would clearly have been helpful, Chilcot revealed that the inquiry had not requested the declassification of any material up to that point. The protocol appears to have had the effect of limiting some fields of questioning in the public sessions. Since then, evident delays in the release of some requested material, especially that already in the public domain through leaks, generated confusion and suspicion about the openness of some witnesses and of the Brown government. Several of the more important documents have been validated elsewhere by their originators or by members of the government, and the necessity for the committee and witnesses to refer obliquely to information that is well known to many has undermined one of the declared purposes of the public sessions – to convince the public that the matter is being properly investigated. Whether the public release will be adequate to satisfy public opinion by the time the inquiry concludes remains to be seen.

Chilcot noted that the inquiry was not a court of law but, although nobody was on trial, it would not shy away from making criticism or highlighting mistakes. He explained that the opening weeks of public hearings, which began on 24 November 2009, were used to provide a framework on which subsequent analysis could be built in a second phase. That phase commenced with Alastair Campbell's evidence on 12 January 2010 and was characterised by more detailed and at times more aggressive questioning.

The main part of the second phase was completed with evidence from Jack Straw on 8 February covering the period from 2001–2006, when he was Foreign Secretary. Although it had been anticipated that public hearings would then stop until after the pending general election, Gordon Brown

offered to give evidence earlier and did so on 5 March, covering his positions
first as Chancellor of the Exchequer and then as Prime Minister. On the
same day Douglas Alexander testified, and on 8 March David Miliband also
gave evidence relating to their ministerial duties from 2007–9, after which
the election break from public hearings was taken.

The election was held in May with the Labour being replaced by a
Conservative–Liberal Democrat coalition government. Although public
hearings were not resumed until 29 June, the inquiry remained active,
visiting the United States to gather information and seeing a number of
witnesses behind closed doors in the UK. The Chilcot committee appears
to have 'met' about twenty 'people' in the US and of those named the two
'heads of the Iraq Survey Group', David Kay and Charles Duelfer, are the
most likely to have given evidence that would have been of relevance to this
volume.

The witnesses that the inquiry had seen in private were not announced
until 8 July, after public hearings had recommenced. It was explained that
the reasons for privacy were to explore issues that might still have affected
national security or the national interest, or because of the personal
circumstances of witnesses in relation to the organisations for which they
had worked or because of their junior status at the time. Some more senior
officials appear to have been seen in private because their witness sessions
included more junior staff.

Three of the four witnesses who had given evidence on intelligence issues
in public were interviewed again in private. They were Sir John Scarlett,
Sir William Ehrman and Tim Dowse. Additional witnesses in important
intelligence posts during or shortly after the war were seen only in private.
They were Sir Richard Dearlove ('C'), Julian Miller (head of the Assessments
Staff) and Martin Howard (DCDI from 2003–4). In addition the committee
heard from six unidentified members of the SIS, although no indication has
been given of the periods that were being studied or the general nature of
their work at the time. It may be that one of these SIS representatives was
the person who briefed the senior DIS officials on Report X in the final
stages of the approval of the 2002 dossier.

It could be significant that no intelligence analysts were called to give
private evidence.[3] This would suggest that the inquiry may rely heavily on
the intelligence evidence accumulated by the Butler review, to which I and
the section heads from my branch gave evidence. Two significant officials
appear not to have been interviewed by this or any of the previous inquiries.

The WMD desk analysts on the Assessments Staff who drew up the various drafts of the dossier and related JIC papers could probably provide important background: for example, did they have visibility of Report X, and subsequent intelligence assessments? I remain concerned that several important issues may not have been re-examined.

Other witnesses who gave evidence in private which might be relevant here if it were available are Sir Jeremy Greenstock and Major General Tim Tyler, deputy commander of the Iraq Survey Group in its later stages. Evidence was also provided by Ian Lee, who was the MoD's director general for operational policy from September 2002 to May 2004 and the inquiry posted his written evidence on its website. Lee wrote that he 'saw the intelligence and attended some JIC meetings' and was provided with a personal oral briefing from DIS experts in which he describes the prevailing certainty about Iraq's possession of WMD to be strong and seemingly unanimous. It is to be hoped that the inquiry has established exactly what intelligence Lee saw, who briefed him and when they did so. Otherwise, I am not sure that his somewhat superficial general comments on intelligence add significantly to our state of knowledge.

The following discussion of the public evidence up to July 2010 focuses mainly on the intelligence aspects of the justification for the war.[4]

Intelligence issues

The evidence of the five intelligence officials who have appeared in public at Chilcot revealed little that was new, except for a nuanced shift in the degree of certainty attached to the existence of chemical and/or biological weapons in Iraq before the war. This could be inferred from their denials that they or the JIC had endorsed Tony Blair's declared belief in the foreword to the September 2002 dossier that the intelligence on this was unequivocal.

Sir William Ehrman and Tim Dowse, two senior Foreign Office officials, spoke from a perspective that was right at the interface between intelligence and policy.[5] They distanced themselves from the foreword and made it clear they had not been consulted before other similar statements had been made, but they accepted that the intelligence advice allowing the impression that Iraq possessed significant stocks of WMD was wrong. In a subsequent letter to the inquiry,[6] Dowse suggested that the drafters of the dossier, with whom he appears to associate himself, believed the intelligence and acted in good faith. He insisted he did not regard it as making a case for war. He did not say that he recognised its potential for making such a contribution, nor did he refer to the well-documented unresolved objections raised by the DIS members of the dossier drafting group.

Dowse and Ehrman implied that there was no reason to doubt the validity of the 45-minutes intelligence and the subsequent sensitive intelligence on chemical and/or biological weapons production (Report X), providing no suggestion that the primary sources were not established as reliable nor referring to the absence of any significant collateral. Although Sir Lawrence Freedman displayed a degree of incredulity at some of their comments on intelligence, they were not pressed hard in public but may have been further questioned in private session.

The two witnesses seemed to suggest, without being explicit, that the government's case for war was based on two related arguments – that Saddam retained WMD which threatened the UK in some way they did not define, and that Iraq was in breach of related UN Security Council resolutions. Whilst the asserted possession of stockpiles obviously implied such a breach, other less significant compliance failures would also constitute one. The witnesses spun these two distinct strands cleverly and confusingly, as had been done so often since 2002, making it difficult for any but the dedicated to divine which element of the argument applied to which assertion. For example, only one direct WMD-related breach based on intelligence was discovered by UNMOVIC before the war – a find of hidden documents connected with the former nuclear weapons programme. But it was suggested that in some way this provided convincing validation of both the intelligence that Iraq possessed chemical and/or biological weapons, which of course it did not, and the decision to go to war because failure to disclose the documents was itself a breach.

Sir John Scarlett's evidence showed some minor but important variations compared to what he had told the Hutton inquiry.[7] He had previously stressed that he had direct access to the Prime Minister, but now emphasised that, in the main, his access was through Sir David Manning, Blair's foreign policy adviser. Scarlett even went so far as to say:

> If I saw something happening or we saw something happening which didn't look right or something was being said which we didn't think was quite right, then one could always go back, but it would be to, in this case,

> David Manning, [and say,] 'You need to be aware of this, you need to be
> aware of that, I want the Prime Minister to be aware of this or aware of
> that.'[8]

This detail was confirmed by Jonathan Powell, who later told the inquiry
that 'David Manning was the foreign policy and defence adviser and
intelligence adviser, so he would mastermind all of that'.[9] The significance
of this was emphasised in evidence from Alastair Campbell, who noted
that in terms of advice to Blair, Manning was far more important and
influential than he, Powell, Scarlett and Sir Richard Dearlove were.[10]

Whether or not Scarlett drew Manning's attention to Blair's exaggeration
of the certainty of the intelligence about Iraq's WMD was not clarified.
However, it is not a comfortable thought that someone in Manning's
position, with a strong commitment to the policy of the day, might be in
a position to apply a filter to such a message. From Scarlett's own words it
appears that the fundamental safeguard of direct intelligence access to the
Prime Minister may have been compromised by the arrangement in place
in 2002 and 2003. It is not known whether the inquiry pursued the issue
with either or both of the witnesses when they were seen in private.

Responding to a question from Lyne about the changing intelligence
assessment on Iraq's WMD capability, Scarlett's recollection was not
entirely accurate on Saddam's assessed capability.[11] He acknowledged
that in March 2002 the intelligence was not clear on whether Iraq
possessed chemical or biological warfare agent or whether they were
currently producing them.[12] He suggested that a report was subsequently
received that had supported earlier intelligence on mobile biological
agent production facilities, and as a result of new intelligence in August
and September, the JIC instructed the Assessments Staff to firm up the
assessment on Iraq's possession of chemical and biological weapons in the
paper that was issued on 9 September 2002. Scarlett's statement implied
that all the latest intelligence reports had resulted in significant shifts in the
JIC assessment but examination of the paper shows that the Assessments
Staff afforded them no great prominence.[13] They offered an indication of
what might be the case, rather than allowing firm assessments to be made.
Continuing the practice of government witnesses, Scarlett neglected to
mention the uncertainty inherent in the description of the source of
perhaps one of the two most significant of these reports – the 45-minutes
intelligence – or the meagre detail it contained. But he did say more clearly

than any government witness had done previously that the significance
of this report was that it indicated Iraq possessed actual weapons. On
the other intelligence report – the sensitive report on agent production
(Report X) – he did not mention Dearlove's description of the source as
being new and on trial, or explain how the content of the report had been
checked.

When questioned by Sir John Chilcot about the words Blair used in
his foreword to the dossier, 'What I believe the assessed intelligence has
established beyond doubt. . .', Scarlett said he thought it was an overtly
political statement, and that he had not paid the same attention to the
wording in the foreword as he had done to the text of the dossier itself.

Sir David Omand, meanwhile, challenged Chilcot's assumption early in
his evidence of 'the primacy of intelligence in justifying the Iraq strategy',
pointing out that 'Saddam's past behaviour' and 'obstructionism of the
United Nations' were also factors.[14] Omand suggested that in preparing the
dossier, the JIC had overlooked the likely influence of Britain's adversarial
political system, which leads politicians to disregard the equivocation in
background advice when advocating policy. When challenged that this
was really no excuse, he offered the defence that 'more broadly across
Europe, the other side of the Atlantic, we did all believe that Saddam
was hiding illegitimate programmes'. In reducing the issue to a 'belief'
about 'programmes', Omand blurred the matter because, on the basis of
intelligence, there could be no more than a *suspicion* about the existence of
the stockpiles that Blair said he believed there was no doubt about.

Omand then quoted from what he called 'the now rather famous
minute' I had sent to warn my bosses of my concerns in September 2002.
What he said appeared to be intended to downplay both its significance
and thrust. Not only did he not properly represent the context in which
the minute was written, but he quoted selectively and inaccurately from
it. In particular he did not acknowledge the uncertainty I was reflecting
about whether specifically chemical agent production had occurred. He
also modified a phrase from it when suggesting I had written that we were
'more than ever convinced that Iraq has continued to produce BW agent'.
In doing this he suggested I had a growing conviction or certainty based
on the new intelligence. He omitted completely the qualification 'we
would not go so far as to say we know this to be the case'.[15] The growing
conviction Omand attributed to me conveniently matched the assertion
made by Scarlett and others that the assessment that Iraq had chemical

and/or biological weapons had been firmed up by new intelligence received in August and September 2002. The point of my minute had been to warn my bosses that we had seen no intelligence to justify such a change of assessment.

Omand recalled, reflecting Scarlett's evidence, that not much attention was paid by JIC members to the Prime Minister's foreword to the dossier. Contrary to his recollection, I remember the foreword was in place in the draft circulated on 19 September 2002 and that it was unclear as to whether comment was required. My colleagues' more detailed comments on the 20 September draft of the dossier included specific criticism of the foreword.[16]

Although he did not go quite as far as he had on a previous occasion when he suggested the 45-minutes intelligence was not of the first order,[17] Omand hinted at its insubstantial nature and said that, with hindsight, he could see that its inclusion was asking for trouble. This observation appears not to take account of the significance ascribed by some, including Scarlett, to this intelligence because it appeared to demonstrate the actual existence of agent and weapons which had previously been much less certain.

Sir Lawrence Freedman asked whether, if the material upon which the dossier had been based had been put into the public domain, people would have been more or less impressed. 'How actually strong was the evidential base upon which so much of this was based?' Omand thought they would have been less impressed, but he avoided giving an answer to the question of whether he agreed with Butler that the intelligence was 'thin'.

Omand appeared to endorse some of the points I made in my written evidence to Butler,[18] supporting what Butler had recognised when he stressed the 'national role as well as defence role' of defence intelligence, and described the DIS as a 'national jewel in our crown' that had to be protected when there was pressure on defence expenditure. If Omand supported the suggestion of the Butler review that additional funding should be made available to the DIS from the central intelligence pot to provide it with some independence from MoD priorities in financial matters, he appears to have lost the argument in his Butler Implementation Group. Omand also acknowledged the ascendency of MI6 within the intelligence machine when he said:

SIS were very much in the inner council. They had proved their worth to the Prime Minister in a number of really very, very valuable pieces of work, not just delivering intelligence, but of course conducting back channel diplomacy, and that, I'm sure, would have weighed heavily on the Prime Minister's sort of calculation that 'these are people I should be listening to'.

And, apparently pointing out the danger inherent in this, he continued:

But there was a sense in which, because of past successes – very, very considerable successes – [for] this government, SIS over-promised and under-delivered, and when it became clear that the intelligence was very hard to find, it was a very hard target, they really were busting a gut to generate intelligence.

Baroness Manningham-Buller, director general of the Security Service (MI5) from 2002–7 and previously its deputy head, gave evidence on 20 July. She had given evidence in private to the Butler review in 2004. Recalling her membership of the JIC at the time, she thought the intelligence on Iraq was fragmentary and incomplete. With regard to MI5 responsibilities she said that from early on it was clear that the Iraq policy being followed would lead to an increase in the threat from terrorism, although that would not be directly from Saddam or Iraq. Manningham-Buller said, with respect to a letter she had written in March 2002 noting the terrorist threat from Iraq was low, that she was responding to a pre-Crawford perception that going to war with Iraq was a possibility.

She drew attention to the fact that a threat from al-Qaida was recognised before 9/11 and that her service had contributed largely to the dossier that the government had published in October 2001 which made no reference to Iraq. There was no evidence of Iraqi involvement in 9/11, an assessment also held in the US by the CIA. She said this judgement was not held in favour by some parts of the US machine and was why 'Donald Rumsfeld started an intelligence unit in the Pentagon to seek an alternative judgement'. She was dismissive of the quality of what that unit produced. However, once the US was committed to war with Iraq she thought the increase in the terrorist threat might have been unrelated to direct British military involvement because Britain would, in any case, be perceived as a supporter of the US. But she refuted the notion that the removal of Saddam eliminated or significantly reduced the potential threat of terrorists acquiring and using WMD, recalling that 'after all, Osama bin Laden said it was the duty of members of his organisation or those in sympathy with it to acquire and use these weapons'. Manningham-Buller regarded as hypothetical the question of whether the post-conflict failures in Iraq had increased the motivation of Islamic extremists to mount terrorist attacks but thought it a possibility.

It became clear that neither she nor her predecessors had regular access to the Prime Minister although she had that right in law. Taken with the evidence of John Scarlett and David Omand, this suggests that on Iraq Blair's only direct interaction with the intelligence community was with 'C'. On the JIC she painted a picture not of a truly coherent body in which joint decisions were made on assessments, so much as a disparate group of experts each dealing independently with their own speciality and bowing to the judgement of other specialists. If this is truly the situation for those members who are intelligence professionals, the presence on the committee of those with related policy axes to grind is all the more worrying, especially if there is the need, as she identified, for the JIC to calibrate any raw, unassessed intelligence that might be distributed to ministers and lead to wrong decisions.

Manningham-Buller concluded by saying that the intelligence on which the decision to go to war was based was not substantial enough to support it, and the link that the government made between the medium-term increases in the threat, and the immediate imperative to forestall Saddam Hussein, was not real.

Political and legal issues

Sir Christopher Meyer, who had been British ambassador in Washington, had not given evidence to any of the previous inquiries.[19] Much of what he said had appeared in his 2005 book.[20] It was entirely compatible with the evidence of his and Manning's leaked memoranda of March 2002 which I discussed in Chapter 5. Meyer was slightly more expansive on the clever or 'cunning' plan he had referred to in his memorandum. It appeared in fact to be a clever plan within a clever plan. There was a plan to persuade the Bush hawks through Paul Wolfowitz that Britain was determined to support regime change by military action in such a way as to gain wide international support for an invasion and perhaps even UN approval. This was to be achieved through a clever plan to wrongfoot Saddam by obtaining UN approval to insist on the return of inspectors. The American hawks were not told, at least in the first instance, that the British government hoped that regime change could be achieved without military action. However, subsequent witnesses suggested that the President was aware of this possible outcome even to the point of leaving Saddam in power but now agreeing to abide by UN resolutions. Clearly, Vice President Cheney and Defence Secretary Rumsfeld and their senior staffs were never fully on board and whilst they acceded to Bush's wish to go to the UN, military planning proceeded.

Meyer said he advised London that a core problem with the Blair plan involved timing and the need to operate within a timescale fixed by the logistical requirements of a ground invasion of Iraq. The necessary limit on that timescale meant that whereas the original onus had been on Saddam to prove his innocence on the WMD charges, now it was shifted to the US/UK-led coalition, which needed to demonstrate that Iraq was in breach in order to gain support at the Security Council.

Related to the plan was the UK requirement to establish a legal basis for possible military action through the United Nations. Sir Jeremy Greenstock, the British ambassador to the UN, thought that after President Bush's speech on 12 September 2002 there had to be a new Security Council declaration that Iraq was in material breach of Resolutions 678 and 687, because he thought the reaffirmation in Resolution 1205 had lapsed.[21] He decided he could not support a US/UK agreement about the use of force unless there was a new resolution and let this be known to London.

Greenstock thought Resolution 1441, which the Security Council adopted in November, was vital to the UK's participation in the invasion of Iraq. Some, especially in the legal department of the Foreign Office, questioned the lawfulness of the action and gave detailed and complicated evidence to Chilcot in this regard, but Greenstock's view offered an important degree of clarity on a matter that is likely to remain the subject of different legal opinion. Greenstock thought:

> If you do something internationally that the majority of UN member states think is wrong or illegitimate or politically unjustifiable, you are taking a risk, in my view, and increasingly. . . and I think one of the lessons you may want to look at as an inquiry is on the importance of legitimacy in geopolitical affairs nowadays. I regarded our invasion of Iraq – our participation in the military action against Iraq in March 2003 – as legal but of questionable legitimacy, in that it didn't have the democratically observable backing of a great majority of member states or even perhaps of a majority of people inside the United Kingdom. So there was a failure to establish legitimacy, although I think we successfully established legality in the Security Council in the United Nations for both our actions in December 1998 and our actions in March 2003 to the

degree at least that we were never challenged in the Security Council or in the
International Court of Justice for those actions.

Sir David Manning's evidence to Chilcot was complex and at times seemed
contradictory. His references to the meetings he had in Washington in March
2002 do not accord closely with the detail and tone of the memorandum he
sent to Tony Blair on 14 March.[22] He told Chilcot he considered his trip to the
US capital a reconnaissance visit for Blair's Crawford summit and, although
his meetings covered much more, he thought Iraq was given a 'salience'
because the US administration was determined to confront the international
community over a perceived threat. He said he was particularly interested
in what Condoleezza Rice could tell him about the perceived nature of the
threat from Saddam in the US and beyond, but did little to explain what he
heard and what he believed. The memorandum was not mentioned in the
public hearing but it would be interesting to hear Manning's interpretation
of it and Blair's reaction to it may have been discussed in private session.
Manning's description of Blair's line to Bush at Crawford indicated higher
hopes of avoiding military action than either the Options paper or his
memorandum had. He suggested Blair's approach had a different emphasis
when he told Bush, 'Yes, there is a route through this that is a peaceful and
international one, and it is through the UN, but if it doesn't work, we will be
ready to undertake regime change.' But when Manning saw Rice and Bush at
the end of July he told them the *only* way UK could take part in any regime
change policy would be through the United Nations.

Touching on the intelligence, Manning told the inquiry:

> Throughout the time I was involved in this it was quite clear our policy was
> to disarm Saddam Hussein, that we were convinced that he had weapons
> of mass destruction or that he certainly had the capability – and probably,
> I should say, that he had the capability to manufacture weapons of mass
> destruction and that this had to be dealt with.

He very deliberately attached certainty only to the capability to manufacture
WMD and not to their existence. Ironically, it is virtually impossible to
remove such a capability from a country like Iraq that has, and will retain,
the required intellectual capacity, experience and physical resources.

But Manning said he believed that Blair was determined that the US
should not go it alone on Iraq. He recalled that the Prime Minister first

asked for military options in June 2002 but insisted that knowledge of this should be tightly held, not least because he did not want the US to gain the impression that Britain would consider anything other than the UN route. He explained how, in the face of these constraints, cross-Whitehall coordination was achieved on the official side. The Overseas and Defence Secretariat organised two groups: one a restricted group with access to all the sensitive material, and another which had a more limited view. I was not aware of the existence of these groups nor that the DIS was ever asked to contribute to an assessment of the possible chemical or biological threat to our forces before the JIC 'Scenarios' assessment, conducted in parallel with the drafting of the dossier. Manning said that as the invasion approached in March 2003, it was his view that Saddam should have given a 'more sensible declaration' to UNMOVIC but that 'inspections should be given more time to work'.

Sir Peter Ricketts, who had been political director at the Foreign Office, gave evidence on 1 December 2009. He appeared to confirm the veracity of the leaked minute from the Foreign Secretary, Jack Straw, to Blair on 25 March 2002, and to go some way to confirming his own leaked minute of 22 March to Straw.[23] He also seemed to prevaricate on whether WMD existed when he said, 'We had, in Whitehall, been seriously concerned about the threat from weapons of mass destruction and the risk that they would be *reconstituted* as the sanctions regime broke down and Saddam got access to more money, and it had been a consistent worry [my emphasis].'

When Alastair Campbell gave evidence on 12 January 2010 he said he had no doubt that Blair thought the transatlantic relationship was of fundamental importance to his analysis of the British national and strategic interests. He avoided answering several questions from Sir Roderic Lyne about whether Blair believed Saddam had to be confronted, even if this was not supported by the United Nations. However, Campbell did seem to suggest that after the UN route had been explored and exhausted, and blocked by the French, Blair thought it was a reasonable next step. Blair wrote Bush a note in 2002 in which, as paraphrased by Campbell, he said that the British government 'was absolutely with you in making sure that Saddam Hussein is faced up to his obligations and that Iraq is disarmed. If that can't be done diplomatically and it has to be done militarily, Britain will be there.'

When Campbell was pressed with questions on the dossier and the intelligence that underpinned it a major difference of opinion between witnesses emerged and was explored by the inquiry. Officials had been telling Chilcot that they considered the foreword overtly political and did not feel they could comment on it; therefore they had not paid it as much attention as they perhaps should have. Campbell told the inquiry he was sure they would have spoken up if they had not agreed with it. It is difficult to know if this is genuine misunderstanding or whether it is a deliberate avoidance of responsibility by one side or the other. However, in either case it indicates the need for a greater degree of separation between the intelligence assessment authority and the policy/political authority.

Lyne grilled Campbell on Blair's 'beyond doubt' statements, pointing out the many apparent inconsistencies and the contradictions in earlier evidence. Campbell justified them in terms of the approval, or failure to object, of the intelligence officials. He also clarified that a good deal of detail on Iraq was withheld from some of the Cabinet, singling out Clare Short for special mention.

On 18 January, Jonathan Powell told the inquiry that he had no doubts that Iraq had weapons of mass destruction. Surprisingly, he thought that too much emphasis was being put on intelligence in relation to that belief. He said that when Blair formed his government, it was dealing with an Iraqi regime that could not be trusted on WMD and that the reason 'we bombed Iraq in 1998, together with the Clinton administration, was that we believed they had weapons of mass destruction. So it would have taken something pretty dramatic to persuade us that he had got rid of those weapons.'

On the intelligence case made in the dossier, he said that the right thing, looking back, would have been to publish the JIC reports themselves. But he continued:

> The specific state of Saddam's WMD was simply not the essence of our concern. What concerned us was the threat he could potentially pose. The decision to topple Saddam was not intelligence driven, it was based on an assumption about the weapons of mass destruction, the holdings that he had, but how this could develop in the future.

On 29 January, the witness everyone had been waiting to hear at last made his appearance: the former Prime Minister Tony Blair. In a long session, he provided a typical performance in which strong statements were supported by arguments in which the general and strategic were stirred together with the specific and tactical in a chronological sequence that was difficult to understand.

Sir Martin Gilbert tried to confirm that the basis of the case and legal justification for military action against Iraq was WMD rather than human rights or any other issue. Blair immediately blurred the boundaries between them. He appeared to acknowledge there were uncertainties about Iraq's possession of WMD in early 2002 but insisted that by September that year there was a lot more information. However, echoing Powell's evidence, he subsequently resorted to an argument that leaned more heavily on historical evidence and inferences from Saddam's behaviour than on intelligence reporting. When questioned on his argument that an important factor in his decision related to a need to confront what he described as the twin threats of WMD and terrorism, Blair was unable to offer a definitive link in the case of Iraq, but outlined the general concept of WMD leaking from states to terrorists as being the idea that concerned him.

Asked by Sir Lawrence Freedman about the intelligence base, Blair insisted the significance of the 45-minutes intelligence was painted greater in retrospect than it had been before the war. Blair said he did not focus much on the detail of this intelligence. However, Scarlett's evidence had already explained its significance in firming up the JIC's view. It was a vital factor in the assessment presented in the dossier, emphasised in the Prime Minister's foreword and his Commons speech, and important to our objection to the dossier.

When pressed on the overall quality of the intelligence and his interpretation of its assessment, Blair suggested he made it clear he represented his own 'belief' about its certainty and, again like Powell, said he wished the actual JIC assessments had been released rather than the dossier. The implied assertion that the JIC assessments were more convincing than the dossier is without foundation, and indeed was contradicted in the evidence of Sir David Omand.

Lyne said the committee had read the JIC assessments and asked Blair if the intelligence was telling him that the WMD threat from Iraq was growing. This prompted Blair to refer to 'mobile production facilities for biological weapons', which he said he had heard about at a meeting on 12 September 2002 and which had an impact on him, although they were not in the JIC assessment of 9 September. All previous evidence about the intelligence discussed at the 12 September meeting, including that in the Butler report, suggests that the mobile production facilities were not the key issue. The intelligence reports on those facilities were received well before this date and were included in the JIC assessment. The important new information was in Report X and was on the recent production of chemical and/or biological weapons. The impression is that Blair paid little attention to the detail of the intelligence assessment on which his justification of the war was originally based, that he asked few challenging questions about it at the time, and that his recollection of it at Chilcot was poor.

When asked if he had any regrets about Iraq, Blair said he had none, and he accepted responsibility for what happened. He said:

> I genuinely believe that if we had left Saddam in power, even with what we know now, we would still have had to have dealt with him, possibly in circumstances where the threat was worse and possibly in circumstances where it was hard to mobilise any support for dealing with that threat.

Gordon Brown, giving evidence on 5 March, was possibly the most evasive witness seen by the inquiry. He said firmly that the decision to go to war with Iraq was the right one and for the right reasons – a phrase he repeated several times. He explained that the reason was Iraq's continued defiance of the will of the international community but, despite being asked repeatedly in a number of different ways whether the decision was based primarily on the perceived threat from Iraq's possession of WMD, he avoided giving a direct answer. For example, on one occasion Lyne tried by asking, 'From five briefings that you had and the JIC papers that you read and received like other members of the Cabinet, were you convinced that the threat from what was being reported as Iraq's programmes of weapons of mass destruction was growing?'

Brown's reply was typical of the others he offered: 'I was convinced of a more basic fact. I just say to you: for me, I repeat, the major issue was that a breach of the international community's laws and decisions was unacceptable.'

Carne Ross, who had been the first secretary responsible for the Middle East at the UK mission to the UN from 1997–2002, gave evidence on 12 July. He felt that during that time he was on the front line of UK policy on Iraq. The thrust of his evidence was that it was wrong to claim that in 2002 that the containment of Iraq was failing and that sanctions were collapsing. He believed that the government did not consider, let alone pursue, non-military alternatives to the 2003 invasion. He suggested these would have involved diplomatic efforts to close off sanctions-busting activities and provided numerous examples. He expressed great scepticism of the intelligence case presented to the public on Iraq's WMD, arguing that it did not conform to any previous reporting or assessment he had seen.

Ross was the first, and so far the only, witness to challenge the inquiry on the way in which the government was controlling the release of important documents, implying that by not protesting the inquiry was allowing the effectiveness of its work to be constrained. He seemed to feel that the quality of his own contribution was being affected by this. Not surprisingly, the committee was annoyed by this charge, and the attitude it took, at least in the early period of questioning, was notably aggressive.

The executive chairman of the United Nations Monitoring, Verification and Inspection Commission, Dr Hans Blix, was interviewed by the inquiry on 27 July. He thought UNMOVIC, which had existed since 1999, finally received an offer to allow its inspectors into Iraq on 16 September 2002, as a result of the threat of US military action which was underpinned by the new Bush doctrine of pre-emptive deterrence.

When Freedman asked about the modulation of evidence that might be found, ranging from significant stocks of weapons, to trivial quantities, to just documents or plans to reconstitute a capability, Blix was quick to point out that the UK September 2002 dossier really was not talking about anything other than the actual existence of the biological and chemical weapons he was responsible for, bearing in mind that the IAEA continued to deal with nuclear weapons, about which no similar claims had been made. When Chilcot clarified on the basis of previous evidence to the Butler review a comment Blix made about Iraq's attempted acquisition of uranium oxide from Niger, explaining that the British assessment in this regard had not been based on obviously forged documents, Blix commented sarcastically that he was 'glad they didn't manage to misinterpret that one'.

On the Iraq Survey Group, Blix was doubtful about the motives of its two leaders, Kay and Duelfer. He pointed out that both had been appointed by the CIA and thought that, having failed to find actual weapons, they were keen to offer the US government straws. Blix seemed doubtful about the quality of the evidence on the existence of programmes and Iraq's future intentions to reconstitute a capability.

Lord Prescott, who had been deputy Prime Minister to Blair throughout his premiership, was possibly the last witness to give public evidence to the Iraq inquiry on 30 July. Although his evidence was often disjointed and difficult to follow, it did shed important light on the nature of the Blair administration. The impression he gave was that Cabinet government had ceased to operate in the expected sense of objective collective decision-making as well as collective responsibility. He appeared to acknowledge that there had been no comprehensive discussion on Iraq, due in part to the high workload and time constraints on Cabinet members, and in part to the lack of trust that all members would respect the strict confidentiality of what was said.

At the personal level Prescott's duty to support the Prime Minister, at least on Iraq, seemed to exclude any responsibility he might have to challenge policy decisions. In that regard he seemed not to be alone in Cabinet. He said he had doubts about the intelligence but failed to register them in Cabinet, and that he was not interested in the detail of arguments about the legality of an invasion but just wanted a simple positive or negative statement from the Attorney General, despite recognising the enormous pressure he was under.

The committee's questions appeared to expose that Prescott was not as well informed on the Prime Minister's plans and actions as he claimed to be and may have thought he was. For example, he seems not to have seen the 'Iraq Options Paper' in March 2002.

When talking about the link between terrorism and WMD, Prescott took the opportunity to state his belief that it was the JIC that clearly identified the threat to which Blair was responding and was particularly critical of the evidence given to the inquiry by Baroness Manningham-Buller, implying she was trying the duck her responsibility as a member of the committee that provided that advice. When pressed he offered a thinly veiled criticism of her motives, implying that the assessments generated by MI5 were influenced by a desire to obtain increased resources. This clearly acknowledges that a situation in which the intelligence agencies are required to compete for money has the potential to undermine their credibility with their paymasters, especially when their assessments are inconvenient or unpopular.

PART IV

CONCLUSION

CHAPTER FIFTEEN
Bigger issues

Introduction

Iraq remained at the forefront of international attention in the decade following the war, owing to the failure of post-war planning to deliver an improved environment for ordinary Iraqis and the violence, suffering and death that continued in Iraq for many years, combined with instability in the surrounding region. The impact of the Iraq experience is likely to be of long-term significance globally as well as for Britain.

Blair and Bush cast their decision to invade Iraq in terms of a policy context centred on WMD arms control and international terrorism – describing these issues as the security challenge for the twenty-first century. The suggested use of intelligence in a more proactive way to guide critical political, military and security decisions was also part of the thinking. Tony Blair had sympathised with and supported Bill Clinton in the late 1990s as he tipped the balance in arms control and counter-terrorism away from diplomacy and towards deterrence with limited attacks on the Sudan, Afghanistan and Iraq in 1998. But it was George W. Bush's Vice President, Dick Cheney, who concluded after 9/11 that much more significant policy adjustments were needed to meet the risks that had continued to increase in the intervening years and had now resulted in a strike at the very heart of the American homeland. Cheney believed that the growing background threat of mass destruction had to be met pre-emptively by responding at a lower level of risk based on a reduced standard of proof.[1] Presumably, the limitations of intelligence were well understood when Bush delivered Cheney's concept as the doctrine of pre-emptive defence early in 2002.[2]

There can be little doubt that the overriding aim of using extreme measures to remove the regimes in Afghanistan and Iraq was to achieve wider deterrence relating to terrorism and WMD in order to preserve and enhance America's freedom of political and commercial activity across the globe. The Taliban and Saddam Hussein were judged 'guilty' of these two distinct, if slightly overlapping, transgressions (overlapping because al-Qaida was known to be seeking WMD, not because there was really any serious danger of Iraq supplying them). Military aggression tending towards 'shock and awe' was intended to dissuade other states from becoming involved in either hosting terrorists or acquiring WMD and to reduce the chance of the two things coming together as the nexus so dreaded by Blair and Bush.[3]

So, if these were the objectives, how has Iraq affected them?

Nuclear, biological and chemical arms control

The eternal tension between the instinct for survival and an altruistic desire to contribute towards some more universal good is clearly reflected in national attitudes to WMD and arms control. It produced the 1968 Nuclear Non-proliferation Treaty, the 1972 Biological Weapons Convention and, eventually, the 1993 Chemical Weapons Convention.

Even before the CWC was in place, many in the West came to doubt the adequacy of diplomatic attempts to limit the proliferation of WMD. As the Iron Curtain came down it gradually yielded visibility of the size and sophistication of the Soviet chemical weapons capability, which although not strictly illegal had been carefully concealed, and, more importantly, its biological weapons programme, which was in direct contravention of the BWC. During the same period a proliferation of WMD programmes in a number of other countries had been detected. The significance of what was happening could no longer be avoided by policy makers and military commanders as they prepared to fight the Gulf War of 1991. The emergency planning necessary for that war was a siren warning for many of them. Then, having been challenged for the first time with the difficulty of defence and protection in a conflict with a non-nuclear enemy that had WMD, their distress continued through the 1990s as they discovered how difficult it was to ensure that Iraq's programmes were closed down. Meanwhile, in 1998 India and Pakistan conducted surprise underground nuclear tests which rocked the foundations of the NPT and conjured visions of a domino chain of new nuclear states across the globe.

All of this prompted a decision in Washington that was evident not only from its subsequent attitude to treaty-related negotiations but also its other activities. It decided that proliferation had to be tackled by means beyond diplomacy. It is not clear whether the minds of politicians and policy makers simply could not embrace the idea of a future with many more WMD-capable states, or whether the objective was to delay that eventuality. Where diplomacy had failed, it was decided that the development of such capabilities should be prevented by military action and, where necessary, by regime change. Saddam's Iraq presented itself as the first 'doable' example of a perceived belligerent WMD proliferator and, whilst this may not have been the only driver for regime change in Iraq, it was undoubtedly a major factor. Propaganda based on intelligence was now required to confirm the existence of WMD. The diplomatic approach had required information at one level of certainty to make a case for concerted action with foreign governments on sanctions, for example. But now more detailed and persuasive intelligence of an actual threat was needed to justify military action by persuading public opinion that a war was worth paying for with lives and money.

The quality of information demanded was not available in the intelligence that existed on Iraq or could be reasonably guaranteed to be available in any other situation. Unfortunately intelligence leaders were too concerned about the preservation of their domain to acknowledge this. There was a more sustainable case that could have been made about the problem of Iraq and WMD, but it involved potential threats and future weapons, rather than actual threats and existing stockpiles, and there was neither the inclination in Washington nor the time in London for politicians to explain this more subtle alternative.

The bald accusation that Iraq possessed major quantities of such weapons and was a threat proved to be without foundation.[4] The consequence was to set back the cause of non-proliferation. The limitations of intelligence have been painfully and dangerously exposed. Whereas previously an exaggerated perception of Western intelligence capabilities may have served to dissuade would-be proliferators from even starting a programme, they are now more aware of what can be hidden. The demonstration by the US that it was prepared to take military action before it was in possession of good-quality evidence will have increased the likelihood that some of those countries already in America's bad books will go for WMD in the hope of acquiring a deterrent themselves before they are attacked. As a consequence a larger number of countries around the world will probably feel threatened and reconsider their options. In acting without the endorsement of not only the United Nations in general, but also significant Western partners within it, Britain and the US will have reduced the inclination for such countries to offer support in future attempts to limit proliferation.

Finally, in demonstrating its inability to establish stable replacements for changed regimes with which the West can work to prevent proliferation, and by exposing the limits of its ability to establish and sustain control by military means, America has probably reduced its capability to deter those who oppose it. The consequences of that will be felt by all its allies.

Terrorism

In distracting the focus of attention away from efforts to establish a more liberal regime in Afghanistan, where there was much wider international support and sympathy compared to Iraq, America and Britain have failed to consolidate the success of removing the Taliban government that had provided a safe haven for al-Qaida. Supported by elements of al-Qaida, since 2007 the Taliban had been reasserting itself in parts of Afghanistan and, increasingly, across the border in north-east Pakistan. Ironically, since the removal of the strict Taliban government and the failure to establish a significantly improved economy, opium poppy growers have expanded production to fuel the illegal trade of narcotics in Europe, which in turn has implications for the funding of terrorism. The stability of Pakistan itself has reduced and its future cooperation with the West is less certain.

Amongst the chaos of an Iraq riven by religious and ethnic difference, insurgents thrived, who included al-Qaida sympathisers and foreign operatives, inciting terrorism, rehearsing its black arts and recruiting new members. Across the West, and especially in Britain, tolerance of and support for the Islamic fundamentalist cause have grown in the relevant communities as a consequence of what has happened in Iraq. This has resulted in an increase in the small minority of British Muslims who are prepared to take terrorist action in support of al-Qaida or related Islamic groups. A problem that lurked beneath the surface of Britain's changing society but was previously contained has been unleashed by the perception of a dishonest government which, with the endorsement of the British electorate in 2005, continued to contribute to death and chaos in an important Islamic community. Blair used the 'intelligence on Iraq's WMD' as an excuse, rather than the reason, for joining the US invasion in 2003, in much the same way as he subsequently claimed that Islamist fundamentalists used the invasion of Iraq as the excuse, not the reason, for the London bombings on 7 July 2005.

Whilst the election in the US of President Obama, who had opposed the Iraq War, has heralded a shift to a less aggressive foreign policy, the coalition government established in Britain in 2010 is led by a party that supported the war and still believes it was just. The report of Sir John Chilcot's Iraq inquiry and the government's response to it will be important factors in determining Britain's future reputation in the world.

Intelligence

The intelligence community has emerged from the Iraq War with its reputation severely damaged. Credibility with its political and military masters has always been the major factor, but with the rise of the terrorist threat its reputation with the public at large is more important than ever. It remains at a low ebb.

Iraq has helped crystallise much of what is wrong with British intelligence and it is important that the opportunity to understand it is not lost. Unfortunately, the previous government's inclination to obscure important elements of the background to its decision to participate in the war has masked many of the underlying intelligence problems. Few, if any, have a complete overview of intelligence, but the Iraq experience convinces me that such an overview is worth striving for.

British intelligence has evolved rather than been designed. Consequently, it comprises a confused and incoherent assembly of disparate centres of expertise and experience, the full value of which is denied to the nation through a poor definition of its overall function and an inadequate understanding of its potential by those who run it and use it.

An important issue at the core of the problem with British intelligence is the absence of a clear statement of its primary function. Intelligence does two main things: it provides the government with information to shape policy decisions and support the implementation and conduct of programmes related to those decisions; it also organises and participates in activities flowing from that information, which can assist the government more directly. Whilst the first function requires inputs from the whole intelligence community, the second is mainly organised and often conducted by compartmented elements within MI6 and MI5.

It may be because the second function is in the nature of providing politicians with solutions to problems, whereas the first is more in the nature of bringing problems to them, that the second attracts greater kudos and reward. It follows that the most powerful organs in intelligence are the problem solvers. They are the ones that gain a louder voice in the ear of government. It is no coincidence that many who should know better see 'C', the head of MI6, as the senior person in British intelligence. Sometime in the mid-1990s, a senior member of MI6 confided in me that he was disappointed that his organisation set much greater store by achieving operational activities in support of government policy rather than by providing information that might help form it. It was what an intelligence officer had to do to reach the highest ranks.

In 2002–3, when Iraq rose to the top of the political agenda, there also arose a coincidence of personalities. The government was led by an action-man Prime Minister in danger of being overshadowed by his Chancellor and rival on matters of domestic politics and frustrated on European policy who turned his efforts increasingly to foreign policy as a means of sustaining his authority and making his mark. MI6 was led by a charismatic intelligence 'collector' who inherited an organisation which had lost influence, partly as a result of having to yield up its share of the 'peace dividend'. The Joint Intelligence Committee was led for the first time by another intelligence 'collector' who 'belonged' to MI6 and aspired to be its next head. Thus when the opportunity arose to 'solve' a major problem for the Prime Minister it was irresistible to these combined forces. It would serve to reduce 'the risk of irrelevance' that had been the greatest fear of the intelligence community in general, and MI6 in particular, since the end of the Cold War.

Part of that solution lay in familiar territory for the agency – influencing foreign opinion in favour of British interests.[5] Unfortunately, another part of the solution involved persuading public opinion to deliver parliamentary support for British participation in the invasion of Iraq. There was a need, if not to fix intelligence around the policy, then to mould it close enough to do a good supporting job. A quiescent intelligence community would have allowed this to happen without a murmur but the organisation was sound at its roots, requiring the leadership to take exceptional measures to override its experts.

Another consequence of the 'peace dividend' had contributed to the problem. A defence review in the mid-1990s, masquerading as a study of options to meet the change demanded by reduced budgets, did two things to the community of intelligence analysts (lodged almost exclusively in the MoD). It reduced numbers, coverage and quality, and also determined a subtle shift in culture so that intelligence would not just 'inform' policy but also be more supportive of it. These changes, which took place under the Conservative government of John Major, were not reversed or modified by Blair, despite the additional pressure placed on defence and its intelligence arm by his policies towards the Balkans, Sierra Leone and Afghanistan. Military action in these countries meant that the chief of defence intelligence was focusing on operational and battlefield intelligence, which also bore down on the time of his deputy, who would normally have spent more of it managing the strategic aspects of intelligence analysis, such as the work on WMD. By this time the occupant of the deputy chief post had become an imported expert on policy to better align the analytical product with the policy makers' needs. As a consequence he was a relative novice on intelligence matters who was easily led, outranked and outgunned on the JIC by the 'collectors' from the agencies. Because of this a hectically busy and unnecessarily naive Defence Intelligence Staff was persuaded to ignore the advice of its own experts in favour of whispered reassurances that everything was in order from an ascendant MI6.

Of course, efficient and effective organisations, and appointments to them, should be designed to prevent the short circuits in process which so often cause great damage. The organisation of British intelligence is demonstrably not fit for purpose in this regard. The fact that this has not been recognised or acknowledged seven years on from a calamitous failure indicates that the oversight of intelligence is also ineffective. Therefore, a thorough review of all aspects of British intelligence is needed. Such a review would require guidance from a clear political and policy statement on what is expected of intelligence. The Butler review focused specifically on WMD intelligence but some of its recommendations have wider relevance and represent a good springboard for further work to which the Chilcot inquiry could make a contribution.

Contrary to Butler, I believe there is a strong case for the establishment of a single overarching intelligence agency. It would retain the excellent existing agencies with few changes, and would embrace major elements of the analytical capability locked in the DIS, as well as the Assessments Staff and other elements of the central intelligence machinery. Individual departments, such as the MoD, would retain the right to fund their own intelligence organisations to meet their own specific needs. The oversight offered by a single accountable head of intelligence, operating a single budget, would contribute to a better balance between collection, analysis and 'other activities'. The head of the organisation would be responsible for producing, by whatever means were deemed appropriate, authoritative intelligence assessments to meet customer demands or stimulate their interest. Individual departments should be afforded good visibility of an assessment and a right to advise during its production, but no right of veto over the intelligence experts. This would eliminate the need for the Joint Intelligence Committee as it currently exists, in which the authority over assessments is, bizarrely, shared with policy customers.

The JIC might be replaced by a senior committee which jointly considered the implications of intelligence assessments for government policy across departments. This would give policy makers the opportunity to interrogate intelligence officials on their assessments and ensure they understood the significance of their pronouncements. The government itself should have control over the tasking of the intelligence community in setting down its requirements and priorities with an appropriate degree of flexibility. However, the performance of the intelligence community against those tasks should be judged by a specially cleared but independent panel of senior people with experience embracing intelligence, government, policy and military service. That panel should, in turn, be answerable to Parliament.

The biggest of issues

Although I consider myself no more qualified than the next man, I offer in closing a personal view of the overriding implication of the Iraq experience. It has challenged the suitability of our democracy, as presently constituted and operated, to resist the pressures placed upon it by the demands of modern national and international society. Up to 2010, the process by which Parliament constrained the government and the Cabinet constrained the Prime Minister appeared to have broken down. Tony Blair was not the first modern Prime Minister to become more than the first amongst equals. He maintained an embargo on the release of relevant information on an impending war even to his own Cabinet, the vast majority of which seemed not to be offended. Parliament set aside the fact that it was misled by the government in favour, presumably, of a conflation of party and personal interests which it allowed to outweigh consideration of its duty to the electorate. It is ironic that our own democracy has been so badly served as the consequence of a purported attempt to introduce a more enlightened approach to government in a country where a repressive regime held sway. Time will tell whether the changes to process proposed by the coalition government led by David Cameron, and the shift in political culture that will be necessary for a coalition government to succeed, herald a more acceptable form of democracy for the governance of our own dear land. Iraq above all has shown that is what is needed.

NOTES

Chapter 1: 1987–90: Intelligence, chemical warfare and biological warfare

1   R. V. Jones, *Reflections on Intelligence* (Mandarin, London, 1989) describes the dilapidated state of the interior of the Metropole Building at that time.

2   US National Intelligence Estimates are the nearest equivalent of JIC assessments. There are some similarities but also major differences in the mechanism by which they are produced.

3   Gruinard Island, off the west coast of the Scottish Highlands, had been used to test biological weapons in WWII. Parts of it remained contaminated with anthrax until it was declared safe in 1990 after a four-year decontamination campaign.

4   *Report of the Presidential Commission on the Intelligence Capabilities of the United States Regarding Weapons of Mass Destruction*, 31 March 2005.

Chapter 2: 1990–2000: The First Gulf War and its consequences

1   It is likely that some Iraqi officers, who by the 1980s would have been in senior positions, trained in the US and obtained relevant background information in the 1960s. Subsequently, Egypt, or at least some Egyptians, appear to have contributed significantly to aspects of the Iraqi programme.

2   Judith Miller, Stephen Engelberg and William Broad, *Germs: The Ultimate Weapon*, Simon & Schuster, London, 2001.

3   Rt Hon. Sir Richard Scott, *Report of the Inquiry into the Export of Defence Equipment and Dual Use Goods to Iraq and Related Prosecutions*, London, HMSO, 15 February 1996.

4   Neil Mackay, 'Revealed: the secret cabal which spun for Blair', *Sunday Herald*, 8 June 2003.

5   Representatives of UNSCOM also interviewed Kamil.

6   Some believe that Israel conducted a nuclear explosion in the south Indian Ocean before this time but the evidence is sparse. North Korea is suspected of having conducted underground nuclear tests since 1998. It is unclear whether they were successful.

7   Two US officials who served UNSCOM in the 1990s have separately suggested this. See Scott Ritter, *Iraq Confidential: the Untold Story of America's Intelligence Conspiracy*, London, I. B. Tauris, 2005, pp. 4–5, and Charles Duelfer, *Hide and Seek: The Search for Truth in Iraq*, Public Affairs, New York, 2009, pp. 86–7, 468. President Clinton eventually signed the Iraq Liberation Act on 31 October 1998, giving tangible substance to an undeclared policy goal that had apparently existed since 1991.

8   Charles Duelfer, who led the Iraq Survey Group's investigation into Iraq's WMD from February 2004 until its conclusion, thinks this was the case (see Duelfer, *Hide and Seek*, pp. 86–7, 468). He believed WMD issues were 'a surrogate for national policies between Washington and Baghdad' in the 1990s and again in 2002–3.

9   Ritter, *Iraq Confidential*, pp. 269–77.

10   *Proliferation Issues: A New Challenge after the Cold War – Proliferation of Weapons of Mass Destruction*, Russian Foreign Intelligence Report translation, Joint Publications Research Service, 5 March 1993.

11   *Defending against the Threat from Biological and Chemical Weapons*, Ministry of Defence, London, 1999.

12   Hans Blix, *Disarming Iraq*, Bloomsbury, London, 2004, p. 38.

13   Ibid.

14   The 2000 Foreign Office Iraq Strategy paper was acquired by *The Independent* in February 2010 and posted on the Iraq Inquiry Digest website on 3 March 2010 (http://www.iraqinquirydigest.org/?p=7964).

Chapter 3: 2001: 11 September

1   Richard Preston, *The Cobra Event*, Orion, London, 1997.

2   It was not until 2008 that the FBI publicly identified the likely/possible perpetrator. Bruce Ivins, a long-serving US government scientist at the US biodefence laboratory at Fort Detrick, Maryland, committed suicide shortly after learning of the intention to charge him with the offence. Of course, the case against him could not be tested in court. In February 2010 the US Department of Justice closed the investigation of the incident and published a summary of its conclusions and a large number of related documents. It concluded that Ivins was solely responsible for the attacks. Some argue that the evidence supporting this is not conclusive.

3   Bob Woodward, *Plan of Attack*, Simon & Schuster, London, 2004, p. 30.

4   This and other Blair speeches can be found on the official 10 Downing Street website. An interesting background to the speech is discussed by John Kampfner in *Blair's Wars*, Simon & Schuster, London, 2003, pp. 50–53.

Chapter 4: January–July 2002: Iraq ascendant

1   'Iraq Options Paper', 8 March 2002. This was one of a total of eight papers
    (the Downing Street papers) obtained by the journalist Michael Smith.
    They have subsequently been reproduced elsewhere; see for example
    www.michaelsmithwriter.com.

2   Robin Cook, *The Point of Departure*, Simon & Schuster, London,
    2003, p. 116.

3   Alastair Campbell, oral evidence to Chilcot inquiry, 12 January 2010 (see
    http://www.iraqinquiry.org.uk/transcripts/oralevidence-bydate/100112.
    aspx) and *The Blair Years: Extracts from the Alastair Campbell Diaries*,
    Hutchinson, London, 2007.

4   2000 Foreign Office paper 'Iraq: Future Strategy', available at http://
    www.iraqinquirydigest.org/?p=7964.

5   Memorandum, Manning to Blair, 'Your Trip to US', dated 14 March
    2002; see 'The Manning Memo' at www.michaelsmithwriter.com/
    memos.html. In Prime Minister's Questions on 13 October 2004 Blair
    confirmed the veracity of this memorandum (Hansard, HC Deb, vol.
    425, col. 279).

6   Memorandum, Meyer to Manning, 18 March 2002; see 'The Meyer
    Memo' at www.michaelsmithwriter.com/memos.html.

7   Christopher Meyer, *DC Confidential*, Weidenfeld & Nicolson, London, 2005.

8   Cabinet Office briefing paper, 21 July 2002 for Prime Minister's
    23 July meeting; see 'The Cabinet Office Briefing Paper' at www.
    michaelsmithwriter.com/memos.html.

9   Minutes dated on the day of the Prime Minister's meeting on 23 July
    2002; see 'The Downing St Minutes' at www.michaelsmithwriter.com/
    memos.html.

10 *Review of Intelligence on Weapons of Mass Destruction, Chairman the
    Rt Hon. the Lord Butler of Brockwell*, HC 898, The Stationery Office,
    London, 14 July 2004 (the Butler report), pp. 163–71.

11 Brian Jones, 'Intelligence, Verification and Iraq's WMD', in Trevor
    Findlay (ed.), *Verification Yearbook 2004*, Vertic, London, 2004.

12 Memorandum, Ricketts to Straw, 'Iraq: Advice for the Prime Minister',
    22 March 2002; see 'The Ricketts Memo' at www.michaelsmithwriter.
    com/memos.html.

13 Memorandum, Straw to Blair, 'Crawford/Iraq', 25 March 2002; see 'The
    Straw Letter' at www.michaelsmithwriter.com/memos.html.

14 A transcript of the interview is in the archive of Blair's speeches on the
    No. 10 website at http://www.number10.gov.uk/output/Page1709.asp.

15 Cook, *The Point of Departure*, p. 135.

16 Cabinet Office briefing paper, 21 July 2002; see 'The Cabinet Office
    Briefing Paper' at www.michaelsmithwriter.com/memos.html.

17 According to Bob Woodward's *Plan of Attack* (Simon & Schuster, London, 2004, p. 144), the briefing actually took place on 5 August.

18 See, for example, the evidence of Air Chief Marshal Sir Jock Stirrup to the Chilcot inquiry on 1 February 2010, when he was questioned about his time as deputy chief of the Defence Staff (Equipment) from April 2002–May 2003 and discussed problems with the availability of advanced body armour (http://www.iraqinquiry.org.uk/transcripts/oralevidence-bydate/100201.aspx#am).

19 Minutes, Iraq: Prime Minister's Meeting, 23 July 2002; see 'The Downing St Minutes' at www.michaelsmithwriter.com/memos.html.

20 The list of attendees is identified in an odd mixture of post titles and names. For clarity, I have added the alternatives in square brackets.

21 One or all of the following, or their representatives, might have been expected to be present since there were clear implications for homeland safety arising from the matters under consideration: the Home Secretary, David Blunkett; the head of the Security Service (MI5), Eliza Manningham-Buller, a member of the JIC; and the intelligence and security coordinator, Sir David Omand, also a member of the JIC. All had relevant responsibilities. Manningham-Buller is reported as saying that she had repeatedly warned ministers and officials that an invasion of Iraq would increase the terrorist threat (Richard Norton-Taylor, 'Ex-head of MI5 among new witnesses at Iraq inquiry', *The Guardian*, 12 June 2010, http://www.guardian.co.uk/uk/2010/jun/11/iraq-inquiry-chilcot-head-mi5).

22 The Prime Minister and the Cabinet secretary were responsible for ensuring all facets of policy implications were considered. Jack Straw had been Home Secretary until 2001.

23 According to Thomas Powers in a review of George Tenet's book, *At the Center of the Storm*, Dearlove and other British intelligence officials visited the CIA in Langley on Saturday 20 July (*New York Review of Books*, 19 July 2007).

Chapter 5: August–September 2002: The road to the dossier

1 JIC(02)181. See *Review of Intelligence on Weapons of Mass Destruction, Chairman the Rt Hon. the Lord Butler of Brockwell* (the Butler report), HC 898, The Stationery Office, London, 14 July 2004, p. 163.

2 Cheney's first speech was to the Veterans of Foreign Wars 103rd National Convention in Nashville on 26 August; the second was to veterans of the Korean War in San Antonio, Texas on 29 August (see http://georgewbush-whitehouse.archives.gov/news/releases/2002/08/20020826.html and http:// georgewbush-whitehouse.archives.gov/news/releases/2002/08/20020829-5.html).

3   Dilip Hiro, *Secrets and Lies: The True Story of the Iraq War*, Politico's, London, 2005, p. 537.

4   Air Marshal Sir John Walker explained in written evidence to the FAC inquiry (see Chapter 7) dated 7 July 2003 that he had spotted the change in targeting from media reporting. The FAC appears not to have published this evidence. However, it emerged in the BBC's evidence to the Hutton inquiry and can be found on its website (www.the-hutton-inquiry.org.uk) as item BBC/6/0129-0135.

5   http://webarchive.nationalarchives.gov.uk/+/http://www.number10.gov.uk/Page3001.

6   Butler report, p. 163.

7   See ibid.

8   See ibid.

9   During the summer, I had been under pressure to provide my MoD customers with more specific guidance on Iraq's WMD capabilities to assist in their contingency planning and the provision of defence equipment against nuclear, biological and chemical weapons for the anticipated military campaign.

10 See the archive of Blair's speeches at http://webarchive.nationalarchives.gov.uk/+/http://www.number10.gov.uk/Page1725

11 Allen described what had happened in a speech in the House on 2 April 2008. See Hansard, HC Deb, vol. 490, col. 1092.

12 Robin Cook, *The Point of Departure*, Simon & Schuster, London, 2003, p. 203.

13 Hans Blix, *Disarming Iraq*, Bloomsbury, London, 2004, p. 74.

14 Butler report, p. 36.

Chapter 6: September 2002–March 2003: Concern and departure

1   I reproduce here the redacted version of the text of my minute that was supplied to and published by the Hutton inquiry. It can be found on the Hutton inquiry website (http://www.the-hutton-inquiry.org.uk/content/evidence/mod_22_0001.pdf).

2   I am unable to disclose which country because that information is classified.

3   Hansard, HC Deb, 24 September 2002, vol. 390, cols 1–7.

4   It is possible that this version had been sanitised to some degree to protect sensitive intelligence that the US did not wish to release to the UK.

5   Butler report, p. 88.

6   Greenstock's evidence to the Chilcot inquiry on 27 November 2009, www.iraqinquiry.org.uk.

7   Al-Sa'adi had overseen the Iraqi WMD programme and been involved in disarmament negotiations over the previous decade.

8   Hamish Killip told me that later interviews with al-Sa'adi, who had overseen the declaration, gave him the impression that al-Sa'adi thought the exercise pointless because Iraq's credibility had been lost through the prevarication of the 1990s.

9   Hans Blix, *Disarming Iraq*, Bloomsbury, London, 2004, p. 104.

10 Intelligence and Security Committee, *Iraqi Weapons of Mass Destruction: Intelligence and Assessment*, Cm 5972, September 2003, p. 33.

11 As opposed to radiological weapons or 'dirty bombs', which do not have such devastating effects but do have the potential to cause widespread panic in a public that has not been appropriately informed about the limits of their impact.

12 After the Iraq War, the concern that was highlighted in relation to the objective of Iran's nuclear activities was rarely described as a 'WMD' problem, despite the fact that issues existed with respect to both Iran's biological and its chemical warfare capability.

13 Eventually, in November 2003, I presented a paper dealing with this issue at a 'Sussex Day' organised at Sussex University as part of the Harvard Sussex Program. A version of the paper can be found online at http://www.sussex.ac.uk/Units/spru/hsp/documents/17-11-03%20Jones%20 Paper.pdf. Similar arguments were made in my submission to the FAC inquiry into global security: see House of Commons Foreign Affairs Committee, *Global Security: Non-proliferation*, HC 222, 14 June 2009, Ev. 97–106.

14 Milton Leitenberg, 'Further Information Regarding US Government Attribution of a Mobile Biological Production Capacity by Iraq', Federation of American Scientists website, 3 August 2006 (www.fas.org/ irp/eprint/leitenberg.html).

15 This became known as the 'dodgy dossier' because it plagiarised academic work produced some years earlier on Iraqi deception and concealment programmes. It was disowned by the JIC, and Alastair Campbell later accepted responsibility for this when he appeared before the FAC. In his 2007 and 2008 diaries he claims not to have kept his eye on this particular ball (Alastair Campbell, *The Blair Years: Extracts from the Alastair Campbell Diaries*, Hutchinson, London, 2008).

16 A series of documents tracing the background to the advice offered by the Attorney General has been published on the Chilcot inquiry website at www.iraqinquiry.org.uk/transcripts/declassified-documents.aspx.

17 This was referred to in the evidence of former Defence Secretary Geoff Hoon to the Chilcot inquiry on 19 January 2010.

18 Hansard, HC Deb, 18 March 2003, vol. 401, col. 797.

19 In evidence to the Chilcot inquiry on 27 November 2009.

20 ISC, *Iraqi Weapons of Mass Destruction: Intelligence and Assessment*, p. 34.

21   Blix, *Disarming Iraq*, p. 194.

22   Zinser was interviewed for *Panorama*'s 'A Failure of Intelligence', broadcast on 11 July 2004.

Chapter 7: March–July 2003: The war and after

1   *Review of Intelligence on Weapons of Mass Destruction, Chairman the Rt Hon. the Lord Butler of Brockwell* (the Butler report), HC 898, The Stationery Office, London, 14 July 2004, pp. 163–71; US National Intelligence Estimate, October 2002 (www.gwu.edu/~nsarchiv/NSAEBB/NSAEBB129/nie_first%20release.pdf).

2   George Tenet, *At the Center of the Storm: My Years at the CIA*, HarperCollins, New York, 2007.

3   See Bob Drogin, *Curveball: Spies, Lies, and the Man behind Them – The Real Reason America Went to War in Iraq*, Ebury Press, London, 2007, pp. 198–9.

4   Brigadier John D. Deverill, 'A Personal Experience with the Iraq Survey Group', *British Army Review*, no. 134, Summer 2004. See also transcripts of the evidence to the Hutton inquiry of Wing Commander John Clark and Dr Bryan Wells.

5   Andrew Gilligan, 'I asked my intelligence source why Blair misled us all over Saddam's weapons. His reply? One word . . . CAMPBELL', *Mail on Sunday*, 1 June 2003.

6   Peter Beaumont, Antony Barnett and Gaby Hinsliff, 'Iraqi mobile labs nothing to do with germ warfare, report finds', *The Observer*, 15 June 2003.

7   Although Chidgey tended to conflate chemical and biological weapons, the potential threat posed by chemical weapons is not so challenging. In the limit a chemical stockpile could be produced from scratch in weeks or months, but very much larger quantities would be needed. They would be much harder to hide. Any amounts that could be easily hidden would not be very significant.

8   See for example, G. B. Carter, *Chemical and Biological Defence at Porton Down 1916–2000*, The Stationery Office, London, 2000.

9   *Iraq's Weapons of Mass Destruction: A Net Assessment*, International Institute for Strategic Studies, 9 September 2002.

10   Paper subsequently released to the Hutton inquiry and available on its website (www.the-hutton-inquiry.org.uk). See Intelligence and Security Committee evidence item ISC/1/0003.

11   Such briefing minutes are a typical requirement and provide the minister with background details, advice on 'the line to take' and suggestions for answers to possible questions. This one was subsequently released to the

Hutton inquiry and is available on its website: see MoD evidence items MOD/4/0006–0010.

12 Intelligence and Security Committee, *Iraqi Weapons of Mass Destruction: Intelligence and Assessment*, Cm 5972, September 2003.

13 Ibid., p. 28, para. 99.

Chapter 8: August 2003: The Hutton inquiry begins

1 The oral and documentary evidence obtained by the Hutton inquiry is available on the inquiry's website, www.the-hutton-inquiry.org.uk.

2 See JIC(02)181: 'Iraq: Saddam's Diplomatic and Military Options', reproduced in *Review of Intelligence on Weapons of Mass Destruction, Chairman the Rt Hon. the Lord Butler of Brockwell* (the Butler report), HC 898, The Stationery Office, London, 14 July 2004, p. 165: 'Although we have little intelligence on Iraq's CBW doctrine. . .'

3 See JIC(02)202: 'Iraq Use of Chemical and Biological Weapons: Possible Scenarios' (9 September 2002), reproduced in the Butler report p. 164. It referred to the 45-minutes intelligence as telling us something we did not already know about Iraq's doctrine for use of such weapons.

4 As acknowledged by Sir John Scarlett in his evidence to the Chilcot inquiry on 8 December 2009.

5 A full copy of the message can be read on the Hutton inquiry website (www.the-hutton-inquiry.org.uk/content/evidence/cab_23_0015.pdf).

6 Minutes, Iraq: Prime Minister's Meeting, 23 July 2002; see 'The Downing St Minutes' at www.michaelsmithwriter.com/memos.html.

7 Foreign Affairs Committee, Ninth Report, Session 2002–03, HC 813-I, Minutes of Evidence, 24 June 2003, Q. 755.

8 Blair said he could not say when Saddam would use his weapons: 'this month or next, even this year or next'. Hansard, HC Deb, 24 September 2002, vol. 390, col. 5.

9 It was not publicly available until December 2009, when I decided to publish it on the internet. It can be found at www.iraqinquirydigest.org/ ?p=4577.

Chapter 9: 3 September 2003: My day in court

1 Iraq Inquiry Digest website, www.iraqinquirydigest.org/?p=4577.

2 Hutton inquiry website, www.the-hutton-inquiry.org.uk/content/ transcripts/hearing-trans28.htm and www.the-hutton-inquiry.org.uk/ content/transcripts/hearing-trans29.htm.

Chapter 10: September 2003: ISC reports and Hutton hearings end

1   Intelligence and Security Committee, *Iraqi Weapons of Mass Destruction: Intelligence and Assessment*, Cm 5972, September 2003.

2   The term 'single source' as used here is shorthand for 'information from a single source' and is not about an individual. An individual source can provide information that is 'single source' if he/she is the only source of that specific information, but he/she can also provide other information that is 'multi-source' when the same or overlapping information has been provided by an independent source. The greater the overlap, the greater the confidence in the information. The greater the quantity of secret information from an individual source that is supported by independent sources, the greater the confidence in the individual source. However, if the individual source is repeating information from a sub-source in addition to information he/she has acquired directly, it is the sub-source that has to be validated.

3   Some officials would argue or imply this was the case in later evidence to Hutton and to the Chilcot inquiry.

4   Hansard, HC Deb, 11 September 2003, vol. 410, cols 491–2.

5   The transcript of evidence is available on the Hutton inquiry website, http://www.the-hutton-inquiry.org.uk/content/transcripts/hearing-trans31.htm.

6   The words here are taken from the transcript of Dearlove's evidence on the Hutton website, http://www.the-hutton-inquiry.org.uk/content/transcripts/hearing-trans32.htm.

Chapter 11: October 2003–January 2004: the Hutton report

1   Blair gave an interview to the BBC Arabic Service that received wider coverage. The transcript can be read at http://webarchive.nationalarchives.gov.uk/+/http://www.number10.gov.uk/Page5021.

2   See Chapter 10.

3   Hansard, HC Deb, 28 January 2004, vol. 417, col. 337.

4   *Government Response to the Intelligence and Security Committee Report on Iraqi Weapons of Mass Destruction: Intelligence and Assessments, 11 September 2003*, Cm 6118, February 2004.

5   Liaison Committee, Session 2003–04, oral evidence given by the Rt Hon. Tony Blair MP, 3 February 2004, HC 310-i. (http://www.publications.parliament.uk/pa/cm200304/cmselect/cmliaisn/310/4020301.htm).

6   Brian Jones, 'There was a lack of substantive evidence. . . We were told there was intelligence we could not see', *The Independent*, 4 February 2004.

7   Parliament endorsed the decision to go to war with Iraq in a debate on 18 March 2003; see Hansard, HC Deb, vol. 401, col. 760.

Chapter 12: December 2003–April 2004: The Iraq Survey Group and the Butler review

1   I have had long discussions separately with Hamish Killip and Rod Barton, two of the most experienced WMD inspectors to serve in Iraq and elsewhere over many years. They explained what had happened. Killip had been with the ISG in Iraq from July 2003, shortly after it came into being. Barton had initially resisted becoming part of the ISG despite repeated requests to do so because he could not obtain from the Australian government a clear definition of the terms and conditions under which he would work in this potentially dangerous environment. I understand that British inspectors suffered similar problems. Since my discussion with him much of what Barton told me has appeared in his book *The Weapons Detective: The Inside Story of Australia's Top Weapons Inspector* (Black Inc. Agenda, Melbourne, 2006).

2   Statement by David Kay on the interim progress report on the activities of the Iraq Survey Group before the House Permanent Select Committee on Intelligence, the House Committee on Appropriations, the Subcommittee on Defense and the Senate Select Committee on Intelligence, 2 October 2003.

3   George Tenet, *At the Center of the Storm: My Years at the CIA*, HarperCollins, New York, 2007, p. 407.

4   Hamish Killip, private communication.

5   Tenet, *At the Center of the Storm*, p. 406.

6   Charles Duelfer, *Hide and Seek: The Search for Truth in Iraq*, Public Affairs, New York, 2009, p. 333.

7   Hearing of the Senate Armed Services Committee, subject: Iraqi weapons of mass destruction programmes, chaired by Senator John Warner, witness: David Kay, former head of the Iraq Survey Group, Washington DC, 28 January 2004.

8   See also Brian Jones, 'Intelligence, Verification and Iraq's WMD', in Trevor Findlay (ed.), *Verification Yearbook 2004*, Vertic, London, 2004.

9   Duelfer, *Hide and Seek*, p. 337.

10 On 1 August 2004 Tom Mangold had provided some background to the affair in an article in the *Mail on Sunday*.

11 The late Dr John Gee was an expert in chemical weapons who joined the ISG to help with the report in January 2004. He was an Australian diplomat and had been an UNSCOM commissioner and the deputy director general of the Organisation for the Prohibition of Chemical Weapons (the body charged with the oversight of and verification of compliance with the Chemical Weapons Convention).

12 *Washington Post*, 9 December 2007, p. B01.

13 My submission in full can be read on Chris Ames's Iraq Inquiry Digest at www.iraqinquirydigest.org/?p=4577.

14   Cabinet Office briefing paper, 21 July 2002; see 'The Cabinet Office
      Briefing Paper' at www.michaelsmithwriter.com/memos.html.

Chapter 13: May–July 2004: Panorama *and the Butler report*
1   *Panorama*, BBC1, 11 July 2004.
2   *Review of Intelligence on Weapons of Mass Destruction, Chairman the
      Rt Hon. the Lord Butler of Brockwell* (the Butler report), HC 898, The
      Stationery Office, London, 14 July 2004.
3   Hansard, HC Deb, 24 June 2009, vol. 494, col. 850.
4   I learned this, along with about a hundred other people, at an invitation-
      only conference conducted under 'Chatham House rules', which means
      that attendees can refer to, but not attribute, what is said.
5   See the Iraq Inquiry Digest website (http://www.iraqinquirydigest.
      org/?page_id=5255).
6   Anthony Glees, Philip H. J. Davies and John N. L. Morrison, *The Open
      Side of Secrecy: Britain's Intelligence and Security Committee*, Social Affairs
      Unit, London, 2006, p. 105.
7   See 'The Cabinet Office Briefing Paper' and 'The Downing Street Minutes'
      at http://www.michaelsmithwriter.com/memos.html.
8   Scott Ritter, *Iraq Confidential: The Untold Story of America's Intelligence
      Conspiracy*, I. B. Tauris, London, 2005.
9   Hansard, HC Deb, 14 July 2004, vol. 423, col. 1431.
10   Hansard, HC Deb, 14 July 2004, vol. 423, col. 1438.
11   Hansard, HC Deb, 20 July 2004, vol. 424, col. 195.
12   Hansard, HL Deb, 7 September 2004, vol. 664, cols 448ff.
13   *Comprehensive Report of the Special Advisor to the DCI on Iraq's WMD*, 30
      September 2004. This is a three-volume report running to several hundred
      pages to which a short addendum was later added. It can be found at
      www.globalsecurity.org/wmd/library/report/2004/isg-final-report/.
14   Hansard, HC Deb, 12 October 2004, vol. 425, col. 151.
15   At the end of col. 152 Straw began by noting the suspicions about the
      MI6 WMD intelligence reports mentioned in Butler before saying, 'The
      House will now wish to be aware that the chief of the Secret Intelligence
      Service has written to my Right Hon. Friend the member for Dewsbury
      [Ann Taylor], the Chairman of the Intelligence and Security Committee,
      formally withdrawing those two lines of reporting.'
16   Hansard, HC Deb, 13 October 2004, vol. 425, col. 279.
17   *Review of Intelligence on Weapons of Mass Destruction: Implementation of Its
      Conclusions*, Cm 6492, March 2005.
18   Peter Hennessy, 'Intelligence reforms rely on political will', *The
      Independent*, 14 January 2005.

19 Anthony Seldon, *Blair*, Simon & Schuster, London, 2005, p. 648; Anthony Seldon, *Blair Unbound*, Simon & Schuster, 2007, p. 270.
20 Brian Jones, 'Blair's integrity', letter to the editor, *The Independent*, 14 February 2004.

Chapter 14: 2005–2010: Intelligence oversight and the Chilcot inquiry

1 Iraq inquiry website, www.iraqinquiry.org.uk/about.aspx.
2 See www.cabinetoffice.gov.uk/reports/iraq-inquiry-protocol.aspx.
3 The writer was asked to give public evidence to the committee in July but when the inquiry learned this book was about to be published they decided to read it before deciding whether this would be necessary. The inquiry was supplied with an advance copy of a late draft manuscript and it advised that it would put written questions back to the writer when the committee had read the book.
4 The original transcripts of evidence discussed here can be located through the Iraq Inquiry website at http://www.iraqinquiry.org.uk.
5 Ehrman and Dowse gave evidence on 25 November 2009. Ehrman had spent a period on secondment to the Cabinet Office as chairman of the JIC, and Dowse had served as a deputy chief and subsequently as chief of the Assessment Staff. Neither had given public evidence on Iraq before, although both had contributed to the ISC and Butler inquiries.
6 Letter from Dowse to Margaret Aldred, secretary to the Iraq inquiry, dated 14 December 2009 (see http://www.iraqinquiry.org.uk/media/41144/tdowse-evidence-addendum.pdf)
7 Scarlett appeared at the inquiry on 8 December 2009. As chairman of the JIC from 2001 until 2004, he had given evidence to all the Iraq inquiries, except for one conducted by the Foreign Affairs Committee. He was subsequently made head of MI6 before retiring in 2009.
8 See the transcript of Scarlett's evidence to Chilcot, www.iraqinquiry.org.uk/media/40665/20091208pmscarlett-final.pdf.
9 See Powell's evidence to Chilcot on 18 January 2010, www.iraqinquiry.org.uk/media/44184/20100118pm-powell-final.pdf.
10 See Campbell's evidence to Chilcot on 12 January 2010, www.iraqinquiry.org.uk/media/42384/20100112am-campbell-final.pdf.
11 Scarlett suggested Iraq had 'a proven ability to weaponise chemical and biological agents onto . . . ballistic missiles'. Although there may have been some trials with chemical warfare agent on Scud missiles their effectiveness was not entirely clear. Whilst some other chemical weapons were 'battlefield proven' in the war with Iran, there was no indication that biological weapons had been used. It will be recalled that in 1991, Iraq's attempts to deliver conventionally armed ballistic missiles against Israel

had been unsuccessful, with the missiles breaking up in flight. Iraq had conducted no further trials after 1991.

12 A JIC assessment showing this was distributed on 15 March 2002. On 3 April 2002 Blair told NBC News, 'We know that he [Saddam] has stockpiles of major amounts of chemical and biological weapons.'

13 *Review of Intelligence on Weapons of Mass Destruction, Chairman the Rt Hon. the Lord Butler of Brockwell* (the Butler report), HC 898, The Stationery Office, London, 14 July 2004, pp. 163–71.

14 See the transcript of Omand's evidence to Chilcot on 20 January 2010 (http://www.iraqinquiry.org.uk/media/44187/20100120pm-omand-final.pdf). Omand had been the security and intelligence coordinator, a member of the JIC, from 2002 until 2005, and Scarlett's line manager for much of that period.

15 As explained in Chapter 7.

16 This minute of 20 September 2002 is also reproduced in Chapter 7.

17 Anthony Glees, Philip H. J. Davies and John N. L. Morrison, *The Open Side of Secrecy*, Social Affairs Unit, London, 2006, p. 105.

18 See the Iraq Inquiry Digest website, www.iraqinquirydigest.org/?p=4577.

19 Meyer gave evidence to Chilcot on 26 November 2009; see www.iraqinquiry.org.uk/media/40453/20091126am-final.pdf.

20 Christopher Meyer, *DC Confidential*, Weidenfeld & Nicolson, London, 2005.

21 Greenstock gave evidence to Chilcot on 27 November 2009 (www.iraqinquiry.org.uk/media/40456/20091127am-final.pdf). He had been involved in achieving UNSCR 1205, albeit with notable abstentions, which 'enabled' Operation Desert Fox in December 1998.

22 Manning gave evidence to Chilcot on 30 November 2009 (www.iraqinquiry.org.uk/media/40459/20091130pm-final.pdf). For discussion of his memorandum see Chapter 5.

23 See Chapter 5.

Chapter 15: Bigger issues

1 Bob Woodward, *Plan of Attack*, Simon & Schuster, London, 2004, p. 30; Ron Suskind, *The One Percent Doctrine: Deep inside America's Pursuit of Its Enemies since 9/11*, Simon & Schuster, London, 2006.

2 President's Graduation Speech, United States Military Academy, West Point, NY, 1 June, 2002; *National Security Strategy of the United States*, White House, September 2002.

3 See Blair's speech in his Sedgefield constituency, 5 March 2004 (http://webarchive.nationalarchives.gov.uk/20041109040811/number10.gov.uk/page5461).

4 According to Bob Woodward in *Plan of Attack*, on 2 February 2004

Secretary of State Colin Powell commented on whether he would have recommended an invasion if he had thought there were no actual stockpiles of WMD: 'It was the stockpile that presented the final piece that made it more of a real and present danger and threat to the region and to the world. The absence of a stockpile changes the political calculus. It changes the answer you get.'

5 For example 'Operation Mass Appeal', as discussed in Chapter 13, and the attempt to persuade the Mexican ambassador to the UN to support a stronger Security Council resolution in 2003 as revealed on *Panorama* in July 2004 (Chapter 6, note 22).

INDEX